Lacan and the Subject of Law

LACAN AND THE SUBJECT OF LAW

Toward a Psychoanalytic Critical Legal Theory

DAVID S. CAUDILL

HUMANITIES PRESS
NEW JERSEY

First published in 1997 by
Humanities Press International, Inc.,
165 First Avenue, Atlantic Highlands, New Jersey 07716.

© 1997 by David S. Caudill

Library of Congress Cataloging-in-Publication Data
Caudill, David Stanley.
   Lacan and the subject of law : toward a psychoanalytic critical legal theory / David S. Caudill.
     p. cm.
   Includes index.
   ISBN 0-391-04009-X (cloth : alk. paper). —ISBN 0-391-04010-3 (paper : alk. paper)
   1. Lacan, Jacques, 1901– . 2. Critical legal studies.
3. Sociological jurisprudence. 4. Law—Methodology.
5. Psychoanalytic interpretation. I. Title.
K230. L282C38 1997
340'.1—dc20   96–24792
                                                                                            CIP

All rights reserved. No part of this publication may be reproduced or transmitted, in any form or by any means, without written permission.

Printed in the United States of America

10 9 8 7 6 5 4 3 2

To Chris

CONTENTS

Preface and Acknowledgments   ix
Introduction   xi

PART I: COMING TO TERMS WITH LACAN

1. Trafficking in Lacan: The Next Intervention of Psychoanalysis in Law?   3
2. Networking with the Big O[ther]   25
3. Legal Language: Meanings in the Gaps, Gaps in the Meanings   42
4. Schlag's "Problem of the Subject": Law's Need for an Analyst   66

PART II: LEGAL ANALYSIS IN LACANIAN TERMS

5. Social Hysteria, Social Psychoanalysis, and Modern Witch-Hunts   85
6. "Name-of-the-Father," the Logic of Psychosis, and Real Estate   101
7. Two Ideological Monsters: The Subject of the Bar and the Object of Desire in *Bleak House*   116
8. Lacanian Ethics and the Debate over Religion in Politics   129
9. Concluding Remarks   152

Notes   154
Index   205

PREFACE AND ACKNOWLEDGMENTS

When I was an undergraduate philosophy major in the early 1970s, Jacques Lacan (1901–1981) was already a major figure in French philosophical and psychoanalytic circles. When I was a graduate student in philosophy in the late 1970s, Lacan's work began to appear in English translations. When I graduated from law school in the early 1980s, Lacanian theory was familiar to many American scholars in literary theory, film theory, comparative literature, and psychoanalysis, and his influence was growing steadily. Nevertheless, I do not recall hearing of Lacan's life and work until the late 1980s, when I had completed a doctoral dissertation on critical legal philosophy and I was asked to deliver a paper (at a political science conference) on the influence (mostly indirect) of Freud within the American Critical Legal Studies movement. I was familiar at the time with the interest in psychoanalysis on the part of neo-Marxian Critical Theorists (e.g., Horkheimer, Adorno, Fromm, Marcuse, and the early Habermas), whose work was foundational to contemporary critical legal theorists, but I was not a student of French critical theory (which also informed and inspired many in the Critical Legal Studies movement). In my survey of the appropriations of psychoanalytic theory by radical social theorists generally, the influence of Jacques Lacan was readily apparent; the more I read about him the more interested I became in the relevance of his work for critical legal theory. Though I concluded that the Lacanian perspective was not, in contrast to the work of Foucault and Derrida, particularly influential in American Critical Legal Studies, I was convinced it should be.

For the last six years I have delivered papers and published essays on the significance of Lacan for critics of legal processes and institutions. The materials in chapters 2–8 of this book are substantial revisions of eight such essays, and I appreciate the permission of the editors of *Legality and Illegality* (New York: Peter Lang, 1995) to reprint (in modified form) the materials in chapter 7, and the permission of the following journals to reprint (in modified form) the materials comprising most of the remaining chapters of this book: *Studies in Psychoanalytic Theory* (chapter 2), *Law and Critique* (chapters 3 and 5), *Cardozo Law Review* (chapter 4 and portions of chapter 8), *Legal Studies Forum* (chapter 6), and *The Psychoanalytic Review* (portions of chapter 8).

I would also like to thank Nancy Stutesman and Sheri Kubasek for invaluable editorial assistance, and the following colleagues and friends for their moral support and critical comments with respect to this project: Peter Goodrich, Peter Rush, Costas Douzinas, Richard Delgado, David Gray-Carlson, Ellie Ragland, Richard Weisberg, Shaun McVeigh, Steven Friedlander, L. H. "Lash" LaRue, David Millon, Dragan Milovanovic, James Skillen, Denis Brion, Joan Shaughnessy, Louise Halper, Tyler Lorig, Mark Bracher, Hugh Crawford, Kareen Malone, Sanford Levinson, Pierre Schlag, and Jack Balkin. I am grateful as well to the Frances Lewis Law Center at Washington and Lee University for a series of summer research grants in support of this project. Finally, I want to thank Keith Ashfield, president of Humanities Press, for making things happen.

In the end, it was Penny Pether who taught me that the last mile can be the first.

INTRODUCTION

While many legal scholars—and I include in this category not only law school professors but also philosophers of law, sociologists of law, criminologists, law and literature theorists, and other inter-disciplinarians concerned with the theory and practice of law—are familiar, in varying degrees, with Jacques Lacan's psychoanalytic theory, and even as the relevance of Lacanian categories for social theory and cultural studies is becoming obvious, Lacan is not yet a fixture in the theory and criticism of legal processes and institutions. My primary intention in this book is to explore the promise of Lacanian theory as a critical supplement to the discipline of law. In recognition of the fact that some readers interested in Lacan and law have not studied his own and his followers' work, I have divided this book into two parts. Part 1 is intended as an introduction to several Lacanian conceptions that are particularly significant for any attempt to employ Lacan's methodology in the service of contemporary legal theory. (Part 2, an exercise in applied psychoanalysis, builds upon the conceptions introduced in part 1 by reference to several current legal controversies.) Given, however, that the term "introduction" is ambiguous with respect to an author's assumption of the understanding of his or her readers, a few qualifications are in order.

First, while I do not in part 1 assume any familiarity with Lacan's analytical framework, and while I introduce Lacan's notions of the "Other," the symbolic order of language, and the decentered subject in what I believe to be their ascending order of complexity and unfamiliarity for critics of law (from any disciplinary perspective), I do assume some familiarity with (1) the ongoing debates over postmodern approaches, (2) the so-called hermeneutic or interpretive "turn," and (3) the challenge to human agency known as the problem of the subject or "self" (i.e., its supposed disappearance), each of which has affected and/or divided almost every discipline of contemporary academia. Examples include the debates in literary theory over whether the meaning of a text is determinable by reference to the author's intention, the text itself, or the reader; the debates in historiography over whether an historical account always involves fictional "emplotment"; the debates in the natural sciences over the sociality or narrativity of science; the debates in philosophy over the rationality of human knowledge; and the debates in law concerning the indeterminacy of legal doctrine. The extreme positions in these debates—like the belief in objectivity or the belief that all knowledge is illusory—are less than helpful, as are the exaggerated caricatures of traditional thinkers as ideologues or postmodern thinkers as nihilists. One of the primary aims of this book, alongside my identification of some implications of Lacan for legal theory, is to demonstrate that the most helpful cultural criticism takes place between the extremes in contemporary debates over postmodernism—that theme predominates in the first and last chapters of this book, with the remaining chapters focused on Lacanian theory as an example of avoiding the extremes. Nevertheless, Lacan is a radical thinker and is critical, for example, of Enlightenment ideals of rationality and freedom, of most post-Freudian psychoanalytic theory, and of scientism. To the extent that we may speak, perhaps more heuristically than descriptively, of an ongoing struggle between traditional (or mainstream) thinkers and postmodern (or critical) scholars in law schools as in English or Comparative Literature or History Departments, my own (and most existing) discourse concerning Lacan will be most accessible to nontraditional scholars and their sympathetic critics.

Second, while I explore several elements of Lacanian theory by reference to contemporary legal theory and practice, my examples in part 1 (regarding legal education and contract law) are quite simple and are included primarily to explain Lacanian theory to readers interested in law. I reserve for part 2 my more developed applications of Lacan's work to concrete legal problems, thus the examples in part 1 are merely suggestive. Readers familiar with Lacanian theory may therefore choose to skip or perhaps skim part 1, though the basic legal applications in the early chapters may be of interest to students of Lacan who are less familiar with the critique of legal institutions and processes.

Third, while Lacan's training and approach is decidedly psychoanalytic, I do not attempt in this study to *place* Lacan in the history of—French or otherwise—psychoanalysis, nor do I attempt to compare and contrast Lacanian theory with existing "schools" of psychoanalysis, such as American ego psychology, self psychology, object relations theory, and so forth. (The implications of each such school for legal theory is likewise not a subject of this book.) Readers familiar with various psychoanalytic theories will make their own compari-

Introduction xiii

sons, and will find similarities and differences in Lacan's reading of Freud. Lacan is neither completely unique nor ultimately attuned with American "schools" of psychoanalysis; Lacanian analysts themselves belong—informally or formally—to a school of psychoanalysis that is dominant in southern Europe and in South America, but again that phenomenon is not a focus of this book.

Finally, while my intention in part 1 is to demonstrate selectively how Lacan's analytic framework relates to legal theory and law practice, the controversial character of his work requires that I acknowledge first (in chapter 1) the ostensible barriers to any intervention of Lacanian theory into law. I identify, for example, the current hesitance and skepticism (regarding Lacan) among literary and psychoanalytic theorists, which responses are predictable among legal scholars. The inconsistent critiques of Lacan, however, suggest that his psychoanalytic approach may provide bridges between the antinomies of traditional and critical theory, mainstream and leftist analyses of culture, and modern and postmodern paradigms. Moreover, while Lacan's focus on individual (or *clinical*) analysis might appear to limit his relevance for social and legal theory, the brief legal analyses in part 1 will show how Lacan's emphases on language and identity establish the contours of a radical sociolegal psychoanalysis.

Another seeming "barrier" to the intervention of Lacanian theory into legal studies—the difficulty of reading Lacan's and his commentator's texts—bears special mention. That difficulty cannot be overlooked, and though I begin my first chapter by highlighting Lacan's style and complexity, I conclude early in the book that little is gained by endless references to the esoteric, almost secret, features of Lacanian theory. I would not have written this book if I believed that Lacan cannot be popularized, in the sense that James Joyce, or Hegel or Kant, are studied in spite of the difficulties encountered. In the case of Lacan, I believe, the complexity is justified by the ambitious nature of his critical project.

In chapter 2, for example, after briefly discussing some current examples of psychoanalytic approaches to law, I present a lengthy, detailed commentary on Lacan's *Schema L* (a graphic representation of the "relational" subject or self), drawing from law my examples of its elements (e.g., the Other). Though my intention is to be clear and concise in my introduction to Lacan, *Schema L* offers an opportunity to explore some novel aspects of Lacanian theory. Similarly, in chapter 3, after describing the conventional role of doctrinal "gap-fillers" in contract interpretation, I discuss in some detail Lacan's symbolic order, his notion of the signifier, the tropes of metaphor and metonymy, the linguistic structure of the "clinical" symptom, and parallels to Lacan's views in legal semiotics and deconstruction, in each case to give the reader more than a facile sense of Lacan's unique theory of language as highly determinative and sometimes unconscious. Finally, in chapter 4, after summarizing the problem of the subject or self in legal theory, I pay particular attention to the possibility of agency, especially resistance to what might appear in Lacan to be a deterministic symbolic order. (Interestingly, Lacanian theory is not only a critique of those who posit a rational, autonomous subject and of those who [with some difficulty] posit cultural determinants as irresistible, but also of those who acknowledge a restrained subject but then forget that problem in their theorizing, including legal pragmatists in Schlag's account [see chapter 4], ideology critics in Zizek's account [see chapter 7], and liberal theorists like Rawls [see chapter 8].) All of these details are important, I think, to understand Lacan's potential contribution to ongoing debates in legal theory about the sources of law, the operation of legal language, and the basis on which any social critique proceeds.

Part 2 is a series of studies, in Lacanian terms, of some current legal controversies. I begin with two psychoanalytic clinical notions to demonstrate their applicability in social and legal analyses. Chapter 5 revives the clinical category of hysteria—Lacan is known for his own revival of that category—for the analysis of false accusations of child abuse. My approach in chapter 5 is intentionally comparative; rather than emphasizing Lacan's texts, I highlight traditional Freudian, historical, and legal analyses of hysteria and then compare them to feminist views influenced by Lacan, all in an effort to construct a new interpretation of an old legal category. Another clinical category—psychosis—and another Lacanian notion—the "Name-of-the-Father"—are explored in chapter 6 in the context of the "takings" controversy in property and constitutional law. In contrast to chapter 5, I explicitly use Lacanian theory as explanatory of certain legal phenomena.

My focus changes in the next two chapters, where I turn from courtroom legal disputes to the more abstract question of ideology in law. The "legal controversies" I address in chapters 7 and 8 include the use of literature in legal analysis, the problem of self-critique in ideology-critiques, and the arguments over the place of religion in legal and political decision making. I view Lacan's work primarily as a psychoanalytic supplement to the critique of legal ideology, which critique attempts to disclose the inevitable political tilt of legal processes and institutions, even when—especially when—they appear rational or neutral. Chapter 7 provides an example of ideology-critique

Introduction

in the style of the "law-and-literature" movement now popular in legal theory, using Dickens's *Bleak House* as an allegorical text. In chapter 8 I discuss Lacanian ethics in the context of two contemporary notions of pluralism. Lacan's complex notion of desire, introduced in chapter 7, is central to my analysis in chapter 8.

I conclude in chapter 9 that the barriers to the appropriation of Lacan in law are not barriers at all, but reasons to reconsider some of the deadlocks in legal theory in terms of Lacanian psychoanalysis. Those deadlocks, the numerous debates among legal scholars about specific legal subfields and about the nature and operation of law generally, are not exhaustively described in this book. Nor do I attempt systematically to compare Lacanian thought with the various "movements" in legal theory today. From the outset, however, I do align Lacan with critical legal scholarship and with its proponents who appreciate psychoanalysis. Moreover, when appropriate to clarify an aspect of Lacanian theory, I compare Lacan's method to other approaches—in chapter 2 I describe traditional and skeptical appropriations of Freud in law; in chapter 3 I introduce a law-and-economics-style analysis, followed by references to legal semiotics and other language-centered analyses of law; chapter 4 includes an appraisal of legal formalism, legal neopragmatism, and "cultural conservatism," and even a (self-)critique of Critical Legal Studies; chapter 5 is based on a feminist appropriation of Lacanian theory, while chapter 6 acknowledges the feminist critique of Lacan (as well as acknowledging the conflict between property rights and environmentalist camps that appears in cases involving constitutional land-use jurisprudence); chapter 7, an example of law and literature scholarship, includes a critique of traditional psychoanalytic literary criticism; finally, chapter 8 highlights the debate between Rawlsian proponents of "public reason" and their communitarian and religious critics. In each such comparison, I intend not only to elucidate Lacanian theory but also to demonstrate (1) its unique contribution to social theory, (2) its potential as a critique of various philosophies of law, and (3) its usefulness in mediating the types of controversies that arise nowadays in legal scholarship.

In the process of writing about—introducing, defending, applying, extending—Lacan's work in the context of contemporary debates over cultural determinism and human freedom, a certain rhythm is unavoidable and is reflected in the structure of this book. The symbolic order, interrupted by imaginary and real relations, exhibits gaps and leftovers (chapter 2), even while its determinative function is primary, unconscious, and inescapable (chapter 3); and yet, in the multiple and contradictory discourses that construct the subject, there is space for resistance (chapter 4), which sounds good but is perhaps exemplified by the position of the hysteric (chapter 5), which sounds bad but is to be preferred to the failure of the symbolic in psychosis (chapter 6); just as the symbolic order begins to sound like a bad lover you can't live with or without, the analogy with ideology (not as *false* consciousness but as *consciousness*) is complete (chapter 7), but Lacanian psychoanalytic theory provides a compelling account of ethical responsibility that honors diversity and pluralism (chapter 8). Lacanian theory is thus framed by the rocks and hard places we are between and seek to avoid.

My method—an attempt to isolate (roughly) and then to discuss one by one a selection of Lacanian themes most relevant to law—reflects my own study of Lacan over the last several years. While I start with unconscious language and the problem of the subject, and later deal with hysteria, psychosis (and the "Name-of-the-Father"), desire, and ethics, other students of Lacan may believe that Lacan's notion of desire is the appropriate starting point for social theory and cultural analysis, or that the "Name-of-the-Father" is the primary marker for any Lacanian legal analysis. Moreover, some followers of Lacan may believe that a more thorough introduction to Lacan should precede any "applications" to concrete legal and social problems. Anticipating both criticisms, I should explain my concern that readers interested in the implications of Lacan for law might grow impatient with a preliminary, abstract presentation of Lacan's entire analytical framework, which presentation, after all, is available in Lacan's own texts and in other books introducing Lacan. My goal of establishing several exemplary meeting points between Lacan and legal theory is reflected both in my choice to refer to legal controversies in every chapter and in my choice to highlight (in part 1) the Other, the symbolic, and the subject as the *place(s)* of law. In any event, I hope to encourage all readers to confront Lacan on his own terms, in his own texts, and to consider his relevance for legal theory and practice well beyond the boundaries of my own commentary, examples, and analyses.

PART I:

Coming to Terms with Lacan

1

Trafficking in Lacan: The Next Intervention of Psychoanalysis in Law?

> One doesn't see oneself as one is, and even less so when one approaches oneself wearing philosophical masks.
> —Jacques Lacan, "Science and Truth"

> Take a leaf out of this book if you think it could do well in other kinds of discourses. Although I doubt it [will].
> —Jacques Lacan, *Television*

> His comment... asks, and I quote, "Is [Lacan's] take on psychoanalysis worth the trouble of deciphering his oracular jargon?" Malevolent as it is, it's nevertheless judicious, and I do not even discard his words, because you could as well ask this about the unconscious itself.
> —Jacques-Alain Miller, "Introductory Remarks before the Screening of Television"

When, at last, Lacanian theory is established as a methodological approach available to students and theorists of law, having overcome both self-imposed and its critics' obstructions, it will be bruised and beaten. It already is; for while the Lacan "industry" in America is flourishing—new English translations of Lacan's seminars appear with regularity, commentaries (in books and journal articles) abound, conferences are held, and interest continues among practicing analysts and professors of literary and cultural studies—a counterindustry of criticism of Lacan grows in the shadows. The answer to the frequently asked question, Why bother with Lacan? is not at all clear for many psychoanalysts, literary theorists, and social critics, much less legal scholars.[1]

The fact that Lacan's name is often dropped alongside the names of Derrida, Foucault, Lyotard, and other influential French critics is no reason to receive Lacan into law—surely following French fashion is out of fashion among serious scholars. Even apart from the French connection, the mere fact that Lacan has a unique, "fancy" theory—unmined in legal theory—is no longer inviting for the risk-averse scholar: the danger of being accused of "intellectual voyeurism" is ever-present.[2] Thus the only reason to appropriate Lacan for legal studies is the potential for new understandings of legal processes and institutions, for clarifications of existing controversies, and so forth. Certain features of Lacanian theory, however, suggest that the process of evaluation will be complicated. For reasons I will explain, one cannot simply distill the essence of Lacan for law, then run it up the flagpole and see how it flies. Not only do barriers to such a project appear at the "distill the essence" and the "for law" stages, due to the character and focus of Lacan's (and his disciples') work, but the (justifiable or unjustifiable) biases against Lacan's radical psychoanalytic approach may ensure that the flagpole, much less the test flight, is not easily reached.

Framing an argument (for appropriating Lacan) with such concerns might seem counterproductive, but exploring the confrontations between disciples and critics of Lacan actually helps clarify the aspects of Lacanian theory that hold promise for legal scholarship, and also provides an opportunity to begin to fill in the details of that theory. I do not, of course, purport in this opening chapter to summarize Lacan or the substantial body of literature that explains, develops, applies (in various disciplines), or criticizes his work. Nevertheless, introducing Lacan in a brief chapter is no more difficult than introducing any complex and unfamiliar philosopher, literary theorist, or linguist who intends "to bring about a reconceptualization of the conventionally assumed and unquestioned words by which Western people have come to describe themselves."[3]

Barriers, Resistances

Two sets of barriers (or, ennobling Lacan, "resistances"), which might be termed "internal" and "external," stand between Lacanian theory and its appropriation for legal studies. In the first category, I include stylistic and systematic difficulties that would exist *even if* a substantial number of legal scholars wanted to initiate a Lacanian Legal Studies movement. The second category captures several arguments, sometimes contradictory, why Lacan is not a likely candidate for resolving problems faced in analyses of legal processes and institutions—*even if* the internal barriers are overcome.

INTERNAL FACTORS

Style, References

> Stylistically, the Lacanian discourse has entered an esthetic of pronounced indirection, whose asides hopelessly confuse . . . the "train" or "thread" of thought. With Lacan, psychoanalytic discourse cools to—becomes indifferent to—its prior overarching schemes, plans, and objectives.
> —Henry Sussman, "Psychoanalysis Modern and Post-Modern"

Books written to introduce Lacan all seem to begin with a warning about Lacan's elusive and enigmatic presentations, and first-time readers of Lacan know why; even longtime readers find Lacan exceptionally difficult. Lacan admits that these difficulties are intentional—he wants "to leave the reader no other way out than the way in, which I prefer to be difficult"[4]—and sympathetic readers grow to appreciate that what "his texts give voice to and in a certain sense 'stage' is not simply something represented, an object that would be self-identical, but is itself representation, translation, staging."[5]

This "something" that is not simply represented by Lacan, but is "itself representation," is the unconscious, the focus of psychoanalytic inquiry. In Lacan's reformulation of Freud, the unconscious is structured like language, thus the unconscious speaks; the phenomenon described in Lacan's theoretical discourse is unconscious discourse—for example, the discourse that we glimpse in dreams and slips of the tongue. This is not to say that the difficulty of Lacan's texts—whether written by him for publication or transcribed from his recorded seminars—is due to an effort on Lacan's part to mimic or reproduce the seemingly nonsensical discourse of the unconscious; nevertheless, most readers of Lacan are faced with an unstable text that resists familiar understandings and conventional categories, a text that is often out of control:

> To make one's way under conditions that can never be entirely controlled is part of what constitutes psychoanalytic truth. To learn how to read Lacan involves making one's way in this sense. The pace of such *reading* is laborious, if also often exhilarating; it has little in common with the rush to judgment that often goes by the same name.[6]

Another problem for readers of Lacan is his presumption of familiarity not only with Freud, but with all of the classical sources, modern French fiction, and philosophical movements with which Lacan himself is familiar. Lacan is rarely in the introductory, overview mode of exposition, which creates problems of conceptual vocabulary. In fairness to Lacan, his seminars do include close readings of Freud and extended discussions of some major Western thinkers (for example, Hegel, Kant, Saussure, Jakobson), but the treatment of their ideas is always at a fairly sophisticated level, and is often accompanied by passing references to various other philosophers, artists, analysts, and scientists.

Despite these stylistic and contextual difficulties, interest in Lacan continues to grow. To the extent that Lacan challenges entrenched notions of the subject, language, and cognition, he will be forgiven (as any critical thinker would be) for running up against the limits of language as well as for disturbing familiar concepts in the process of reconceptualization. Besides, reading Lacan may not be as complicated as first appears. Some of the difficulties encountered by American readers may result from poor translations, or from translation itself.[7] Moreover, the characterization of Lacan's writing as "baroque" and "dense" should not eclipse "his capacity to be memorably simple"—for example, Lacan's dictum "the unconscious is structured like a language," as well as his didactic models and graphs, offer to readers frameworks, or markers, for the barrage of details that appear in his work.[8] Finally, while critics of Lacan may find his texts confused and careless,[9] or perhaps (intentionally) surrealistic,[10] more sympathetic readers are often awestruck at the systematic and logical character of these texts:

> Lacan's careful attention to detail and his painstaking elaboration of a formal structuration of the unconscious make it possible to support any aspect of his thought by randomly choosing from any text and from any point in chronological time. The consistency of Lacan's epistemology has all the aesthetic beauty of a mathematical theory or the cantos of Dante.[11]

Whether Lacan *is* so utterly consistent is a matter of some debate among commentators, some preferring to historicize Lacan's theory as developing in stages: "Although self-consistency is not a virtue Lacan particularly prizes, he is so skilled in the reintegration of early views into late that his writings can easily seem all of a piece, a progressive revelation that has the force of a single event."[12]

The force of Lacanian texts, whether by elegant logic or clever rhetoric, would allow interested readers in law (and has allowed those in other disciplines) to overcome stylistic barriers. Moreover, the problems of translation and referential context are simply obvious in, but not unique to, Lacan. Yet the outlines of another barrier to appropriating Lacanian theory loom large—namely, that the theory is *so* large.

Grand Theory

> Lacan's seminars took place in Paris every week for approximately thirty years. They were recorded.... In the bulk of twenty-five volumes [, about half of which have been published], and when they appear in English [, five to date], you will see for yourselves... a complete and very careful reading, not only of Freud, but of [psycho-]analytical literature in every language.
> —Jacques-Alain Miller, "How Psychoanalysis Cures According to Lacan"

The "size" barrier is not, in my view, a function of the number of pages of Lacan, though there are many (and there will be—as seminars are transcribed, edited, and translated—many more). Rather, the problem is the theoretical space occupied by Lacanian theory, the sheer number of issues addressed and disciplines crossed. I have seen various "Lacan's single aim (or focus) was" statements, but I remain skeptical. For example, "His particular aim was to elaborate the notion of the human subject";[13] or "He never pretended to be anyone else other than a pupil of Freud";[14] or (speaking of Lacan's epistemology): "There is... a single ideology of which Lacan provides the theory: that of the 'modern ego', that is to say, the paranoic subject of scientific civilization, of which a warped psychology theorizes the imaginary, at the service of free enterprise."[15] If there is one such theme, one central feature to Lacanian theory, then it has thousands of parts. Consider, for example, the field covered by the three (related) inquiries suggested above: the subject, Freudian psychoanalysis, and theories of knowledge and of ideology.

First, Lacan's account of the subject is a critique of popular, Freudian, post-Freudian, Cartesian, and most modern psychological, scientific, philosophical, literary, and sociological notions of the "I," ego or self. Indeed, Lacanian theory at times appears to have no subject at all—subjected as it is to language, to Law, to the unconscious, to others, and to the Other. Each of those aspects of subjectivity is in Lacan's seminars described comprehensively, but with a high degree of originality that denies to readers the enjoyment of conventional categorizations (such as "I see, Lacan is a [reductionist, behaviorist, determinist, Freudian, etc.]"). Lacan's subject is—but is not *only*—a network of relations among—at least—the speaking subject, the subject of identificatory (mis)recognitions, other people, and the Other—the latter term (discussed in chapter 2) a notoriously ambiguous reference to the "place" of unconscious discourse, the outside-within-us, culture, and (in dozens of senses) that to which the subject is in a dialectic relationship. Far beyond a mere de-centering or split, Lacan seems to shatter the subject and then attempt to keep up with each shard.

Second, Lacan's professed fidelity to Freud is integral to his analysis of the subject, and one might also characterize Lacan not as a theorist of subjectivity but as a rearticulator of Freud (though the projects are, for Lacan, the same). Lacan retools the theory of the unconscious, reformulating each element—for example, desire (replacing drive), repression, resistance, transference—and drawing out the implications of each both for clinical practice (Lacan was an analyst) and for his theory of the subject. Freud's Oedipal drama, his classifications of disorders, his techniques of analysis, and his topology of the subject are invariably praised as brilliant and then substantially modified. As with all revisionists in the psychoanalytic tradition, one is never quite sure whether their approach is Freudian, or whether the answer to that question even has any significance. For better or worse, Lacan's reinterpretation appears total, but then the entire framework of his work is built on Freudian texts.

Finally, the expansive theory of the subject and the accompanying (or foundational) return to Freud integrates, or is integrated into, a theory of cognition which identifies three interrelated planes or spheres of thought and experience: the imaginary, the symbolic, and the real. *Imaginary* relations include the subject's identification with images, with others and with the signifiers located within (or, in another formulation, associated with the desire of) the Other; but recall that the subject is in part constituted by those relations, so the first part of my sentence presumed a distance (between subject and image) that is only didactic. The *symbolic*, which can be said to include language (including unconscious discourse) and all its operations, gains a certain primacy in Lacan that leads both to the recognition (by Lacanians) of our utter dependency on language, and to the criticism (by anti-Lacanians) that Lacanian theory risks linguistic reductionism. While recourse to the other two "orders" allays that risk, Lacan argues that "Freud's discovery was that of the field of the effects in the nature of man of his relations to the symbolic order and the tracing of their meaning right back to the most radical agencies of symbolization in being."[16]

Following that passage are aphorisms, like "It is the world of words that creates the world of things" and "Man speaks ... but it is because the symbol has made man,"[17] confirming that Lacanian theory is, or includes, a theory of language (which is indeed developed in great detail beginning with and substantially revising the signification theories of Saussure and Jakobson).[18] Lacan's controversial conception of determinative signifiers (linked into signifying chains) and his downplay of signifieds (in contrast to Saussure)—controversial because it appears to some critics as dated—serves to prioritize the symbolic, which explains why Lacan elicits interest from many literary theorists. The notion of the *real* is one of Lacan's most difficult conceptions, and for good reason, since it designates that which is outside both language and the realm of images, and is therefore unknowable—the real, which resists representation and cognition, is not to be confused with knowable "reality." The real functions instead as a limit, as that which we are up against or as the impossible, and may thus appear to be the element least accessible the theoretical discourse:

> In the last two decades, however, a general shift occurred in the field of Lacanian theory, a shift from the predominance of the Symbolic to the predominance of the Real: the inertia... of the *drive* instead of the dialectics of *desire*. The accent is now being put on the [nonsymbolic] left-overs.[19]

Without attempting here to penetrate the density of Lacan's (and his commentators') description of the three orders, note that the identification of something left over—some residue after the imaginary and symbolic screen out (or "interpret") the real—introduces an incongruity between the personal unconscious and what might be seen as a determinative order of language and society;[20] Lacan thus wavers between realism and idealism, satisfying neither school and keeping readers off guard and unable to "classify" Lacan.

I share with Malcolm Bowie the sense that Lacanian theory is not just an attempt to describe the subject of analysis and then to update Freud for clinicians: "Lacan's three orders [are] presented as the foundation for a new science of man.... The three orders *are* the human world, and if they are aligned, interconnected and disjoined with appropriate subtlety they will tell the whole story of mind in action."[21]

To the extent that Lacan presents not only a psychoanalytic theory, but a philosophy of language, a metaphysics, an ontology, and an epistemology, then the project of appropriating Lacan for law seems to call for a new "law and everything else" subdiscipline. Making matters worse, all of the categories and conceptions mentioned above are, in Lacanian theory, interconnected—all seem to be in play at once, so that no starting point or "fundamental" thesis is evident. Such a theoretical framework, even if it was to some degree mastered by a legal scholar with a light teaching load, raises concerns over its transmissibility within a discipline already full of theoretical debates and practical problems. The difficulties in summarizing Lacan distinguish, I think, a third barrier to his reception in law.

Limited Texts, Unlimited Summaries

> Anglophone readers ... express the hope that someone will explain Lacan to them on their own terms. This is simply impossible. To do so would permit an interlocutor to retain assumed meanings, providing the comfort of resolution, but only the *illusion* of understanding.
>
> —Ellie Ragland-Sullivan, *Jacques Lacan and the Philosophy of Psychoanalysis*

The difficulties commentators encounter in the effort to "encapsulate" Lacan are, of course, related to the two barriers discussed above. Lacan's challenge to established ways of discussing the subject, Freud, and language require, adherents say, a jarring and unfamiliar theoretical discourse—any rendition in familiar terms would miss the point. Hence Malcolm Bowie's half-joke that Lacan's students feel a moral obligation to be difficult.[22] As to Lacan's referential context, which I identify as part of the first barrier alongside stylistic complexities, anyone doing intellectual history knows the significance of a thinker's training, sources, intellectual "circles," and concerns; Lacan is a foreigner—in time, geographically, and by discipline—to American law, and even his scanty references to legal processes and institutions usually involve French law. Finally, given the scope of Lacan's critical interests, and the interrelationships between his analyses of the words, texts, psychical disorders or philosophical problems he seems to isolate, commentators fear reductionism even as they write books about Lacan, and even when the summation of one of Lacan's seminars well exceeds the original text.

Consider, for example, Samuel Weber's description of the risks and challenges of introducing Lacan:

> As is often the case when a work emerging from one intellectual field—in this instance, that marked by French Structuralism—is transposed to a different linguistic and cultural area, the contextual underpinnings tend to disappear.... [Proper] names [like "Lacan"], far from rendering what they name accessible, function as *screens*, isolating rather than simply repressing, by seemingly arresting the movement of signification.... The difficulty ... is not just that of translating a difficult text ... but even more, of *rendering a sense of signifying movement* that is irreducible to conceptual discourse. And yet, reduced it must be by a style informed ... by the conventional rules and norms of academic discourse.[23]

Alongside such limits, Weber questions whether Lacan's work even constitutes a "whole": "I doubt that it can be assembled into anything like a system without the most incisive and pathbreaking aspects... being lost in the process."[24] The implication that Lacan challenges conventional systematization is echoed by Jacques-Alain Miller: "Just to have a close-cut picture which everyone is going to learn in one hour or one year, and then apply or mix it with other things [is no] ideal."[25] If the reference to "one year" sounds like a joke, Lacan remarked that "ten years is enough to everything I write to become clear to everyone."[26] What I have termed the style and size barriers, and the difficulties of systematization, were for Lacan altogether necessary. Thus Anthony Wilden, translator of Lacan's landmark Rome Discourse, places an introductory essay *after* the translation of Lacan's text,[27] implying (in my words) that "you've got to read Lacan first or you'll think I'm exaggerating."[28]

The resistance of Lacanian texts to the construction of models that might be transferred to and applied in disciplines like law forms the basis of my fourth and final internal barrier—the absence of an isolatable social theory in Lacan.

The "Culture as Clinic" Conundrum

The utility of psychoanalysis for social theory remains an open question, though the project of social psychoanalysis is not new. The "social Freud" belongs to his later works—in the 1920s and 1930s—which are often considered the most speculative and philosophical. Lacan never *turns* to the social per se, but his persistent critique of "individual" psychology and his notion of constitutive imaginary and symbolic orders suggest that an account of culture pervades his theory of the subject. The Other seems to function, at times, as the collective unconscious of social relations. Predictably, however, those who *read* Lacan as a social theorist are often accused of misreading, of minimizing Lacan to fit *another* social-theoretical framework.

The most famous example of appropriating Lacan into a critique of culture is Louis Althusser's neo-Marxian account of ideology. In *Lenin and Philosophy and Other Essays* (1971), Althusser embraced psychoanalytic theory and credited Lacan with discovering how the "transition from (ultimately purely) biological existence to human existence (the human child) is achieved within the... Law of Culture... confounded in its *formal* essence with the order of language."[29] This conception of Lacan's symbolic order, which seems to work so well in describing ideological discursive formations, has been repeatedly attacked by Lacan scholars as mistaken. Paul Smith, for example, argues that Lacan's symbolic order does not take on the characteristic of the historical real as Althusser wants it to, and in Lacan it is certainly not this place of an "absolute effectiveness" where the human person is anchored.... Lacan might suggest that the symbolic is not ever completely used up in ideology.[30]

Recall that Lacan's subject is determined as well by imaginary and real relations; Althusser, significantly, also appropriates those terms but gives them Marxian connotations—the imaginary is a sort of false consciousness and the real refers to material conditions.[31] The resulting framework is therefore not Lacanian.

The initial difficulty here, designated as my fourth "barrier," is not that Lacan offers no theory of culture, but that it is not isolatable from the rest of his "system." Lacanian criticism of Althusser reveals the exclusiveness of Lacanian theory, its thematic unity. If that barrier is overcome, as I believe all the "internal" barriers I've identified can be, there is another reason that progressive social theorists like Althusser may not want to appropriate all of Lacan: Lacan is depressing. Lacanian theory tends to "collapse into an account of a universal, albeit contradictory, subject who is not situated historically, who is tied and bound by pre-existing language, and is incapable of change because of it."[32] Thus the appropriation of Lacanian theory for social and legal theorists often tends (as in Althusser's interpretation) to be tentative and partial, not wholesale.

For example, John Brenkman, in *Culture and Domination* (1987), argues that the impasses reached in critical social theory call for a psychoanalytic, and especially Lacanian, account of the subject. Nevertheless, neither

> Freud nor Lacan adequately integrates a conception of human autonomy into the theory of psychological development.... Lacan is constrained, on the one hand, by [his strategy to free psychoanalysis] from its mechanistic and biological tendencies; ever after he must also continually denounce the construct of the autonomous ego.... On the other hand, Lacan's ... structuralism never completely escapes the ... tendency to reduce or exclude the question of the subject.[33]

Among legal theorists, Peter Gabel draws upon Lacan for certain insights, especially concerning the alienation or splitting-off of the subject from his or her own desire, but for Gabel Lacan's "insistence on the unintelligibility of desire leaves him as unable to capture what we are alienated *from* as Freud was."[34] Dragan Milovanovic's recent book,[35] the first major attempt to appropriate Lacan for legal criticism, is in fact a synthesis of Lacanian theory and neo-Marxian social theory. All three scholars—Brenkman, Gabel, and Milovanovic—are careful and knowledgeable students of Lacan's texts, but each finds lacking (in Lacanian theory) the basis for social critique.

Other students of Lacanian theory, however, are slower to revise or to seek to "exceed" Lacan. Ellie Ragland, for example, acknowledges the "tragedy of natural being" conveyed by Lacan—we must choose between "alienation into language, social conventions, and rules" and "failure to evolve an identity adequate to social functioning"[36]— but she also sees optimistic implications in the "potential for modifying the fixity of the symbolic order" (e.g., "redefining the meaning of gender").[37] Paul Smith, likewise, contrasts the seemingly powerless subject (or "absent" subject) in Lacan with a flexibility on the part of Lacan's "subject" that revisionists often ignore:

> Subjectivity is always a product of the symbolic in an instance of discourse; thus, Lacan leaves room for a consideration of subjectivity as contradictory, as structured in divisions and thus as never the solidified effect of discursive or ideological pressures. [The] "subject" is a divided and provisional entity.[38]

Whether Lacanian theory leaves room for resistance on the part of the subject, because of multiple (and contradictory) discursive formations with variable effects, or on the contrary "leads to a form of pessimistic determinism"[39] that requires a supplement from elsewhere, Lacan is in any event often appropriated by critical social theorists as "the most radical critique from within psychoanalysis of essentialist assumptions of human integrity, and with this [Lacan] lays the groundwork for a provocative dismantling of the powerful assumptions surrounding 'human nature' with which we are saddled."[40] Such evaluations, of course, are beyond the scope of my discussion of the "internal" barriers to the appropriation of Lacan—his style, the scope of his theory, the problem of summation, and the absence of a pre-packaged social theory. Assuming, as I do, that legal scholars are perfectly capable of reading, discussing with clarity, and discovering the implications for law in the texts of Lacan, several reasons exist why they might choose not to do so.

EXTERNAL FACTORS

> One way of characterizing the compendium of approaches and interventions known as "Lacan" would be to say that it [brings] the discourse of psychoanalysis... into its post-modern phase.
> —Henry Sussman, "Psychoanalysis Modern and Post-Modern"

> [Lacan's] motto was "the return to Freud."
> —Jacques-Alain Miller, "How Psychoanalysis Cures According to Lacan"

> [Lacan's work] is a logophallocentric, nostalgic countertransference to rationalism, a marked regression from Freud's prescient distaste for philosophy.
> —William Kerrigan, "Terminating Lacan"

Critical reaction to Lacanian theory is striking in its variation. One suspects that the reception of Lacan in law will also be resisted on numerous, though not necessarily consistent, grounds. I focus below on two sets of barriers that appear with clarity given (1) the history—both promising and problematic—of pre-Lacanian psychoanalytic interventions in law, and (2) the new interest—both optimistic and critical—in so-called postmodern approaches. Lacanian theory has attracted and will continue to attract criticism that it is too Freudian, not Freudian enough, too postmodern, and too traditional.

Why Return to Freud?

> The meaning of a return to Freud is a return to the meaning of Freud.
> —Jacques Lacan, "The Freudian Thing"

In one sense, no reader of Lacan will take seriously his recurrent claims of fidelity to Freud. When Lacan says, in a particular exposition of a Freudian text or conception, "All I've done is rerelease what Freud said," or "this is me speaking here, but you can look it up and you'd see it" in Freud,[41] readers familiar with Freud often see little in the exposition that even remotely resembles traditional Freudian theory. Lacanian theory is, on the surface, a thorough rereading, revision, or reinterpretation of Freud. In another sense, however, Lacan's return to Freud is a critique of our familiarity with Freud—that is, Lacan seeks the "true" meaning of Freud, and Lacan is happy to acknowledge that his own Freud may not be recognizable within popular, traditional, and neo-Freudian understandings:

> [T]he project of a return to Freud ... involves for me ... not a return of the repressed, but rather taking the antithesis constituted by the phase in the history of the psychoanalytic movement since the death of Freud, showing what psychoanalysis is not, and seeking ... the means of revitalizing that which has continued to sustain it, even in deviation, namely, the primary meaning that Freud preserved in it.[42]

Not surprisingly, for Lacan, the primary meaning of Freud has not only been eclipsed by decades of Freudianism, but was even hidden at times to Freud himself.

Putting aside (until my discussion of the next external "barrier") the question of whether Lacan's Freud is closer to the original (or its *meaning*) than others' Freuds, Lacanian theory is quite transparently constructed within a Freudian framework—Lacan's referential anchors are the unconscious and its mechanisms, the analytic situation and its disorders, and the desire of the subject. Lacan is comprehensive in his interpretation and defense of Freudian texts, as if their authority is ultimately, if not immediately, uncontroversial. Such an evaluation, of course, is not likely to generate enthusiasm among the majority of contemporary scholars.

While the originality and influence (both academically and culturally) of Freud's work are generally acknowledged, Freud is viewed in mainstream psychology "as, at best, an interesting relic."[43] The same view persists in mainstream law and psychology scholarship. Some of the criticism of Freud as unscientific identifies psychoanalysis as a hoax, but most critics are satisfied to condemn Freudian theory as out of date or as speculative, as empirically unverifiable.[44] Throughout the social sciences and the humanities, Freud fares better, but scholars who take him seriously are often at the margins of their disciplines; the field of literary theory may appear to be an exception, but even there the growth of psychoanalytic approaches remains to many "something of an embarrassment."[45] Feminist recourse to Freud, for example, is problematic due to Freud's apparent misogyny. Within the Marxian tradition, itself a marginalized enterprise, Freud is often rejected as a bourgeois ideologue.[46] Even in the relatively small psychoanalytic establishment, Freud's own invention, he is celebrated then overrun by neo-Freudian revisionists. Short of trying to prove a flat earth, Lacan could not have constructed—by his return to Freud—a bigger stumbling block to his popularization.

Turning to the discipline of law, where "psychoanalysis has been and remains at most a marginal tool,"[47] the conventions of science, Marxism, and clinical psychoanalysis are perhaps less relevant. Leonard Kaplan and Vincent Rinella's sympathetic assessment of past and present psychoanalytic approaches in law makes a compelling case for the relevance of Freud's legacy, but identifies a resistance that is not based in science:

> [It] is the potential despair uncovered by the psychoanalytic that has limited its appropriation by legal theoreticians who feel the need for a theoretical analysis that reinforces unrelated utopian hopes. However, a refusal to appropriate psychoanalytical insight will continue to insure that legal analysis remains, at best, superficial and limited and, at worst, potentially dangerous.[48]

Even if a consensus could be reached on the productive value of Freud in law, however, the place of Lacan in legal scholarship would remain insecure—the barrier against psychoanalysis would be quickly replaced by critics of Lacan's alleged *anti*-Freudianism.

Lacan's Burial of Freud

> I want out of the traffic in Lacan because I don't like what he did to Freud, I don't want him to replace Freud.... His so-called "return to Freud" ... effect[s] ... a premature burial, as Freud's wonderful lucidity—modest lucidity—gets covered over and lost.
> —William Kerrigan, "Terminating Lacan"

Just as the impact of Lacanian theory has been greatest among literary theorists, for whom a tradition of psychoanalytic criticism exists, the harshest critiques of Lacan originate there. Norman Holland, an accomplished critic and forerunner of psychoanalytic approaches, has little appreciation for Lacan. The "return to Freud," for Holland, is in fact a synthesis of Freud's early (and later rejected, by Freud himself) notion of the unconscious and an outdated theory of language.[49] Holland's critique, unfortunately, reflects the exaggeration in fashion in literary theory circles, but he confirms that Lacan does not merely "rerelease" Freud, nor even build on a Freudian foundation. Rather, the foundation is reconstructed to accommodate a theory of signification and social relations as determinative:

> Lacan more or less identifies Saussure's signifier with the conscious and the signified with Freud's unconscious.... Thus Lacan renders the *processes* Freud discovered by Saussure's *entities*.... Lacan substitutes this psychological signification for association, memory, learning, and ultimately all other psychological processes.[50]

While I do not think Lacan's story (of language, discussed in chapter 3) is that simple, the Lacanian subject's reliance on language for its very constitution invites Holland's criticism: "What are we to say of a psychoanalyst who does not want to do psychology?"[51] This charge of linguistic reductionism is not new with Holland, and Lacanians remind such critics that (for Lacan) the functions of psychic systems are indeed analogous to, but are not simply, linguistic systems. Moreover, the symbolic is not the *only* order of unconscious meaning:

> The meaning system that makes up any personal unconscious is triggered in conscious life by an Imaginary perception that sets into motion the "text" derived from an interpenetration of Real experience and the "universals" of a given (local) Symbolic, i.e., cultural and linguistic order.[52]

While the above is, I think, a more accurate summation of Lacan, the resemblance to Freud remains faint at best.

William Kerrigan, another psychoanalytic critic, recounts how Lacanian theory, which he once viewed as fascinating or (later on) tolerable, now "looks more and more like a pretentious, personless ... variation on psychoanalysis.... We already have, moreover, a perfectly decent alternative to do for us those limited things that psychoanalysis also can perform—the tradition of Freud."[53] It is not that Lacan is unscientific—Kerrigan concedes that "no genuinely controversial, unobvious, countercommonsensical Freudian idea has ever passed the test of hard-core empirical confirmation."[54] Nor is Lacan's own narcissism, his "Colossal vanity," the problem—"let an ego without sin cast this stone."[55] Rather, Kerrigan argues that Lacan fuses Freud with metaphysical fragments—"He has simply made Kant speak Freud, producing yet another variation on the phenomenon (the imaginary), the noumenon (the symbolic), and the thing-in-itself (the unrepresentable real)."[56] Like Holland, Kerrigan decries Lacan's linguistics, which renders Freud's near-timelessness (Freud's skepticism sounds to Kerrigan "almost brand-new") old fashioned.[57] We ought really, Kerrigan concludes, "to return to Freud, and leave Lacan behind, remembering him as the exorcist who identified with the demon."[58]

The accusation that Lacan is old fashioned, a throwback, is made both by the critics of Freud (because Lacan relies on Freud) and by the Freudians (because Lacan strays from Freud into metaphysics). Such a consensus is curious when Lacan is commonly associated (at least in newspaper and magazine accounts of French critical theory) with postmodernism and poststructuralism, alongside Derrida and others. The charge of postmodernism is, in some quarters of academia, a criticism, just as the mantel of "traditionalist"—one who is locked into old ways of thinking—is never a compliment when it comes from a postmodern critic. Lacan, interestingly, is criticized both for his postmodernism and his traditionalism, which attacks, respectively, are the last two barriers I discuss.

Lacan the Postmodern

> Lacanian [theory has] a distinctly post-modern flavor.... The heavy mechanics of opposition and alternation; the coordination of linear, circular, and vertical movement, segmenting development into

> sequential, discrete phases; the strict division of labor between the genders... —these comprise distinctive traits of Freudian thought and major points of departure from which the Lacanian critique will set out.
> —Henry Sussman, *Psychoanalysis Modern and Post-Modern*

In my use of the terms "postmodern" and "traditional," borrowing a phrase from James Boyle, "my interest is less in intellectual taxonomy"[59] than in roughly distinguishing between two tendencies in contemporary, including legal, theory. With respect to the criticism of Lacan *as* a postmodern or *as* a traditional thinker, I associate the latter with belief in, and the former with challenges to, "Enlightenment desirables such as a decisive philosophical argument,... self-evident truths, or versions of the same thing in moral and political thought";[60] "the reduction of knowledge to propositions and claims rather than actions and power;"[61] and the unified, coherent, or stable subject affected by and often in control of, rather than constituted by, its language, culture, and history. That will have to do as a note on terminology, with all due respect for the understandings (1) that the postmodern is *also* our condition as well as our response to (or the products of) that condition;[62] (2) that the characteristics of the two views I identify as conflicting might properly each (or both) be seen as features of modernity—"we all remain Modernists (despite our desires for a 'post')";[63] and (3) that "the features often ascribed to modernity [e.g., antitraditionalism] are not always peculiar to the 'modern' age, however it is defined [e.g., post-Renaissance, post-Enlightenment, etc.]."[64] While few legal scholars would claim to be strictly traditional or unabashedly postmodern, since ideological precommitments are unbecoming, one often sees a tendency in legal-theoretical discourse either to identify with or to express great concern over postmodern approaches.[65]

Henry Sussman, in what appears to be an intellectual history of psychoanalysis rather than a critique of either Freud or Lacan, argues that they represent, respectively, the modern and the postmodern in psychoanalysis. Freud seems to share with literary modernists both the willingness to "shatter the formal specifications they inherited" and the yearning or nostalgia for coherence; Freud is also a modernist both in his willingness to admit unprecedented conceptual materials—fragments surviving from past cultures, scraps of memory—and in his search for structure "as the new basis for coherence".[66] "Freud begins the century as a structuralist, marshalling repetitive patterns in response to the seemingly impenetrable alogic prevalent within the construction of such phenomena as the dream-work and the joke."⁶⁷ Freud's complex description of the mind as "a field of forces and force transfers" containing material organized in terms of "strata, zones, and (discontinuous) lines" exemplifies, for Sussman, the structuralist project of modernism. Contrast Lacan, who in his selection of

> visual images or insignias for the operation of the psyche, bypasses those that would enforce the closed circuitry of the machine and gravitates toward the "impossible figure," such as anamorphosis, the "interior 8," and the gordian knot—examples leading to the heart of impenetrability, not out of the labyrinth.⁶⁸

All of the discontinuity of Freud's unconscious is carried over into Lacan, "but few of the machine-fittings that would connect various fitful and disparate motions."⁶⁹ Freudian drive (*Trieb*) reappears in Lacan, but not its satisfaction or completion—it "goes precisely nowhere."⁷⁰ The analyst is "no longer the guide and master ... [but] a partner in the discourse with the Other,"⁷¹ which (Other) belongs to no one—we all belong to its linguistic network. No wonder Sussman sees analogies with surrealist art, Beckett's plays, or Joyce's *Finnegan's Wake*: "The angel of history, in the post-modern climate, no longer longingly faces the past. Separations, divergences, and splits do not represent tragic shatterings of various unities, but are merely facts of life."⁷²

Notwithstanding the apparent fashionability of postmodern approaches, Lacanian scholars generally do not view the categorization of Lacan as surreal or post-structuralist as favorable. As to Lacan's surrealism, Jacques-Alain Miller maintains that such analogies are mistaken,⁷³ although he concedes that Lacan's "seemingly inconsistent and cryptic" texts require "hours and hours of reading and rereading."⁷⁴ Upon deciphering, however, the theory is "supported by a tightly woven argument where every sentence is a consistent statement."⁷⁵ Miller often writes of Lacan in such glowing terms, but the polemical tone might be forgiven in the face of contemporary assessments of Lacan as an eccentric artist, not a psychoanalytic theorist.

The association of Lacan with poststructuralism—which movement is associated with postmodern tendencies among literary critics—is also a matter of concern for students of Lacan. Slavoj Zizek's "Why Lacan is not a 'Post-Structuralist'"⁷⁶ is both a critique of poststructural theses and an effort to distinguish Lacan's similar-sounding statements. Both Lacan and the poststructuralists, for example, suggest "there isn't any metalanguage," but, Zizek asks, isn't the poststructuralist position just a little bit too convenient? To put it more rudely, the position from which the deconstructivist can always make sure of the fact that "there isn't any metalanguage," that no utterance can say precisely what it intended to say; that the process of enunciation always subverts the utterance, is *the position of metalanguage* in its purest, most radical form.[77]

Lacan, Zizek argues, eludes this "deadlock" by making metalanguage an entity of the Real, of the impossible—Lacan *really means* there is no metalanguage:

> [In the] post-structuralist understanding.... [o]rdinary language is its own metalanguage. It is self-referential.... "There isn't any metalanguage" is actually taken, then, to mean *its exact opposite: that there is not any pure object-language*, any language that would function as a purely transparent medium for the designation of the pre-given reality.[78]

Lacan, however, takes the impossibility of metalanguage literally—all language is object-language: "Even when the language is seemingly caught in a web of self-referential movement, even when it is seemingly only about itself, there is an objective, non-signifying 'reference' to this movement."[79] In another formulation of Lacan,

> No formalized language ... is epistemologically privileged in relation to what it describes, and no language can be reduced to a superstructure, for it is an infinite web which Lacan described as impossible to scan with any model. What can be ascertained are effects of the unconscious in language. The word can be taken materially as the building cell of identity and cognition.[80]

Even in these fragments taken from the defense of Lacan against poststructuralist affiliations, one might sense that Lacan wants it both ways—just as he out-postmoderns the postmoderns (there *really is* no metalanguage), he seems to reintroduce the dread "metaphysics of presence": the world of identifiable objects, of discernible laws, and of ascertainable effects. This feature of Lacanian theory draws the criticism (a final barrier to the potential enthusiasm among legal scholars in search of fresh insights) that Lacan is not postmodern at all—he's just a traditional thinker in postmodern garb.

Lacan the Traditionalist

> The teachings of Lacan ... appear old fashioned today, like the remote island of science fiction whereon dinosaurs still flourish.... He repeats the most questionable gestures of the major structuralists, especially the staged resignation before some vast systematic

determinism, which turns out to be, since we are supposed to know the "laws" of this system, another way of worshipping reason.
—William Kerrigan, "Terminating Lacan"

The critique of Lacan as traditional takes two distinct forms—the first treats Lacanian theory as postmodern, but then identifies the "traditional" assumptions of postmodern literary theory; the second initiates a postmodern critique of Lacan. Norman Holland, an example of the first type of critic, argues that the disappearance of the self in postmodern theory—the subject is only a fiction—is accompanied by a return to the text as the place of meaning, of "activity," reminiscent of the now old New Criticism:[81]

> True, for the older critics the text creates its own unity, while for the newer ones the text creates its own disunity. For both, however, it is the text that does the work. We are dealing with the old New Critics and the new Old Critics. Or the New Cryptics, to judge from the style which many of them aspire to—and achieve.[82]

Lacan's "New Cryptical" theory of the subject constituted by language, for Holland, is based on an outdated notion of language (Saussure's) and results in an outdated behavioristic psychology—Chomsky already disproved both.[83] The Lacanian response to such charges is predictable—Holland fails, for example, to take account of Lacan's extensive revision of Saussure.[84] Nevertheless, Holland presents a substantial challenge to postmodern theory, basing his critique not on traditional theory, but on contemporary linguistic models, brain research, and cognitive psychology. Holland writes in the unfamiliar—among literary theorists—voice of empirical science.

Postmodern voices—less enamored of the canons of rationalism—can also be heard criticizing Lacan—*as* a rationalist! William Kerrigan, for example, credits Lacan for his structuralist innovations, but then joins those who view structuralism as "the latest edition of western rationalism[:] if we cannot fulfill the rationalist desire to see reality naked because language keeps getting in the way, then perhaps we can develop a special science for seeing language itself naked."[85] Lacanian theory betrays, in this account, the metaphysics of structuralist theory—Lacan turns the obvious and uncontroversial recognition of structure in language into an indefensible quest for Law, for universals. (Derrida's critique of Lacan[86] is, roughly, a more sophisticated but more esoteric version of Kerrigan's argument.) The particular relevance of this evaluation for social theorists is its implication that Lacan is too theoretical, "airy," or global:

> It is increasingly evident today that we ... best appreciate the power of language ... by attending to the local matter of how it is used, what language-games are, how language functions in specific activities. About this down-to-earth, pragmatic sense of discourse Lacan has not an inkling.[87]

Colin MacCabe made a similar argument over a decade ago—briefly, that Lacan ignores the "actual sites of language use (the family, the school, the workplace)"[88]—but MacCabe was later accused of succumbing

> to the temptation of finding fault in Lacan where there is no fault to be found.... Indeed, the aim of Lacanian psychoanalysis is to unveil the specificity of a given Other(A) ["A" is for "*Autre*"] text in its relationship to its own *je* [or "speaking subject"] conventions and to the specificity of its *moi* [or "identificatory subject"].[89]

Adherents of Lacanian theory are anxious to distinguish Lacan from French university intellectuals—"Lacan was a practicing psychoanalyst, after having been trained as a psychiatrist, not as a student in philosophy."[90] Sustaining the argument that Lacan has no inkling of everyday relations is difficult; even among Lacanian literary theorists, I have found an attentiveness to the clinical aspect of psychoanalysis as the source of Lacan's fundamental insights. On the other hand, one cannot talk as though Lacan was not highly theoretical, even philosophical.

Beyond the Barriers

Several different assessments could follow from the foregoing "introduction" to Lacan. Pessimistically, one might conclude that Lacan's enigmatic presentation allows too many (inconsistent) interpretations for his theory to be of any use in law. However, one might also conclude that Lacan challenges those who would seek easily to categorize (and then to dispense with) him. If you dislike Lacan's dependency on Freud or his tendency toward traditional metaphysics, stand by, for adherents of Lacanian theory will demonstrate his careful avoidance of both. If, on the other hand, you dislike postmodern revisions of psychoanalytic theory, consider Lacan's fidelity to Freudian texts and his implied critique of postmodern antifoundationalism. In any event, the successful appropriation of Lacan in law will not likely falter simply because Lacanian theory is the subject of criticism—the question is not whether to become a "disciple," but whether the discourse generated by Lacan's texts offers helpful insights for the discipline of law.

Lacanian theory intersects, quite clearly, some of the major debates in contemporary legal theory. While my purpose in the first few chapters (part 1) of this book is to introduce several fundamental notions in Lacan that are employed in the more complex analyses in part 2, Lacan's relevance for legal theory is identified early on. As I explain in chapter 2, Lacanian theory includes an account of the function of law itself—as "a fundamental category of thought of all known human societies"[91]—which suggests an entry point for Lacan into law and society, law and literature, and critical legal discourses concerning the social, literary, and ideological aspects of law (discussed in chapters 5–7). Moreover, the "interpretive turn" in contemporary legal theory remains controversial, not only because the promised escape from metaphysics is in doubt,[92] but because the stability of law—a textual practice—is called into question. Lacan's current impact in literary theory, discussed in chapter 3, reflects a perceived relevance of his views on the central problems of meaning in language. Finally, Lacanian psychoanalytic theory includes both a sustained critique of conventional presumptions concerning, and a strikingly original account of, subjectivity.[93] Pierre Schlag, discussed in chapter 4, highlights the problem of the subject (more accurately, the failure to examine self-critically the presumed rational and autonomous subject of law) that plagues all major "modes of contemporary legal thought" (rule of law, critical legal studies, neopragmatism, and cultural conservatism).[94]

If the barriers to or misgivings about Lacan can be held in abeyance, several features of Lacanian theory invite reflection upon Lacan's understanding of legal institutions and processes. Patrick Colm Hogan points out, for example, that Lacan uses a juridical model for psychoanalysis—analysis is a *procès*, a proceeding or sort of inquest.[95] The Lacanian analyst attends more to the analysand's relation to the laws of psychic and linguistic structures than to the medical ideal of developmental normalcy. Desire is manifested in speech (for example, in the analysand's speech) as a *demand*, an appeal or legal request. Far more important for law, however, than Lacan's analogy of psychoanalysis to a legal proceeding, are his conceptions of the Other as the place of social convention, of the symbolic *order* of language, of the subject, and of the Law *as*, and not simply *in*, culture and language. The first three of these conceptions are discussed in greater detail in the next three "introductory" chapters, and each conception has its parallel in legal scholarship. My remarks on law as culture appear in the first two chapters of part 2.

Given the breadth of, and the interdisciplinary interest generated by, Lacanian theory, examples of Lacan's relevance for law could easily multiply. Moreover, in addition to the direct engagement with Lacan suggested below (in my limited examples), any successful new interventions of psychoanalysis in law (which are not, of course, ensured) will likely involve recourse to the example of Lacanian theory. Finally, partial appropriations of Lacan in support of critical theories of law as gendered, ideological or textual are evident and may continue (though Lacan often fares poorly as an aid to feminism).[96] None of the aforementioned barriers to Lacan in law is decisive, or even unique to Lacanian theory; and while the conflicting substantive critiques of Lacan might suggest that Lacanian theory is in disarray, they also suggest that our conventional modes of categorization may be oversimplified—the substantive barriers ultimately reveal bridges between the oppositional discourses concerning Freud and postmodernism.

Conclusion

> For nobody is less demanding than a psychoanalyst as to what provides the status of his action, which he himself is not far from regarding as magical. This is because he is incapable of situating it in a conception of his field that he would not dream of according to his practice.
> —Jacques Lacan, "The Function and Field of Speech and Language in Psychoanalysis"

To claim that Lacan offers to legal theorists (unfamiliar with Lacanian theory) a framework of analysis that they've never dreamed of is perhaps misleading—Lacan's texts, for many readers, will be just like their dreams, if we associate dreams with confusing texts and multiple interpretations. Even if a compelling, "latent" interpretation of Lacan stabilizes his "manifest," dreamlike texts, that interpretation will be less than interesting to legal scholars if it simply reintroduces Freud (or established arguments against Freud) or postmodernism (or the traditional analyses challenged by postmodernism). Lacan, however, is clearly not more of the same; whether his differences will ensure his absence from or reception in law remains a question—*the* question for this book.

2

Networking with the Big O[ther]

> Following Freud I teach that the Other is the locus of that memory that he discovered and called the unconscious.
> —Jacques Lacan, "On a question preliminary to any possible treatment of psychosis"

> The fictions in an out-of-sight meaning system—the Other (A)—determine the socioconventional meaning of contracts, pacts, and laws from culture to culture. Meaning... is inherently relational, structural, and "self"-referential. And its roots lie in childhood cognition and resultant unconscious structure.
> —Ellie Ragland-Sullivan, *Jacques Lacan and the Philosophy of Psychoanalysis*

If this inquiry (into the relevance of Lacan for law) is anything—scholarly, scientific—at all, it is personal, implicatory. In trying to maintain a cautious distance from a theory—Lacan's—postulating that objectivity is an illusion, one fears to be only striking a pose. Surely, as I applied for law school admission, the law had not yet *captured*[1] me. Was it, then, in the early months of the first year of law school? Did I, later in my 1980s real estate practice, innocently sleepwalk through deals while speaking the discourse of the law as Other?[2] Do I nowadays (as a law professor) serve in the (unfunded) chair of the gatekeeper?[3] Finally, am I in this exercise approaching "dangerous ground"—"getting too close to" the sudden observation that my "consistency, [my] positivity, is dissolving itself"?[4] In each formulation, the personal is also intersubjective—social—since even the residue of self-dissolution is the network of language and of law.

The technical difficulties of reading Lacan,[5] discussed in chapter 1, are soon eclipsed by his more serious diagnosis of contemporary social, impliedly legal, practices and processes. The pathology of everyday life is comprehensively and yet intricately described, but the analyst of the cure—in the popular sense of the term—is virtually absent.[6] Because of our fundamental "dependency on language and speech,"[7] including unconscious language (the discourse of the Other), the cure is displaced by interpretation, by translation, of a text which "flows, evaporates, and oscillates."[8] Lacan, in a style intended to avoid oversimplifications and illusions of certainty, tells us what we are up against, and that *it is* ultimately indecipherable.

Lacanian theory presupposes an understanding of and return to Freud, yet such observations are alone not very helpful—Freudianism has come to mean too many things,[9] most of which Lacan rejects in his own extensive revisionism. Nevertheless, comparing and contrasting Lacan's Freud with others in the legal psychoanalytic tradition is, I think, an important first step on the way to assessing the value of Lacan for law. To sharpen the contrast, I focus below on certain, but in no sense most or all, Lacanian descriptions of human intersubjectivity, with an emphasis on the place of legal institutions and processes. (Note that Lacan's theories of language and the subject, summarized below, are discussed in greater detail in the next two chapters, and that the Name-of-the-Father, mentioned below in passing, as well as the "takings doctrine" used in my example of law practice, are explored in chapter 6.) At the risk of forgetting "in an intuitive image the analysis on which it is based,"[10] I include a series of didactic schemata that will be inadequate representations of anything other than the outline of this chapter.

Lacanian theory, as it is explicated and proves to be helpful to social theorists, will have meaning for legal scholarship beyond the scope of this book. My purpose in this chapter is to introduce a "concept"— the Other—and consider a slice of its "content"— legal processes and institutions—in order to understand an undeveloped "aspect" of Lacan's work. Each chapter that follows in part 1 will likewise begin with a Lacanian concept and suggest its undeveloped implications for law. Of course, I take seriously the warning of Ellie Ragland, one of Lacan's most lucid commentators:

> Let us beware... of grappling with Lacan's ideas by minimizing or oversimplifying them. Many... do exactly this. They latch onto a single idea; this, then, is erroneously taken to be the sum of Lacan's contribution to psychoanalysis, literary theory, or whatever.[11]

The sum of Lacan for the "whatever" of law is nowhere in sight.

I. APOLOGIES FOR FREUD

> [P]sychoanalysis as method, language and voice represents precisely that disordering or denial of unity and of control over meaning that law and doctrine exist to disallow, to cover over.
> —Peter Goodrich, "Psychoanalysis in Legal Education"

Recall that we credit Freud with many concepts that have become "common sense,"[12] four of which are especially relevant to psychoanalytic approaches to law.

First, we recognize sexuality or sexual desire as a social force; when we pay attention to that which is seemingly an individual and private matter, we realize that sexuality reflects social repression, that "normal" sexuality is not biological (except in the narrowest sense),[13] and that society organizes even our instincts.[14] This is much more than a reduction of life to the erotic, of which Freud was accused.[15]

Second, we acknowledge that our desires, our needs, and our motivations are often hidden. Freud identified an unconscious into which painful or embarrassing desires and ideas are driven or repressed, such that reality is distorted or denied.[16]

Third, we talk about such matters. Freud promised access to the dynamics of mental life through an analytic method; other methods have gained prominence, but Freud's promise remains a turning point in intellectual history.[17]

Fourth, we understand that the first three concepts are significant for our understanding of society. The reason that some social theorists employ psychoanalysis is that a picture emerges as to how the social world constructs the human subject and reproduces ideological patterns—society does not merely affect our otherwise individual and mental experiences, it actually forms them.[18]

TRADITIONAL APPROACHES

With respect to the use of Freud's concepts in legal theory, consider the following representation:

ego--------------------seeks *law* as a
                                father-substitute
_____

  id: desire

In designating this scheme as "traditional," I have in mind Jerome Frank in the 1930s and Professor Schoenfeld nowadays. Frank identified the basic social *myth* that law is precise and coherent, and then analogized (1) a child's search for security and authority in his or her father, and (2) society's craving for finality and rules.[19] We are unwilling,

Frank observed, to concede that law is biased, thus we delude ourselves into thinking that we are governed by reason.[20] Frank acknowledged that his explanation was only partial,[21] and the radical implications of his analysis were thereafter, it seems, ignored by most legal scholars. Psychoanalysis was soon welcomed into sociolegal theory as *just another* helpful insight, and even then it was often regarded as superficial.[22] Much "law and social psychoanalysis" literature betrays an obsessional fear that psychoanalysis will be misused.[23] After all, Freud has been discredited by mainstream psychology and psychiatry.[24] The message is usually: use Freud sparingly.[25]

By the time we reach Schoenfeld, psychoanalytic explanations of sociolegal phenomena are tentative and simplistic.[26] For example, the growing acceptance of judicial review (of congressional law) in the decades immediately following the Civil War *might* be explained by the citizenry's "unconscious wish for parental direction" after a traumatic event.[27] To underscore how speculative this is, Schoenfeld concedes that he has failed in his explanation to consider the insights of sociology, political science, history, and economics.[28] Schoenfeld apologizes for Freud, but is hardly an apologist.

THE SKEPTICAL APPROACH

For want of a better term to describe a much more sophisticated use of psychoanalytic sociolegal categories, I identify as skeptical the contemporary uses of Freud by some legal scholars. I have in mind Charles Lawrence's recent critique of equal protection laws, which takes Freud seriously.[29] I should also mention, in the category of sophisticated analyses, Bienenfeld in the 1950s[30] and Ehrenzweig in the 1960s,[31] both enthusiastic proponents of psychoanalytic jurisprudence, but a current example—represented below—will suffice.

> conscious racism------------eliminated
>   by *law*
> _____
> unconscious racism

Lawrence sees the ideology of equal opportunity as a symptom, a defense mechanism for emotional disturbances.[32] That is, we feel the tensions between (1) a social order in which racism persists, and (2) our ideals of equality, and we resolve those tensions by a selective perception of social and legal realities.[33] When equal protection laws, for example, require a finding of discriminatory intent to establish unlawful discrimination, only conscious racism will be eliminated.[34]

Unconscious racism, due to this intentionalist scheme, maintains unequal treatment throughout society.

Lawrence shows how we repress, that is, how we think and act contrary to, personal and cultural morality. There is a remnant of (the Freudian neo-Marxist) Marcuse here—"repression from without is maintained by repression from within."[35] Nevertheless, Lawrence feels compelled to qualify his argument by clarifying that he is not defending psychoanalysis as definitive—he is only using, he says, its conceptual vocabulary.[36]

CRITICAL LEGAL STUDIES

It is not until the appearance of the eclectic Critical Legal Studies movement that Freudian categories are fearlessly employed. The neo-Marxian and structuralist traditions that inform much that we call critical legal scholarship were less concerned with how psychoanalysis fared within the psychiatric establishment.

social self---------------*established by law*

unconscious desire

I have in mind Peter Gabel's work when I diagram the split between the social self and desire, which is the split between the knowledge the subject has of himself and the subject.[37] (The similarity of this aspect of Gabel's approach with R. D. Laing's "divided self" is worth noting, because Lacan's theory of subjectivity is an indirect critique of the idea of "true" and "false" selves.)[38] The unconscious desire identified by Gabel is the desire for confirmation and connectedness.[39] Families unwittingly throw children into a series of roles that in each case alienate the child from his or her desire, a desire that is repressed to maintain such roles.[40] Politicians, in turn, feed this desire with fantasies.[41] Most important for the present inquiry, legal culture mediates between individual and national needs to create a collective, social denial.[42] Law is seen by nearly everyone as authoritative, which for Gabel evidences a projection by underconfirmed subjects.[43]

Other critical legal scholars have characterized legal thought as a form of denial,[44] or emphasized the *unconscious* self-construction of legal reality,[45] but Gabel is much more systematic in setting forth the contours of a sociolegal psychoanalysis. The social self, in Gabel's scheme, loses contact with unconscious desire; this alienation or blockage results from a *privatization* of desire, that is, a repetitive denial of its social dimension.[46] Significantly, Gabel's work is based in part on the theories of Jacques Lacan, though Gabel is also a critic of Lacan.[47]

LACAN, FREUD'S APOLOGIST

> By way of "fixing our ideas" and the souls suffering here, I will apply the [subject's relation to the Other] to schema L.
> —Jacques Lacan, "On a question preliminary to any possible treatment of psychosis"

SCHEMA L

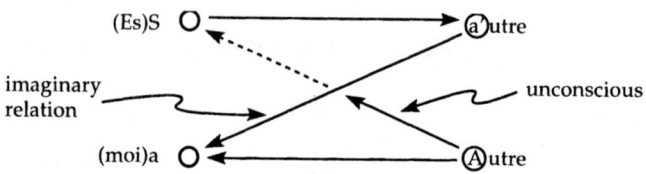

Lacan's quadripartite *Schema L*,[48] while useful to illustrate certain features of (1) his theory of the structure of human intersubjectivity, as well as (2) his famous concept of the "mirror stage" of infant development,[49] in no way *captures* Lacanian psychoanalysis.[50] The Scheme was never intended to be a reductionistic theory in itself.[51] Moreover, dozens of revised schemata appear in the writings of Lacan and his commentators, each one trying to illustrate a few isolated relationships in the overly complex field of human culture.

In a 1955 seminar in Paris,[52] Lacan distinguished the "other," or *autre* ("which is the ego" in the sense that it is coupled with the ego, as an alter-ego), from the "Other," or *Autre*, which concerns the function of speech.[53] Then, turning to Schema L, he identified "(Es)S" as

> the subject, not in its totality, but in its opening up....
> He sees himself in [moi] *a*, and that is why he has an ego. He may believe that this ego is him, everybody is at that stage, and there is no way of getting out of it.[54]

The ego, *moi(a)* on the scheme, perceives "its fellow being," in the form of the specular other, which "has a very close relation to the ego [and] can be superimposed on it, and we write it as *a'*."[55] Notwithstanding this identification with those we see and address (in speech), "authentically intersubjective relations exist," and we in fact speak to true Others, true subjects.[56] But they

> are on the other side of the wall of language, there where in principle I never reach them.

[Thus] analysis consists in getting [the analysand] to become conscious of his relations ... with all these Others who are his true interlocutors, whom he hasn't recognized.[57]

Several years later, Lacan remarked that the subject "is stretched over the four corners of the Schema."[58] Thus the subject is "a network of identificatory and linguistic relations."[59]

Although *Schema L* is superseded by other schemata in Lacan's later seminars,[60] it sketches some of the fundamental features of the Lacanian return to Freud. Instead of attempting to explicate further the notions introduced in *Schema L* by reference to psychic disorders or the pathology of everyday life, the remainder of my discussion of Lacan locates the scheme in the field of law.

I offer below a translation of the *Schema L*, one of many possible translations, that emphasizes the place of legal processes and institutions in Lacanian theory, even though my emphasis was rarely Lacan's, and even though he did not use his *Schema L* in those rare instances.

LAW AS OTHER

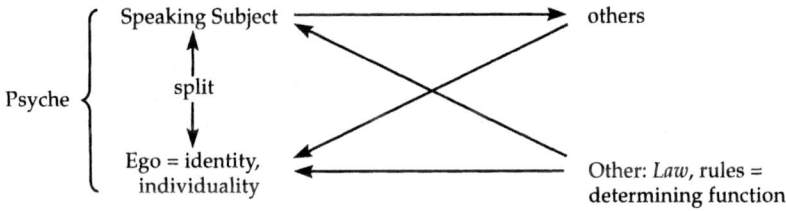

Several features of a scheme I call "Law as Other" are significant for sociolegal theory:

Where It Was

> Where it was, the *Ich*—the subject... must come into existence. And there is only one method of knowing that one is there, namely, to map the network.
> —Jacques Lacan, *The Four Fundamental Concepts of Psychoanalysis*

On the lefthand side of the scheme, there is no simple conscious/unconscious distinction, and no ego in control of an id.[61] Lacan firmly rejected the later Freud's emphasis on a socially adaptive ego that masters its environment.[62] For Lacan, the ego misconstrues, neglects, and ignores—the legendary short session of analysis with Lacan ended, sometimes after a few minutes, when the ego would begin to lie.[63]

The arrowed lines from others/Other in the scheme point *to* the ego or self, which only *assumes* an image of control.

This misrecognizing—*méconnaissance*—function of the Lacanian ego is developed by Gabel in his account of collective repression and denial of our social dimension in the face of legal culture. Legal processes and institutions provide social roles and identities that are assumed, maintained, and reproduced in a cycle of projection (of legal authority) and denial ("privatization" of desire).[64] Thus "the social function of law is not to be found in its direct effect on socio-economic activity, but rather in its effect on people's minds."[65]

Lacan, significantly, is critical of the idea of a "mind" that is "affected," and even of the idea of an ego (even one that distorts reality, that is, not Freud's adaptive ego) that is unified as against the outside world.[66]

The Social Network

> [The] expression *resistance of the subject* too much implies the existence of a supposed ego and it is not certain whether—at the approach of [what Freud calls a] nucleus—it is something we can justifiably call an ego.
> —Jacques Lacan, *The Four Fundamental Concepts of Psychoanalysis*

For Lacan, there is not réally an ego or self at all in the Freudian sense, not only because its fundamental function is misunderstanding (*not* control),[67] but because it is a mirage.[68] The ego is a mere image of a self.[69] (Thus the ego is often termed "zero" by Lacanian theorists, and by the time an identity ("one") is received, the ego has become dependent upon culture, or in sociolegal terms, has been captured by the system of laws.)[70] The subject that appears on the surface to be unified is split in the diagram between the subject of speech and the identificatory function, both of which function at conscious and unconscious "levels," and both of which would more accurately be splintered into hundreds of variations.[71] The subject is a network of relations of need and demand with many *others*—family members, friends, colleagues, boss, analyst. Again, the arrowed lines depict significations *received from* language, from other people, and from the Big "O" *Other*—we are bound to the social structure, the right-hand side of the scheme, the "outside-within-us" that gives us identity and purpose through signs and social practices. We even get an idealized image, a mis-recognition, of autonomy and freedom.

The Other

> I make [a division] by opposing, in relation to the entrance of the unconscious, the two fields of the subject and the Other.
> —Jacques Lacan, *The Four Fundamental Concepts of Psychoanalysis*

As to the "Other," the term has multiple meanings for Lacan and his disciples, but it is typically exterior as well as determinative.[72] It is initially the place of the parents, especially the father as the initial representative of law,[73] and it is therefore the place from which language is received—the outside from which we are named. As parents lose their hold on discourse, the Other is the community, the place of social order or rules of discourse that we internalize.[74] Primarily, for Lacan, the Other is unconscious discourse, the place of Desire, and is therefore analogous to the discourse of our dreams and slips of the tongue[75]—in Freudian terms, the place of clarity and truth.[76]

The ambiguity of the term "Other" appears intentional in Lacan's work, and even its "definitions" (e.g., the unconscious is the discourse of the Other, desire is the Desire of the Other, the mother is the real Other, the father is the symbolic Other, the Other is the locus of the signifier) are ambiguous. Translator Anthony Wilden, sensitive to these ambiguities, nevertheless suspects

> that the substitution of the words "the unconscious" for "the Other" in many of Lacan's formulations will produce an adequate translation, provided it is remembered that the unconscious in question may be the unconscious of [a specific] other or the "collective" unconscious.[77]

In the second sense, "the locus of socially approved hostilities, illusions, and identifications, could not be otherwise than collective."[78] The notion of the Other is helpful in locating hidden or repressed rules that govern discourse, even legal discourse.

In addition, Wilden suggests that Otherness as a methodological category is useful to designate our limited control over the content of our speech and less over its reception.[79] There is also in the term "Other" a sense of "thirdness" in the transindividual mediating function of language between two subjects.[80]

The importance of language for Lacan, not as a theory of communication but as a structure, can hardly be overestimated (unless one views Lacan as reductionistic with respect to linguistics): "[Man] thinks as a consequence of the fact that a structure, that of language—the word implies it—a structure carves up his body, a structure that has nothing to do with anatomy."[81] The unconscious itself "is structured like a language," and the circular relation between the subject and the Other is characterized by the effect of the signifier "produced in the field of the Other."[82]

The Constitutive Signifier

> The Other is the locus in which is situated the chain of the signifier that governs whatever may be made present of the subject—it is

the field of that living being in which the subject has to appear.
—Jacques Lacan, *The Four Fundamental Concepts of Psychoanalysis*

The *moi* (or what I have called the Ego) in the lower lefthand corner includes for Lacan the ego and the id in the Freudian ego/id/super-ego topology.[83] Freud's super-ego, historically associated with internalized social morality and other ideals, is now the mechanism that represses the *moi* and forms the split-off social speaking subject.[84] This mechanism is the equivalent of a system of language and law,[85] and might be represented by the arrowed lines from the Other to the (split) subject. Again, however, the social network is early in life internalized[86] and is not just an *outsider* to which the subject submits.

The focus on the structure of language as constitutive of the subject has its basis in Freud's conception of the unconscious (which discloses itself in the talking cure and in everyday speech), in the effect on infants of their introduction into language, and in the agency of symbols identified by linguistics and semiotics. Lacan designates the "signifier," which is produced in the field of the Other (the locus of the chain of signifiers), as that which governs the subject in his social relations, which reduces the subject "to being no more than a signifier," which petrifies the subject "in the same movement in which it calls the subject to function, to speak, as subject."[87] The signifier here does not represent a signified object, but "represents a subject for another signifier."[88] In another formulation, "subjects meet only through *their* representatives signifiers."[89] Signifiers include language itself ("signifiers proliferate to infinity—sound and concept combinations being infinite"),[90] but in the Other, "the discrete articulations of one's identity exist as 'pure signifiers' concerning birth, love, procreation, and death."[91] The Name-of-the-Father, the *symbolic* father, is such a pure signifier; Lacan identifies this "person" as the figure of law, and remarks that the symbolic father "constitutes the law of the Signifier."[92] In various formulations of Lacan's commentators, the symbolic father "is one of the minimal elements of any signifying network whatever,"[93] it "is equivalent to culture (including language) itself."[94] Note that in Lacanian theory, the subject is dependant on the field of the Other, but that field is reducible neither to conscious discourse nor to an unconscious seat of instincts.

Although "Lacan's use of the word 'signifier' may be more than usually ambiguous,"[95] it is clear that the distinction between signifiers—like "man" or "woman"—and *pure* signifiers does not imply two signifying networks. Lacan is concerned that the subject of analysis find "what signifier—to what irreducible, traumatic, nonmeaning—he is, as a subject, subjected."[96]

Ordinary Language

> When the subject talks to his fellow beings, he uses ordinary language, which holds the imaginary egos to be . . . real.
> —Jacques Lacan, *Seminar*, Book 2

The Speaking Subject functions to *represent* itself, but in fact masks itself. It is a mechanism of defense and denial, pretending to be independent of the Other, while in actuality its language is imprinted with cultural myths.[97]

For Lacan, the Speaking Subject functions primarily to place the desires and identifications of the Ego (*moi*) into the mediating system of language and of "a law which is already quite ready to encompass the history of each individual":[98] "Although the narcissistic and aggressive structure of the *moi* pushes it to obliterate differences and perpetuate identificatory sameness, the subject of language and meaning tempers these intentions by rules and cultural conventions."[99] The subject thus "inhabits the world of the symbol, that is to say a world of others who speak."[100] Collective experience and social needs are preceded by the field of language, which field is activated for each individual by the speaking subject who circulates the signifiers that organize human relations.[101]

Intrasubjective Relations

> In so far as the subject brings them into relation with his own image, those with whom he speaks are also with whom he identifies.
> —Jacques Lacan, *Seminar*, Book 2

Finally, note the arrowed line from others to the identificatory ego, representing the gaze or desire to which the ego responds in constructing its self-image. The momentary distances that are maintained in the scheme, however, are an attempt to map the subject in its own relations, and not in relation to "reality."[102] The network of intrasubjective relations does not divide into inside and outside, nor even into conscious and unconscious functions. Lacan defined the unconscious as "the sum of the effects of speech on the subject, at the level at which the subject constitutes himself out of the effects of the signifier."[103] Language, including the discourse of the Other, is constitutive of Lacan's subject, which is neither a substance nor a biological being nor a "being possessing knowledge."[104] On the left side of the scheme (the Ego and Speaking Subject), there is no independent "self," and on the right side (the other and Other), there is no "otherness" in the sense of an optional relation.

At the obvious risk of rushing to find "practical" applications of Lacanian theory for sociolegal analysis,[105] or, worse yet, of appearing to move "beyond" Lacan before we have come to terms with the richness of his systematic description of our sociality, I begin to consider below the potential of Lacanian theory for analysis of the institutions of legal education and of the practice of law. My tentativeness is not, however, a critique of Lacan, but is rather a self-critical move.

Intuitive Images of Law

> Lacan's teaching requires us to hold many conceptual balls in the air at the same time. How does one align myth, body, organs, cultural ideals, and ideas as they cohere and change in each subject?
> —Ellie Ragland-Sullivan, "The Sexual Masquerade"

Law School

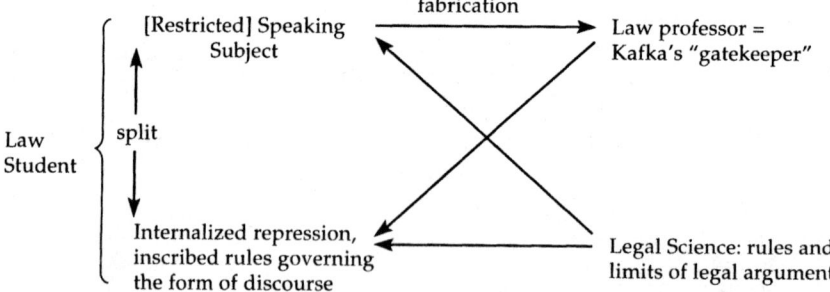

The diagram above is based (roughly) upon Peter Goodrich's analysis (which he did *not* schematize) of legal education in Great Britain.[106] Goodrich uses Lacan (as well as Kristeva and others) to demonstrate that law schools make exemplary patients for social psychoanalysis. The analysand resists such an analysis, of course,[107] but in the everyday discourse of the institution you hear the fabrications of the speaking subject as it attempts to stabilize the ego, as the rules of law are internalized.[108] In the law school context, the professor (allegedly) has what is desired, while the law in the Other provides the empowering signifiers. (Again, the diagram reflects a particular emphasis—mine—on the law professor as an *other*;[109] the relationships would change slightly if the other is a fellow student, a parent, or an interviewer from a law firm.)

The diagram is intended to identify the strange relationships of a split subject with others and the Other, in a context where those relationships really matter. The law student, in his or her desire to be desired, *must* speak to and identify with the professor, and *must* (for that relationship to "work") both internalize the legal conventions of the Other *and* repress extracurricular concerns. Significantly, this is not to say that Legal Science is in fact stable—many critics of legal education who never attended law school erroneously believe that we teach rigorous logic and unchanging rules, that we think in terms of absolutes, and that we require a "single answer" to each of our classroom questions. We clearly do not, but neither do we teach that "anything goes"; the critics are therefore not altogether wrong, because legal education does tend to produce a particular way of thinking and talking about law. Antithetical arguments abound in law, but the form or style of argument is more carefully guarded. An example of how courts stand ready to hear opposing arguments, but will not hear just any argument, may be helpful in clarifying that the dualism between absolutes and "anything goes" is not very helpful.

In his account of the dispute between Western Forest Ltd. and the Haida Indians concerning logging rights on Lyell Island (off the coast of British Columbia),[110] Goodrich notes that the first issue for the Supreme Court of British Columbia was whether the Haida Indians needed legal assistance, that is, "whose speech was to be heard within the institution?"[111]

> Such is always the first question of law, that of authority and qualification for legitimate speech, but here it... was the key question of representation in its fullest sense: how and by what means, by what insignia and in which words... will I appear before the law.[112]

The Haida Indians appeared with "symbolic dress, mythologies, masks and totem poles as well as with... legends, stories, poems [and] songs"; they appealed "to natural justice, to the law of nature"; and they lost:[113] "The court would not compare mythologies... because to do so would raise questions of its 'self,' of the social and mythic constructions of its own body, its social role and actions, its own clothes."[114] The alien and obsolete language and techniques of "a closely guarded and professionally governed register" take years, in law school, to acquire.[115]

Beyond the law school setting, in society generally—as the Haida case illustrates—the law in the Other issues *appropriate* symbolic masks, words, that make social speech possible.[116] Pierre Legendre, whose work is influenced by Lacan, thus explains the importance of psychoanalysis to the study of law:

> [Psychoanalysis] requires one to take note of the mythical side of the subjective order and carefully consider the fact that structural constructions of normativity, which are concerned with the human subject who is endowed with an unconscious, necessarily deal with unconscious representations.[117]

Even so, Legendre warns that psychoanalysis provides no scientific explanation of legal institutions, and he suggests caution with "psychoanalytic theories of social and political—especially juridical life."[118] Freud's theories, nevertheless, allow us to see the link between the Name-of-the-Father (the "metaphor of the Reference" or pure signifier in the Other) and the principle of Reason (that which grounds law), which principle "is a social production."[119]

Legendre's modesty is, to me, appealing, because the promise of psychoanalytic approaches is not to provide an easy answer to the complex question of how law works. It *is* easy to see that legal doctrine is unstable, and that law is a highly political and social affair. Nevertheless, legal doctrine offers, at times, stability, and it is not enough to say that it does so with political and social support (as if that "support" is clearly distinguishable from the genealogy of the doctrine). Citizens rely on law, but are generally not shocked when courts make mistakes, become politicized or reverse prior law. The question is how law works, and anything less than a complicated picture involving education, institutions, social convention, unconscious processes, and the operation of language would be of little value to the inquiry. Turning now to the practice of law, Lacan's psychoanalytic Scheme "takes note" of some of its less obvious features, its mythical side.

Law Practice

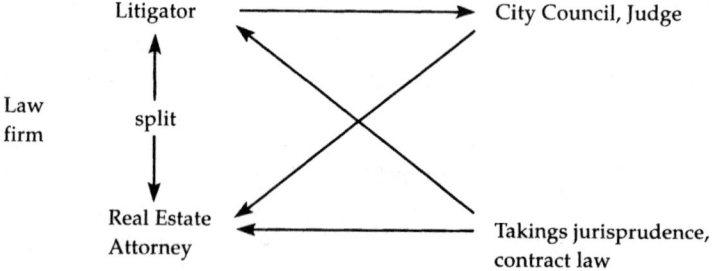

In this diagram I have in mind, first, the problem of the incoherency of the constitutional law prohibiting "regulatory takings" (that is, governmental land use regulations so restrictive as to constitute confiscation) without compensation, an incoherency reproduced in the dozens of law review articles that try to clarify Supreme Court jurisprudence,[120] and reproduced as well in city council chambers wherein litigators fabricate the takings doctrine. Peter Goodrich, informed by Legendre's historical analysis of law, notes that the role of the jurist in the history of the West "was to make the law human, to fabricate a social reality from the Other world of the text."[121] The outcome of regulatory takings cases rests primarily on stories which appeal to unconscious beliefs about greedy developers and helpless municipalities, or vice versa.[122] That is, if the landowner or developer is perceived as desiring to destroy the environment, and the municipality or other regulator is perceived as trying to protect human health and welfare, limitations on land use will not likely be viewed as confiscatory. Likewise, if property rights are glorified and regulation is perceived as interference by overly intrusive government, the regulation may be characterized under the Constitution as a compensable "taking." Any stability offered by law, however, is constructed, since in almost all cases the desire of the developer, the requirement of human welfare, the existence of property "rights," and the limits on governmental intrusion are all contestable, unstable. (I include, in chapter 6, a Lacanian analysis of a recent regulatory takings case.)

In choosing this example, I am following the lead of Joan Copjec, who has attempted to introduce Lacan's theory into discussions concerning the critique of institutions:

> Lacan raises serious questions for those critiques which take institutions—[e.g.,] urban planning ... —as social spaces in which already existing antagonisms are played out, interests are denied or fulfilled, values upheld or denigrated.[123]

Like Gabel, Copjec sees a tendency to "privatize" human intersubjectivity, and thereby "fail to take account of the determining action of the institution itself and of the way its operations exceed any intersubjective intention or effect."[124] Lacanian theory highlights the failures, the accidents, of the conscious intentions of lawyers and judges.

A second example is the myth of equal bargaining power in real estate financing, that is, the rule or presumption of contract law that, with respect to agreements signed by sophisticated parties, certifies that the parties had equal bargaining power.[125] Courts generally believe that a borrower freely negotiates its loan agreement.[126] This myth actually limits the conceivable outcomes of lender liability cases until juries—not educated to believe in the myth—are introduced.[127] *Everyone* knows that loan documents lie in wait for borrowers—the forms are never the result of arm's-length negotiation.

In both examples, the desire of the subject (for a particular outcome) is named or mediated by the order of law and language that encompasses the subject. The result of the litigation is neither in the control of the law firm nor caused in some direct fashion by the text of the law. Rather, a network of identity, fabrication, naming, and signifiers (which represent the subject) limits both the power of the lawyers to rely on legal doctrine *and* the power of the doctrine to govern the outcome. The Other is not only the source of doctrine, but the place of myths concerning developers (innocent business people *or* plagues on the environment) and borrowers (sophisticated negotiators *or* innocent business people). The name given in the field of the Other will constitute the subject of law.

The "split" between litigation counsel and transactional attorneys, which exists in nearly every law firm as a result of specialization trends, can be seen as a split between the Speaking Subject (the function of speech in court is reserved for litigators) and the Ego who assumes the image of control, of planning, of identifying with and desiring the law of those in authority, but who is always "tempered" by the Speaking Subject. Both "sides" of the firm take their cues—the signifiers that will constitute their practice—from the field of the Other, in which (collapsing the scheme) they appear.

The above interpretation is only an attempt to clarify Lacan's theory of the subject, the Other and their network of relations. Such an interpretation is, of course, never a mere description; in another sense, however, Lacanian theory is an attempt at description of our sociality. Once, in a seminar in which Lacan was describing the importance of language in structuring the desires of the subject, a member of the audience commented that human politics comes about on the basis of language, by which knowledge is exchanged; another member of the audience said something about Hegelian logic. Lacan stopped the discussion with the remark: "All this is pre-political. I simply want to help you be clear about the importance of the name."[128]

Conclusion

My primary focus is not on the details of the last three schemata (Law as Other, Law School, Law Practice), but on the observation that each represents a pathological problem, not a solution or cure. Each represents an assessment of what we are up against. Each explains, in a preliminary fashion, why change or progress for Lacan is a slow and complex process. Rational or autonomous control is out of the question—we *need* legal and social processes because they are us, they are the field in which we exist. Unconscious belief is curable, but belief is not. Lacan, however, allows for the possibility of beginning to select what we take from others, from society, and from law.[129] Peter Goodrich identifies psychoanalysis itself as offensive to social systems, and he follows Lacan in recommending self-subversive styles of writing and of life.¹³⁰ Less optimistic Lacanians see only a tragic choice between "alienation into language" and inability to function socially.¹³¹ Lacan, indeed, emphasized the potentially bankrupting price to be paid for knowledge—our consistency, our illusionary substance or enjoyment, might dissolve.¹³²

Does Lacan help those who try to rise above inadequate and simplistic critiques of legal ideology, or does he ruin the project by demonstrating how little self is left in the social-to-the-core subject? That question is addressed in the next two chapters; here I simply note Lacan's attractive willingness to acknowledge our state of affairs.

3

Legal Language: Meanings in the Gaps, Gaps in the Meanings

Consider the idea that Jacques Lacan sees psyche as text ("the unconscious is structured like a language") as opposed to Derrida's understanding of text as psyche (the unconscious is *operative in* language).[1] While many aspects of Lacanian theory are dense and elusive, the contention that the unconscious is made up of words—that it is a place of discourse and not simply desire—is particularly unfamiliar. The purpose of this chapter is to reintroduce, by reference to legal texts, Lacan's notion that texts do not *contain* meaning—a common enough proposition nowadays—but take on meaning in concealment of an unconscious system of repressed meanings.[2]

While I hope to show by my examples (in this and other chapters) that Lacanian theory has important practical implications for analysis of legal processes and institutions, including the language in legal discourse and texts,[3] my primary focus in this chapter is theoretical. Lacan's method is so unconventional, and his terminology so foreign even when the words are familiar,[4] that immediate applications are often misguided and in any event problematical. My own experience in teaching Lacan (to law students) is that by the time Lacanianism is simplified enough to be easily understood, the application to legal problems is so simplistic as to raise the question of why one needs Lacan at all. For example, to point out that the gaps in contract law doctrine are filled in by deeper understandings—unconscious texts—of the law that are not part of the "surface" text (of a treatise or judicial opinion) sounds, in the end, trivial. But it is not really so simple. To say that psyche is textual, that the unconscious is structured like a language, is for Lacan an acknowledgment of a symbolic *order* of logic and law within which human relationships are structured, unconsciously, by language. While we know that there is "something else" informing contract law, besides textual doctrine (perhaps "policy considerations," conventional understandings, "ideological" belief systems, or social relations of power, in various contemporary formulations), Lacan shifts our attention to, and takes into account, not only the hidden or "unconscious" effects on language, but the language of the unconscious.

The primacy given to language by Lacan is familiar ground for legal theorists, but the details of Lacanian theory are new to the discipline of law. My purpose is to describe some of those details that are most relevant to law and language studies. Lacan's methodology, if compelling, will (as it has in literary theory) provide a field of inquiry and applications beyond the scope of this chapter: "As James Joyce said: 'I'm giving work to academics for three hundred years.'... Lacan will give a lot of work... to academics... because the idea is not to get a model, learn the model, and apply it.... It is to re-think the matter everytime."[5] My hope is that some ground is gained in comprehending the complexity of Lacan's language theory, and that his description of where we are and what we have will offer insight as to where we are not yet and what we lack.

As a starting point, I reconsider one of the most significant debates in contemporary contract theory, namely the role of "gap-fillers" in judicial construction of "incomplete" contracts. The problem of filling in the gaps is textual on two obvious levels: first, a written contract inevitably betrays missing provisions (e.g., addressing possible contingencies) that the parties to a contract intentionally or accidentally ignored; second, a court hearing a contract dispute is often called upon (when an unaddressed contingency arises) to apply a generalized "default" (i.e., absent an instruction) rule to a specific contract. A gap in the contract (and sometimes in contract doctrine) is thus filled in by each judicial construction of a contract. This displacement of meaning away from surface texts to an underlying text provides a modest analogy to Lacan's theory of language.

The originality of Lacan's work on language should not be over- or underestimated. On the one hand, genuine similarities are apparent between Lacanian theory and the discourses of the law and literature movement (which emphasizes the literary aspects of law), of legal semiotics (which pays close attention to the underlying structures of meaning in law), and of poststructural criticism (which exposes the social and political character of literary as well as legal texts). On the other hand, Lacan's return to the Freudian unconscious and his conception of its structure (like a language) distinguishes his work from that associated with the above-listed movements. Thus we must read Lacan, first, on his own terms.[6]

The Meanings in the Gaps of Contracts

> [No] metalanguage can be spoken, or, more aphoristically, ... there is no Other of the Other. And when the Legislator (he who claims to lay down the Law) presents himself to fill the gap, he does so as an imposter.
> —Jacques Lacan, "The Subversion of the Subject"

In my own contract law practice (my own story—empirical, but a local phenomenology [in San Diego and Austin, where I practiced during the 1980s, California and Texas representing a sufficient contrast]), I noticed among my clients two extreme responses to contemporary developments in contract doctrine. Some were enamored, and willing to pay the bills, of "thorough" and "experienced" business counsel who tried in each transaction to cover all contingencies by means of a lengthy written contract—one hundred pages was acceptable, even though negotiating such a contract was expensive, and even though the text was difficult to follow even for the most experienced client. However, one hundred pages is not enough, really, to cover all contingencies and thus to avoid litigation over the meaning of the contract. The other type of client, observing this phenomenon, was unimpressed with such efforts and decided to avoid "thorough" attorneys altogether, relying instead on a simple contract,[7] on trusting relationships, and on the litigation section of the law firms with which I practiced. (Litigators, but not transactional attorneys, joke that they love such clients.) The conviction of these latter clients was that if a contractual relationship breaks down, the parties will end up in court whether the contract is long or short, and the court will then rewrite the contract in any event.

Both types of clients, in effect, recognize dangers in contemporary contract doctrine, or more specifically, the dangers of ending up in a court where doctrine will be employed. The first type of client—the believer in long contracts—tries to beat the law at its own interpretive game: to define all ambiguities and to close up all gaps, thereby disempowering judicial discretion to reach into what is popularly perceived as a bag of doctrinal "tricks." The bag contains conflicting principles of law (one of which may be selected to determine the existence or meaning of a contract), such as freedom of contract versus the unenforceability of unfair contracts,[8] or "objectivist" recourse to plain meaning versus "subjectivist" recourse to referential context. The second type of client may feel that the effort to restrain judges is hopeless, or just too expensive. Both types of clients view legal doctrine as risky, perhaps incoherent and indeterminate, and the two types differ only in their degree of confidence that, in Eagleton's terms, one may "nail down" provisionally the fading and evaporating meanings of a bizarre, "modernist" text.[9]

DEFAULT RULES

Randy Barnett notes that the issue of contractual incompleteness, or "gap-filling" rules, dominated contracts discourse during the 1980s.[10] The issue continues to be of interest to legal scholars because written contracts purport to be documents that legally bind consenting parties *in accordance with* their intentions. Yet written contracts are governed by a set of background rules that, irrespective of the parties' intentions, address (1) the propriety of the transaction, (2) how express terms will be interpreted, and (3) what provisions will be implied (because of a gap in the contract or simply in all contracts). Barnett points out that all contracts are incomplete to some degree, either because parties are intentionally silent about a known contingency, or because the parties are unaware of some contingency.[11]

Ian Ayres and Robert Gertner distinguish default rules, which the parties can contract around, from immutable rules (e.g., the rule prohibiting contracts for the sale of children) which cannot be changed by contractual agreement.[12] Gap-filling involves employment of default rules which, borrowing from computer jargon, apply unless the parties choose to fill in a gap with an express provision (or instruction).[13] Default rules are justified, theoretically, (1) because terms are implied that the parties would have wanted if they could have afforded lengthy drafting and negotiation sessions or if they could have foreseen all contingencies,[14] (2) because implied terms offer stability even for parties who prefer to contract around a standard interpretation but do not in fear of misinterpretation,[15] or (3) because terms are implied—as penalties that the parties would not want—in order to encourage parties to reveal information.[16]

For example, assume Airline X expressly agrees to deliver by air an elevator motor from the manufacturer to Y, and the contract does not address damages for X's default. If the airplane carrying the motor breaks down, and Y claims millions of dollars in losses for the delay because the elevator motor was needed for a diamond mine, a default rule will likely be implied where the parties were silent: X is only liable for foreseeable losses. Note that the parties could have drafted around the default rule, and that X would probably have negotiated for a higher payment by Y if X agreed to be liable for *all* of Y's losses in the event of a delay.[17]

From our modern perspective on textual interpretation in law, of course, every contract is "always already" full of gaps, even if there is no "gap" to be filled by a default rule. That is, even the express terms of the contract are subject to conflicting interpretations in the hands of a court.[18] Without denying the theoretical ambiguity of legal language generally, a significant ambiguity in practice persists on the level of the background rules for incomplete agreements, that is, not just on the question of whether "delivery" might in some circumstances mean "nondelivery."

Faced with an incomplete contract, a court may seek to discover the parties' actual intentions or to impose a fair term. While some scholars are not troubled by this formulation,[19] it merely masks the arbitrariness of gap-filling rules. Courts *may* excuse performance on the basis of indefiniteness or mistake, finding not an "incomplete" contract but no contract at all. If a contract is found to exist, the parties' intentions *may* be deduced from a course of dealing or performance.[20] Failing a finding of supposedly "actual" intentions, courts *may* inquire into the fiction of what the parties *would have* wanted, which usually becomes a speculative inquiry into what the majority of parties (similarly situated) would have wanted.[21] Whether this scheme appears doctrinally coherent (because hard cases require judicial discretion) or in disarray (because dozens of outcomes are possible, all in fidelity to the rules), the gap in the contract—that which was not intended—will become determinative of the purported existence of and the "actual" meaning of the contract. The parties' assumption of control over their relationship was unjustified.

Not surprisingly, the dominant discourse concerning default rules takes place in terms of law and economics, not law and literature. The goal of default rules (or "gap fillers") is typically formulated as the efficient distribution of resources or as cost-effectiveness.[22] The economic approach can thus be seen as an attempt to make sense of or stabilize an apparently incoherent set of underlying doctrines. For example, default rules can be justified, formulated and applied in accordance with their potential for creating efficiency in the market.

I have purposely avoided, in the present discussion, recourse to the work of Critical Legal scholars for whom Lacan may seem most relevant. In the critical perspective, doctrine—which is incoherent and indeterminate—is a disguise for differences in power and knowledge.[23] Such a perspective, while helpful in disclosing ideological tilt, eclipses for many the textual operations (the symbolic *order*) of the law that Lacanian theory exposes. I choose, therefore, an unlikely example, if only to confirm that law and economics scholars, as well as Critical Legal scholars, find themselves wrestling with an order of unconscious language.

ECONOMIC PSYCHOANALYSIS

> The apparent disarray that afflicts judicial efforts to interpret contractual agreements results from a fundamental misconception of the purposes of contract interpretation.
> —Goetz and Scott, "The Limits of Expanded Choice"

Goetz and Scott suggest that "much of the apparent incoherence of the case law" on implied terms is explained in great part by the conflict and confusion between objective and subjective theories of contract.[24] Objectivist "textualists" assume that the expectations of the parties is to be found in express contractual language, and that the goal of interpretation is to protect most contracting parties—not the unique interests of specific parties—by recourse to plain meaning. On the other hand, subjectivist "contextualists" assume that what the parties "really meant" is found in their referential context, and that the goal of interpretation is to discover the unique meaning of the contract for specific parties, not the plain or communal meaning of its terms. Courts seem to shift back and forth, sometimes admitting evidence of commercial—contextual—practices but sometimes refusing such evidence since it potentially challenges clear and unambiguous—objective—terms.[25]

On further reflection, however, both approaches can coexist if they are, for the sake of efficiency, recharacterized: "[T]he opposing poles of the interpretive continuum are actually converse to their traditional representations."[26] Attention to subjective meanings should lead to customary norms of *general* application, while textualist or objectivist approaches should protect *particularized* understandings "in the face of contrary inferences from context."[27] Failure to recognize this reversal results in expansive contextual analyses that burden "parties who attempt unconventional expressions," which analyses coexist with counterproductive textualist efforts that ignore "tested, cost-effective formulations embedded in [parties'] contractual context."[28] In short, courts tend to misread the text of the underlying rules—the incoherency of the case law is not just "apparent," in Scott and Goetz's guarded terminology, it is actual. But another meaning is available on closer reading, informed by an acknowledged, faithful presumption of the goal of efficiency in contract law. While theorists in other traditions might seek to impose order on the basis of other interests or commitments, the economic analysts recognize that meaning is in the gaps.

Freud as Scripture

> Supposedly deriving from psychoanalysis, post-structuralism treats Freud's early theories not [as] navigational aids created by a biologist as he sailed into the unknown—but as holy writ.
> —Liam Hudson, "Different Wiring"

Frank Lentricchia's *After the New Criticism*, which appeared in 1980, acknowledged the "major figures" in Continental Critical Theory who influenced the course of the American Critical Theory in the 1960s and 1970s: Sartre, Heidegger, de Saussure, Lévi-Strauss, Barthes, Derrida, Foucault. From our perspective in the 1990s, the name of Jacques Lacan is noticeably "lacking." Even Lentricchia's second string—Adorno, Benjamin, Lukács, Gramsci, Althusser, and Goldmann, who had "a great deal to say to American critics" but were not "shaping influences"—does not include Lacan.[29] Lentricchia was, of course, familiar with Lacan—he mentions the role of Lacan as Harold Bloom's rival sibling (both wayward "children," along with Derrida, of New Criticism);[30] nevertheless, English translation of Lacan's seminars did not begin until the 1970s,[31] and the first English books—*Écrits: A Selection* and *The Four Fundamental Concepts of Psycho-Analysis*—were published in 1977. Prior to 1980, Lacan's influence was minimal in North America.

In the 1980s, however, the situation changed. Lacan is neither popular among mainstream academics nor particularly accessible as a writer, but he is clearly a major figure among critical literary and cultural studies theorists. While Lacan's influence as a training and theoretical psychoanalyst is not negligible, his return to Freud confirms "that psychoanalysis is a work in language, is a 'talking cure,' if it is anything at all."[32] Thus, it is

> no wonder that those ... with backgrounds in literature and literary theory have been drawn to his writings. It is also no wonder that those who were formed in the traditions of the social and behavioral sciences have found him unreadable. Especially when combined with the peculiarly allusive quality of Lacan's ... style, the plethora of [verbal deviations or tropes] gives rise to a prose that is the antithesis of the supposedly transparent, resolutely non-figurative mode of traditional scientific discourse.[33]

Even those workers in language drawn to Lacan, however, are not unified in their assessments of his work—some are enamored,[34] others quite critical.[35]

Freud's own place in literary criticism has always been controversial. David Ellis, in his Freudian reading of Wordsworth,[36] observes that among British literary critics "the most common practice has been to deny that either [psychoanalysis or Freud] has much importance for literature."[37] Ellis seeks, instead, "some intermediate point between the illusion that [Freud] doesn't matter, and enclosure within his system and language."[38] Many psychoanalytic critics (including Lacan), however, are hardly satisfied by acknowledgment of a mere "contribution" of Freud to literary interpretation:

> For reasons very much associated with the allegedly scientific status of [Freudian] thought, the stopping places on the road between repudiation of its relevance for literary studies and wholesale acceptance are few and far between. Freud was the founding father of a way of thinking which summons us to operate more or less exclusively within it.[39]

Before attempting to trace the contours of a psychoanalytic reading of legal texts, I discuss (in the next section) several of Lacan's conceptions of textual interpretation.

THE UNCONSCIOUS AS SCRIPTURE

Lacan identifies the human subject as "the slave of language [and] all the more so of a discourse . . . in which his place is already inscribed at birth."[40] The "elementary structures of culture," which include legal processes and institutions, reveal an order that, "even if unconscious, is inconceivable outside the permutations authorized by language."[41] Culture itself, which alongside nature and society make up the human condition, "could well be reduced to language."[42] The study of the structures and laws of existing languages—Lacan's definition of linguistics—thus occupies "the key position in this domain."[43]

While there may be many senses in which textual interpretation is central to understanding humanity, for Lacan such an exercise is of ultimate significance. The unconscious—seen by Freud to have a structure affecting "in innumerable ways" what we say and do[44]—is structured like, or created by, language. There need be no "extension" of psychoanalytic theory from the individual to society in Lacan's conception, since the socialization of the individual by and into language, including the linguistic structure of the unconscious, *is* the object of inquiry. Thus when Lacan talks about a *patient* (in clinical *analysis*) whose *unconscious* reveals a governing *signifier*, it is never an individual affair, but rather a cultural phenomenon. Conversely, the language and meanings of legal institutions and processes do not *affect* people's lives but *constitute* them.

Of the dozens of fundamental themes in Lacan's writings,[45] I focus below on several notions developed by Lacan in three essays (written between 1953 and 1966) that have been translated (two by Sheridan in *Écrits: A Selection* and one by Jeffrey Mehlman in *Yale French Studies*) and that clarify this fundamental connection between language and the unconscious.

THE SYMBOLIC ORDER

> I may be permitted a laugh if these remarks are accused of turning the meaning of Freud's work away from the biological basis he would have wished for it toward the cultural references with which it is shot through.
> —Jacques Lacan, *The Function and Field of Speech and Language in Psychoanalysis*

Freud identified unconscious texts, portions of which make their way into conscious discourse, in his analyses of dreams, of everyday conversation, and of jokes. Returning to Freud, Lacan reminded analysts (in the so-called Rome Discourse or Rome Report of 1953) that the dream—the "royal road" to the unconscious—"has the structure of a sentence," "of a form of writing."[46] Moreover, as to the phenomena identified by Freud in *The Psychopathology of Everyday Life*—"forgetting familiar names, slips of the tongue, and mistakes in reading or writing"[47]—Lacan remarks that if Freud

> taught us to follow the ascending ramifications of the symbolic lineage in the text of the patient's free associations, in order to map it out at the points where its verbal forms intersect with the nodal points of its structure, then it is already quite clear the symptom resolves itself entirely in an analysis of language, because the symptom is itself structured like a language, because it is from language that speech is delivered.[48]

Finally, Freud's demonstration of the relation of jokes to the unconscious—"the most unchallengeable of his works"[49]—highlights for Lacan both the *ambiguity* conferred by language and the "third listener—the locus of the other," the social nature of unconscious discourse.[50]

Lacan refers to Freud's discovery in such matters as "that of the field of the effects in the nature of man of his relations to the symbolic order and the tracing of their meaning right back to the most radical agencies of symbolization in being."[51] Lacan offers a juridical example to clarify the symbolic order—the marriage tie confronting social anthropologists: "The marriage tie is governed by an order of preference [and taboo] whose law . . . is, like language, imperative for the group in its forms but unconscious in its structure."[52] Unconsciousness of the permanence of the structures of marriage ties, for example, allows belief in freedom of choice. In this formulation, with implications for law and anthropology, the "kingdom of culture" is superimposed on nature. This "law, then, is revealed . . . as identical with an order of language"; more generally, symbols "envelop the life of man in a network so total . . . that they bring to his birth the shape of his destiny; so total that they give the words that will make him faithful or renegade."[53] The symbolic order is, in broadest terms, the unconscious order, and "it designates a symbolic structure based on a linguistic model."[54]

Benvenuto and Kennedy note that for Lacan the symbolic order, concerned with social and cultural symbolism, represents or constitutes the subject.[55] At the outset of his translation of *Écrits*, Sheridan explains that the symbols referred to by Lacan "are not icons, stylized figurations, but signifiers" that radically determine the subject in their effects.[56] Before discussing further the symbolic order—one of the three orders in Lacan's theory of cognition[57] (discussed in chapter 1)—I turn to Lacan's essay (from 1966) on "The Purloined Letter" to consider his use of the term "signifier."

THE PATH OF THE SIGNIFIER

> Do crossword puzzles.
> —Advice to a young psychoanalyst, Jacques Lacan, "The Function and Field of Speech and Language in Psychoanalysis"

Edgar Allan Poe's short story, "The Purloined Letter," illustrates for Lacan that "it is the Symbolic Order which is constitutive for the subject—by demonstrating in the story the decisive orientation which the subject receives from the itinerary of the signifier."[58] The so-called signifying chain of meanings of the displaced letter is seen to dominate the subjects who, in the story, seek to find it.

Recall that Freud's repetition compulsion, whereby painful emotions are often revived, was "ascribed to the unconscious repressed . . . striving for expression, . . . at times overriding" the ego's regulatory pleasure principle.[59] Lacan here finds a model for the *insistence* of the signifying "chain."[60] Moreover, Freud believed that in analysis, the analyst follows "the drift of an arbitrary and purposeless chain of thoughts" when the unconscious takes control of the analysand's discourse.[61] For Lacan, Poe's story provides a picture of how subjects in general are at the mercy of the chain of signifiers.

"The Purloined Letter," a detective story told by an unidentified narrator, involves a compromising letter stolen by a minister from (presumably) the queen; the police, in frustration, eventually seek help from the Sherlock Holmesian Dupin, who successfully recovers the letter. The story is told in two dialogues (among the narrator, Dupin, and the prefect of police), a month apart, the first describing to Dupin the unsolved robbery, and the second concerning Dupin's explanation of his own clever "robbery" of the letter from the minister. The content of the letter, significantly, remains unknown.

Lacan paraphrases the story to show that the second "scene" is a repetition of the story's "primal scene." Initially, the queen receives the letter in her *boudoir*, but the king and the minister enter, and (unable to hide it) she leaves the letter "address up" hoping it will go unnoticed. The minister, seeing the letter *and* the queen's distress, takes the letter (leaving a decoy letter) as the Queen watches helplessly—a protest would draw attention to the letter. The second and final scene is the minister's office in his hotel, searched for eighteen months by the police without success. Dupin calls on the minister, and while secretly inspecting the room by wearing green eyeglasses, sees a crumpled letter in plain view on the mantel. Knowing he has solved the crime, Dupin "forgets" his snuffbox, and returns the next day with a crumpled letter "facsimile" with which he replaces the compromising letter when the minister looks out of the window.

Going beyond the obvious similarity between the two scenes, Lacan identifies a repetition of "intersubjectivity" among three subjects: one virtually blind (the king in scene 1, then the police in scene 2), a second that knows the first's blindness and is thus deluded as to the success of the attempted secrecy (the queen, then the minister), and a third that takes advantage of the first's blindness and the second's delusion (the minister, then Dupin). In each "scene," irrespective of the content or meaning (signified) of the letter (signifier), the position of the letter determines what the subjects in the constellation will do. The

> displacement of the signifier determines the subjects in their acts, in their destiny, in their refusals, their blind spots, their end and fate, their innate gifts and social acquisitions ... [E]verything that might be considered the stuff of psychology ... will follow the path of the signifier.[62]

For Lacan, the symbolic order thus constitutes the subject.[63]

As discussed in the previous chapter, the term "signifier" means, for Lacan, "that which represents a subject for another signifier."[64] Ellie Ragland notes that a subject

> represents himself as a subject for the other who is a signifier (both in his fantasy and in a social context).... [For example, a] subject represents him- or herself to an-other person as signifying something cultural (a title, a profession) within a given symbolic order.[65]

Mark Bracher explains that the word "represent" does not mean a representation or portrayal, but rather "to be a represent*ative*, a stand-in... of the subject."[66]

> [W]hen I encounter another human subject, it is really our representatives, our signifiers, that are communicating and negotiating with each other.... [For example,] when one is represented (to oneself and to others) by the signifier "man" or the signifier "woman," one is prohibited... from enjoying... certain parts of one's own body and the other's body.[67]

Subjects are thus *reduced* by identification with a signifier[68]—in Lacan's words, "the subject is deprived of something of himself, of his very life."[69] Bracher finds in Lacan a methodology of cultural criticism, given the profound "effects produced by the cultural, Symbolic-order definitions" which we embrace.[70]

My own focus is on how Lacan's presentation "is able to make coherent connections between the structure of the unconscious and the interactive signifying practices that constitute a given culture."[71] Lacan concedes that his "fable is so constructed as to show that it is the letter and its diversion which governs [the subjects'] entries and roles."[72] In Poe's "beautiful image" of Dupin seeing through the minister's "bogus finery," we see "the very effect of the unconscious in the precise sense that we teach that the unconscious means that man is inhabited by the signifier."[73] As in analysis, the analysand is unable to see (and the analyst does see) the effects of the unconscious text disclosed to the analyst.[74]

METAPHOR/METONYMY

> Freud constantly maintained that [literary] training was the prime requisite in the formation of analysts.
> —Jacques Lacan, "The Agency of the Letter in the Unconscious or Reason Since Freud"

Lacan's 1957 essay entitled "The agency [or *instance*] of the letter in the unconscious or reason since Freud" was based upon a lecture given to students of literature at the Sorbonne. At the outset of this difficult text, three familiar Lacanian themes are reiterated. First, Lacan suggests that "what the psychoanalytic experience discovers in the unconscious is the whole structure of language," not a mere "seat of the instincts."[75] Second, the term "letter" is defined as the "material support that concrete discourse borrows from language."[76] Third, Lacan emphasizes that "language and its structure exist prior to the moment at which each subject at a certain point in his mental development makes his entry into it."[77] The subject is a "slave of language," and of the "elementary structures of culture" that order his or her life, even unconsciously, through the authority, the *instance*, of language.[78]

The remainder of the essay is a psychoanalytic reformulation of Saussure's (and, in part, Jakobson's) linguistics. Where Saussure emphasized the structural unity of the sign (the object of inquiry for his Semiology), expressed by the algorithm s/S (signified/Signifier), Lacan inverts the algorithm (S/s) and emphasizes the bar (/) separating "the signifier and the signified as ... distinct orders."[79] Instead of illustrating the relationship of signifier to signified with a Saussurean diagram—"TREE/(drawing of an actual tree)"—Lacan draws two identical doors below the bar, and above the bar writes the words "Ladies" and "Gentlemen," respectively, above the actual doors.[80] This shows "how in fact the signifier enters the signified,"[81] in other words, how the signifier *articulates* the difference between identical doors: "The difference in the space above the bar determines a difference in what is below the bar.... It is the signifier that does the work."[82] The diagram sets up another contrast with Saussure's unification of a concept (signified) with a sound-image (signifier), for although Saussure described how shifts occur over time in the arbitrary signified-signifier relationship,[83] there is for Lacan "an incessant sliding of the signifier under the signified."[84]

Acknowledging his debt to Roman Jakobson, Lacan suggests that "the effective field constituted by the signifier" (or, in another formulation, "the effect of the signifier on the signified") has two sides: metonymy and metaphor.[85] Jakobson not only identified metaphoric and metonymic poles as primary in the symbolic process, but suggested a correlation between his categories and Freud's characterization of the unconscious.[86] Taking that analogy seriously, but departing from Jakobson's scheme, Lacan points out that metonymy is based upon a "word-to-word connexion," such as "thirty sails,"[87] which is connected, by association, to a fleet of ships. Lacan's point, however, is

> that there is no connection between word and thing in the way that metonymy operates. We speak of "thirty sail" meaning thirty ships,

but ... for Lacan the connection between ... ship and sail, is totally included in the signifier itself: the relationship is one of ... signifier to signifier, not of word to any reality.[88]

On the other hand, metaphor, the use of "one word for another," takes its creative or poetic spark from two disparate signifiers, "one of which has taken the place of the other in the signifying chain, the [occluded] signifier remaining present through its (metonymic) connexion with the rest of the chain."[89] Metaphor and metonymy are then linked by Lacan, respectively, to the basic unconscious processes identified by Freud as "condensation" and "displacement."[90]

Focusing on Freud's theory of dream interpretation, Lacan remarks that the distorting function of the dream "is what I designated above, following Saussure, as the sliding of the signifier under the signified, which is always active in discourse (its action, let us note, is unconscious)."[91] Freud described condensation as "the fact that the manifest dream has a smaller content than the latent one, and is thus an abbreviated translation of it."[92] Elizabeth Wright explains, in her helpful commentary on Freud, that this

> is far from being a simple process of the mere omission of elements. Composite figures and structures are formed so that as little as possible is left out. Hence the concept of "overdetermination," whereby several latent wishes converge on one manifest item, or the reverse, where one wish is represented a number of times in the same dream-sequence. The result in either case is a superimposition of elements.[93]

Lacan refers to condensation as

> the structure of the superimposition of the signifiers, which metaphor takes as its field, and whose name [*Verdichtung*], condensing in itself the word *Dichtung*, shows how the mechanism is connatural with poetry to the point that it envelops the traditional function proper to poetry.[94]

Displacement, in contrast, "is achieved by the elements in the latent dream thoughts via a chain of associations for the purpose of disguise."[95] Again, Lacan suggests that displacement is close "to the idea of that veering off of signification that we see in metonymy, and which from its first appearance in Freud is represented as the most appropriate means used by the unconscious to foil censorship."[96] The basic unconscious mechanisms that were, for Freud, responsible for the content of dreams are transformed by Lacan into linguistic concepts:

> Thus the formations of the unconscious, in the Lacanian perspective, derive from the workings of metaphor and metonymy, or what

one could also call the play of substitution and combination of signifiers. The dream-work... follows, in Lacan, the laws of the signifier."[97]

In another formulation, the unconscious for Lacan is governed by the "logic of the signifier."[98]

While the metaphor/metonymy distinction might seem a bit too abstract for practical application, Louise Halper's recent analysis of regulatory "takings" law[99] employs Lacan's framework to demonstrate how two inconsistent judicial opinions each "work," rhetorically, by their respective (and *hidden*) recourse to metaphor and metonymy. Specifically, the new metonymic *association* of land with its market value serves to expand the field of compensable takings (a move of which Halper is critical), in contrast to the traditional metaphorical structure of takings analysis (which limits the field of compensable regulating takings to situations that are *similar to* a government seizure of land). Viewed separately, both styles of analysis make sense and instill confidence in the stability of law.

Has Lacan exaggerated the centrality of the signifier by suggesting, in Malcolm Bowie's words, that the "proper object of attention, for the psychoanalyst no less than the linguist, is the signifying chain itself[? For Lacan,] the relationships observable within that chain are the surest guide to psychical structure and to the structure of the human subject."[100] Bowie adds that Lacan's analogies with rhetorical tropes may be "more important for the lessons they teach corporately than for any individual uses they might have as analytic tools."[101] "The enduring appeals that comparisons [between tropes and psychic mechanisms] hold for both Freud and Lacan stems from their [enforcement of] a general truth about the unconscious—that it has, or, in Lacan's view, *is* structure."[102] Predictably, Lacan has been accused of proposing a "linguistic conception of the unconscious."[103] Lyotard, questioning Lacan's fidelity at all to Saussure, Jakobson, and even Freud, argues that the "dream-work is not a language."[104] David Ingleby, following Ricoeur and Norman Coulter, argues that Lacan took the analogy between the unconscious and language "too literally" when claiming that "the unconscious employs literary devices of metaphor and metonymy."[105] Ellie Ragland replies that Ingleby misrepresents Lacan:

> Lacan said that the laws of unconscious—condensation and displacement—work like the principal laws of language (metaphor and metonymy). What the psychic[al] and linguistic systems have in common is an analogous manner of functioning by substitutions, combinations, and references.[106]

In any event, readers of Lacan cannot assume that the formula "the unconscious is structured like a language" is a linguistic reduction:

> So confident is [Lacan] that he has made contact here with something fundamental and universal, that he draws attention to an element of redundancy in his own phrase "structured as a language": "'Structured' and 'as a language' for me mean exactly the same thing."[107]

SYMPTOM/DESIRE

> For the symptom *is* a metaphor whether one likes it or not, as desire *is* a metonymy, however funny people may find the idea.
> —Jacques Lacan, "The Agency of the Letter..."

While the details of Lacan's conception of the symptom and his extremely complex notion of desire are explored in part 2 of this book, note that the identification of the metaphoric and metonymic functions of the unconscious is only the beginning of the Lacanian project. The "untranslated" unconscious meanings revealed by the symptom (through which desire "cries out")[108] are "translatable" due to the symptom's relation to the signifying structure, according to the nature of metaphor and by reference to metonymy.[109]

Symptoms for Freud indicated repression of, or the return of repressed, impulses—Freud refers to symptoms as "symbols of particular (traumatic) experiences," as defensive substitutes for a repressed idea, and as analogous to distortion in dream-formation.[110] For Lacan, the symptom is *not* a symbol, and while the concept of a substitution of the repressed (and the analogy with distortion in dreams) is adopted by Lacan, the symptom is reconceived in linguistic terms.

> The symptom ... is not an isolated meaning, but a relation to a signifying chain—the signifier of a repressed chain of meaning ... [S]ymptoms, like dreams, can be deciphered....
> The symptom is the substitute sign or word—a metaphor—whose "cure" or translation would lie in discovering which meanings are repressed in a person's language.[111]

Clarifying the substitutive nature of metaphor, Anthony Wilden remarks that we see in Lacan

> the "metaphoric" relationship between a symptom and the presentation it replaces, neither of which "means" the other, as in the traditional sense of the meaning of a symbol or symptom, but one of which "stands in" for the other as a result of repression, or rather, as a result of the return of the repressed.[112]

The return of the repressed is mediated within a system of language, thus the "unconscious speaks."[113]

Lacan's conception of Desire is fundamental to his entire project—his return to Freud—and thus the term appears throughout Lacan's texts and those of his commentators. Desire is an indestructible force—a component of Drive (*Trieb*, one of Freud's four fundamental concepts of psychoanalysis); it is the yearning for objects and for the other (or Other); and it "exists at every point in the psychic structure."[114] But desire is also representational and symbolic, referring to images and meanings in a repressed text: "Desire (unconscious desire) is never fulfilled; it is only displaced or substituted for, forming a "chain of signifiers," which always (like the unconscious) leaves traces of itself but eludes us."[115] The displacement from signifier to signifier—metonymy—constitutes desire. The Poe allegory not only introduces the determinative signifying chain, but also the determinative lack that engenders desire: "The desire is forever displaced and disguised as something else (as is the missing letter), and this is evidence of repression."[116]

As to critics of Lacan who claim that desire is not properly characterized as interpretation or textual interplay, but rather by the operation of libidinal (hydraulic or energetic) activity upon sign systems,[117] Ragland replies:

> Lacan's relocation of "drive" in Desire operates a reconfiguration on the aspects of Freudian theory that would distinguish between interpretative and hydraulic models in the first place. Desire ... partakes of energy ... at the same time that it conditions concrete or linguistic meaning in reference to a primary representational chain. ... That the components of Desire may then be analytically decoded in the conscious realm—i.e., hermeneutics—does not make them any less the energetic source and reference point of human meaning.[118]

Note the extreme care taken by Lacanian apologists to avoid any simple reduction of Lacan. That the unconscious is structured like a language, that the subject is inhabited by the signifier, that the meaning of a symptom is derived from its relation to a determinative signifying structure—each can be (has been) read, literally, as a collapsing of two systems—the unconscious and language; but this would be as incorrect as failing to see how each system conditions the other as well as their similar functions.[119]

Law as Scripture

While the language of legal processes and institutions was not a specific subject of inquiry for Lacan, the ordering role of legal language provides a ready example of Lacan's complex notion of the constitutive signifier in human relations.[120] Three immediate and obvious connections between Lacanian theory and legal structures have been acknowledged.

ANALYSIS AS A LEGAL PROCEEDING

First, Patrick Hogan points out that while the tacitly accepted medical model for psychoanalysis "attends to 'developmental normalcy,' Lacan's juridical model considers the subject's relation to the law."[121] Significantly, the term "law" for Lacan refers variously to the superego, to phallic division,[122] to castration, to men, to formalizable psychic and linguistic structuring processes in the symbolic order, to that which "demarcates" the unattainable for desire, and of course to "the laws of the social realm" (which include legal processes and institutions).[123] As such, the suggestion that psychoanalytic "inquests" of the unconscious are similar to legal proceedings provides a starting point for interaction between Lacanian theory and legal theory.

Briefly, recall Lacan's use of the term *demande* or appeal (or request), a term of law (often translated as "demand"),[124] when referring to speech addressed to the Other and creating desire in the gap between *need* and the *demande*.[125]

> Desire is that which is manifested in the interval that demand hollows within itself, in as much as the subject, in articulating the signifying chain, brings to light the want-to-be, together with the appeal to receive the complement from the Other, if the Other, the locus of speech, is also the locus of this want, or lack.[126]

Alan Sheridan, translator of the above passage, explains that (after acquisition of language)

> all speech is demand; it presupposes the Other to which it is addressed, whose very signifiers it takes over in its formulation. By the same token, that which comes from the Other is ... not so much ... a particular satisfaction, but rather ... a response to an appeal. . . . Desire ... is a perpetual effect of symbolic articulation. It is not an appetite.[127]

Note that the "pressure" of unconscious Desire is within language, that biological "man is subjectivised and representationalized in his genesis by the imposition of culture (symbols and language) on his corporal nature,"[128] and that desire is in that sense grammatical, articulable.[129] In the analytic session, the analyst listens to the dialogue with the Other,[130] the *demande* for something that is only a substitute for that which is [insatiably] desired,[131] like a judge "hearing" a request for monetary damages to substitute for something irreplaceable that has been lost. Yet the discourse (and desire) of the Other[132] not only has its analogy in legal proceedings; the discourse of legal processes and institutions can be seen, in an oscillating perspective, to reflect the operation of a social unconscious, structured like legal language. Before considering legal processes as a subject of psychoanalysis, however, the question of Lacan's status as a "semiotician" should be considered.

SEMIOTICS

> Lacan's procedure is to challenge the misreadings of past readers of Freud, by focusing on Freud the semiotician.
> —Elizabeth Wright, *Psychoanalytic Criticism*

In view of the growing literature on legal semiotics,[133] Lacan's attention to the underlying structures of language is familiar to many legal scholars. While Lacan is clearly a semiotician *of sorts*, the label is not terribly helpful given the various "schools" of semiotics generally (American/Peircean, European/Saussurean, and recent variants of each), the variations reflected in the field of *legal* semiotics, and the fact that some writers appear to be semioticians without knowing it.[134] Moreover, while Lacan's symbolic order could be called "a global semiotics of language and society,"[135] semiotics is not known for its attention to the unconscious. For Lacan, "meaning is not anchored (as semioticians suppose) at the level of stylistic figures or of sign and message. Meaning glides perpetually at the surface of language in a constant "translation" of the elements that constitute it in terms of desire."[136] Nevertheless, Lacan *is* an heir to Saussure; some semioticians are, at least theoretically, Lacanians;[137] and some scholars associated with legal semiotics (such as Milovanovic, below) explicitly use Lacan in legal analysis.

LEGAL PROCEEDINGS AS ANALYSAND

> When one interprets a dream, one is always up to one's neck in meaning. What is at issue is the subjectivity of the subject, in his desire, in his relation to his environment, to others, to life itself.
> —Jacques Lacan, *Seminar, Book 1*

The apparent similarity between Lacanian theory and legal semiotics is exemplified in Bernard Jackson's view of legal decision making as "a reflection of the mediating influences of social and psychological frameworks of actors engaged in reality construction through discursive practices."[138] However, Jackson's reliance on Greimasian semiotics—a nonreferential theory of meaning as "constructed at the intersection" of the syntagmatic (grammatical, narrative) and paradigmatic (semantic word choice at each point along the syntagmatic axis) axes—subjects Jackson to a Lacanian critique.[139] For Lacanians,

> the person enters discursive subject-positions which always implicate particular communicative styles and accentuation.... Reality construction has more to do with the effects of insertion in these discursive subject-positions [than] with their attendant bounded semantic sphere (the paradigmatic axis) and the allowable form of expression in grammatical structures (the syntagmatic structure).[140]

Adding a metaphoric dimension to the paradigmatic and a metonymic dimension to the syntagmatic, "the Lacanian construct then becomes a referential construct":[141] "Referentiality..., as an intra-psychic dimension, problematizes any speech act. Stable meaning escapes us; it slips and slides in metaphoric and metonymic displacements."[142] Milovanovic therefore suggests a Lacanian "augmentation" to nonreferential legal semiotics. Although specific legal discourses, as linguistic coordinate systems, do exist with some degree of narrative coherence, gaps inevitably appear:

> Subjects, finding themselves in discursive subject-positions within particular linguistic coordinate systems attempt to "fill-in" missing story elements with materials available, more often consistent with conventional understandings, and, hence... dominant understandings of reality are continuously reconstructed.[143]

Challenging the grammatical-logical closure implied in Jackson, Milovanovic anchors a neo-Marxian critique of legal ideology in Lacanian theory.

Keeping in mind Milovanovic's suggestion, following Lacan, that the subject is both "determined by the interaction of conscious and unconscious processes" and constrained in linguistic structures (including legal discourse), and that rhetoric plays a fundamental role in subverting grammar and logic,[144] I turn briefly to Peller's conception of law as metaphor.

THE METAPHORIC MEDIATION OF PERCEPTION

> When a judge approached a new area, his perception was mediated by... representational metaphors so that, in a sense, the area already was constructed before the judge approached it.... He did not have to make "subjective" judgments or "ideological" choices or ignore the "reality" of the social relations. The representational language constructed reality itself.
> —Gary Peller, "The Metaphysics of American Law"

One of the most compelling accounts of the social power of legal metaphors is in the work of Gary Peller, who is usually associated with American Critical Legal Studies.[145] Relying on a poststructuralist conception of all re-presentation as interpretation, Peller argues that apprehension rests on "particular representational metaphors that mediate or 'tilt' the apprehension."[146] Reminiscent of Lacan's critique of the neo-Freudian unified self or Ego, Peller continues: "Self-consciousness, the representation of ourselves to ourselves, contains traces of social power since we conceive of ourselves in terms of categories provided through social relations."[147] In the so-called liberty of contract era of American law, Peller identifies *spatial* metaphors (e.g., public/private realms) and *temporal* metaphors (e.g., private prior to public) that constructed legal reality, that "naturalize[d] the status quo."[148]

Commenting on Llewellyn's scientific metaphors in his Realist account of law, Peller notes that Llewellyn attempted to focus on the signified, "the concepts or things that were supposed to exist apart from the indeterminate and arbitrary representational practice"[149]—that is, apart from the world of signifiers. However, the "signified concept is never *present* but always already a *re*-presentation. This re-presentation is a signifier containing traces referring to other signifiers within a chain of differentiation."[150] Significantly, Peller is following Derrida, not Lacan, in his "chain of differentiation."[151] Ellie Ragland points out that Lacan not only acknowledged (as do poststructuralists) the Saussurean function of the signifier "to make meaning through oppositions and differences," but posited a second function: "The signifier also functions ... to reappear as misrecognized, enigmatic, unconscious meaning or displaced effect ... imposed on conscious life and daily discourse."[152] Thus when one signifier is substituted for another, "the word or image substituted does not merely disappear on being transformed. It remains present (repressed or signified) by its metonymic connection to the chain of meaning itself."[153] The unconscious chain of associations constitutes a latent text, behind the surface text, that anchors conscious life.[154] We see more clearly why Milovanovic calls Lacanian theory "referential."

POE AS LEGAL SEMIOTICIAN

> [We] maintain that it is the specific law of [the symbolic] chain which governs those psychoanalytic effects that are decisive for the subject.
> —Jacques Lacan, "Seminar on 'The Purloined Letter'"

"The Purloined Letter" is a story about law, about the minister breaking the law.[155] Lacan, in his seminar on Poe, notes that the Minister's sinister and cursed possession of the letter "shatters his vassalage the Law,"[156] just as it did the queen's (in her violation of honor). Thus the king is the law, and upon the letter's *rearrival* at its royal address, it will "reenter the order of the Law."[157] But no one is ever outside the Law—people stand in relationships of vassalage and crime, honor and dishonor, with the Law. Already, of course, "the Law" is the symbolic *order* consisting of "chains" that bind and orient and transform without regard to consciousness. We enter the symbolic order with language, *in place*, and it assigns us our places. In Terry Eagleton's formulation:

> The unconscious is, so to speak, "outside" rather than "within" us—or rather it exists "between" us, as our relationships do. It is elusive ... because it is a kind of vast, tangled network which surrounds us and weaves itself through us, and which can therefore never be pinned down.[158]

The unconscious thus has, or is, structure—like language.[159]

The language of legal processes and institutions is here implicated, not just in the sense of metaphorical mediation of images, but in its metonymic repression of what is not said, of what is displaced or lacking. In terms of literary criticism, "Lacan's analysis of the signifier opens up a radically new assumption ... that what *can* be read ... is not just meaning, but the lack of meaning; ... that the signifier can be analyzed in its effects without its signified being known."[160] In terms of legal discourse, where ordinary meaning is created by metaphor, Lacan shows that such language "as a system is metonymic. Discourse is incomplete, discontinuous, lacunary; as such, it is the sure sign of something more, or of something lacking."[161] The something lacking, the repressed body of signifiers that resists unconscious meaning, makes metaphor possible—it is the "referential base."[162] Lacan shifts our attention from conscious understanding to its discontinuities,[163] from both (1) the mainstream hope for a closed referential system *and* (2) a poststructural contentment of nonreferentiality, to an unconscious meaning system. *All* our discourse, for Lacan, "is in a sense a slip of the tongue."[164]

That we are limited by language (including legal language) and that it structures our lives are common assumptions; and that individual and communal belief-systems (including beliefs about law) are often unconscious is a major legacy of Freud and Freudian social theorists. Lacan collapses these insights in an effort to explain the structure of human thought and interaction. Not only is the unconscious structured like a language, but discourse betrays an unconscious "discourse" that is determinative and analyzable in its effects. Nevertheless, one has to realise that we do our dissecting with concepts, not with a knife. Concepts have their specific order in reality.... The first appellations arise out of words themselves, they are instruments for delineating things. Hence every science remains in darkness for a long time, entangled in language.[165]

Conclusion

A contract dispute over the interpretation of an incompletely written contract (a "surface" text) provides one of the clearest examples in law of recourse to an underlying text. The meaning of the contract is concealed—repressed—in the guise of a formal document that purports to set forth the agreement, but does not. While the knowledge of the parties was limited when the contract was signed, the "knowledge" of the underlying text was waiting—the text in the gaps can handle any contingency.[166] The parties might have believed, naively, that they were free to arrange their affairs, but only because the boundaries of the *order* of contract law were ignored. More sophisticated parties might have intentionally remained silent, creating gaps in reliance, also naive, on the stability of the ground of contract *doctrine*. That ground, however, is another text to be interpreted. Not only future events, but future meanings, were unknown to the parties. In this way, the affairs of the parties are structured by a meaning system beyond their control.

But wait. Default rules can be drafted around with sufficient time and money. Certainly, but like the analysand who risks losing his very "self" in analysis,[167] practicing attorneys do not need law and economics training to know that a deal can be lost in the effort to negotiate *everything*. It is not practicable to try to know everything—thus we say that gaps are inevitable. The contract is a condensation, a symptom, which operates like a metaphor for another contract. The written contract is also a displacement, a disguise, but the censorship will be "foiled"—just as an unconscious slip of the tongue foils our repressions—by the underlying text.

Concerning the purloined letter, which is called "the object of litigation,"[168] Lacan remarks that the "letter" is the unconscious of each of its holders—each becomes "someone else": "One can say that, when the characters get a hold of this letter, something gets a hold of them and carries them along and this something clearly has dominion over their individual idiosyncracies."[169] It takes a Dupin, the allegorical analyst, to see what is really going on.

In psychoanalytic terms, the deep structure or foundation of contract law operates like, or is, language. Not only is the gap in a contract filled by language, and not only are the rules for filling the gap textual, but the ground of contract law is mediated by words. In Lacanian terms, contracting parties are caught in the web of language that will determine who they become.

Judges and legislators attempt to fill in the secondary or incidental gaps of what is assumed to be the primary text of the contract. The gaps, however, contain the meaning of the contract. The contract only hides that meaning. Parties often think of the contract as ordering the situation, but the situation is ordered at the outset by what is not said. Lacan's shift in emphasis teaches that the unsaid is often more important than what is said. Perhaps those parties who choose not to use lawyers have seen through the myth of contractual stability.

4

Schlag's "Problem of the Subject": Law's Need for an Analyst

> The notion that to be a philosopher means being interested in what everyone is interested in without knowing it has the interesting peculiarity that its pertinence does not imply that it can be verified. For it can be put to the test only by everyone becoming a philosopher.
> —Jacques Lacan, "The Subversion of the Subject"

Pierre Schlag's book-length law review article, *The Problem of the Subject*,[1] sets out to reveal, and succeeds in revealing, *nothing*—that is, Schlag reveals a gap in various contemporary legal philosophies with respect to the subject. Of course, the subject itself (i.e., the "I" or self or individual) can be found in legal theory—people reflect on law, make law, and obey or break the law—but most legal theoreticians avoid the question of *who the subject is*. The subject is assumed to be unproblematical. So the subject *is* missing insofar as accounts of the subject are rare in legal scholarship, and the problems (significantly, different problems for different theories of law) that would be raised in such accounts are generally evaded. Ironically, Schlag explains, formalists and Critical Legal Theorists and pragmatists and "cultural conservatives," notwithstanding their disagreements, all seem to share an uncritical attitude toward the subject of law.

Psychoanalytic critics, particularly Lacan and those literary critics and analysts who work within his version of psychoanalytic theory, have not ignored the problem of the subject. The Lacanian enterprise, I think, can provide what Schlag found missing in legal theory—a "rich matrix of intellectual and cultural understandings that would help us inquire into the character of the subject."[2] Of course, the problem of how best to introduce Lacan into the fray remains. If Schlag is correct, however, that legal theorists generally have not recognized and addressed the problem of the subject, then the problem of appropriating Lacan's account of the subject is the same as the problem of the subject—Lacan's field of inquiry is, for legal theorists, new ground.

This chapter is a response to Schlag's invitation to "begin to think about" the problem of the subject for legal theory.[3] My remarks are not *the* beginning, since Schlag and others are well on their way,[4] but the substantial contributions of psychoanalytic critics in articulating the problem of the subject are at least *another* beginning. In describing those contributions, I do not intend to solve the problem of the subject in contemporary legal thought, nor will I suggest that a school of psychoanalytic jurisprudence has overcome the problem that plagues current modes of legal analysis. My efforts are directed at continuing the discussion Schlag began, albeit with a psychoanalytic *turn*, because I agree that "we are missing any convincing accounts of who or what it is that thinks or produces law."[5]

Notably, Lacanian theory is not alone in its attempt to account for the subject. The history of modern Western philosophy, roughly from Descartes on, is characterized by its attention to the knowing subject and its relations to the phenomenal object, the former being explored especially in its consciousness and receipt of sensations. Lacanian theory does not ignore that tradition as much as build upon it, though much of the tradition is rejected along the way. Just as Marx challenged the presumed sovereignty of the subject, and Freud challenged the primacy given to consciousness in modern accounts of the subject, Lacan's revision (or, in Lacan's view, revival) of Freud marks another challenge to modern notions of the subject.

Schlag's "Problem" and Ours

SAMENESS

> There is a recurring sameness to the ways in which the problem of the subject arises within each of [the] modes of contemporary legal thought.
> —Pierre Schlag, "The Problem of the Subject"

There is not one, but three problems of the subject. The problematical assumption that a relatively autonomous subject of law exists, Schlag argues, is common to and is also eclipsed in much contemporary jurisprudence. When that assumption is revealed and articulated, it becomes another problem—the problem of critical inquiry about the subject. Thus, the problem of the subject appears to be two problems: first, a hidden assumption; and second, giving an account of the subject. Schlag is primarily concerned with the first problem—the hidden assumption—but that problem is itself two problems: first, we ignore the problem "of who or what it is that thinks or produces law"; and second, we share a rhetoric or discourse that helps us avoid confronting the problem.[6] Accounting for the subject then becomes the third problem, which Schlag briefly addresses late in his article.

Beginning with Langdell's vision of legal science, Schlag chronicles the disappearance of the subject into the presumably objective order of law.[7] The subject is subordinated and trivialized in Langdell's version of legal formalism, but reappears in the form of judges and legal thinkers who need to be restrained.[8] Self-effacement thus "becomes, through an unseen and undisclosed moment of self-objectification, a kind of fetishism of the order of object."[9] The transcendental order of the object, however, breaks down when the object is seen as constructed by a subject.

In this brief account of Schlag's first analysis (of legal formalism), all three problems of the subject appear. First, the formalist objectifies the legal order without recognizing the role of the subject (i.e., self-objectification);[10] second, legal rules and doctrines appear as stand-alone, "self-sufficient, self-sustaining systems";[11] and third, the strategy breaks down, revealing the subject as maker and interpreter of the law.[12] The response to the breakdown may be resistance—the attempt to restore the order of the object[13]—or criticism of objectivism. The critics, however, also seem to fall back into a new objectivism, leaving an *"untroubled, unexamined* subject in place."[14] For example, Schlag identifies legal realism's "stabilization of the new realm of the object as the realm of social science explanation and functionalist prescription."[15]

Langdellian formalism can perhaps also be understood, Schlag suggests, as a kind of transcendental *subjectivism*—rather than self-effacement to the order of object, the individual subject is subordinated "to the law as a transcendental subject."[16] The law, like a subject, does things; doctrines do things to each other.[17] But whether Langdellian formalism is a transcendental subject strategy or a transcendental object strategy, we are (by the influence of formalism) drawn away from the problem of the subject.[18]

The rule-of-law scholar (the next approach identified by Schlag) attempts to avoid the tensions of subject-object relations by appealing to the appearance that law "works." Doctrines, principles, and policies are *handled* by competent, individual subjects. The problem of the subject is here simply assumed away.[19] Critical Legal scholars may, in their critique of legal formalism and rule-of-law proponents, keep a sharp subject-object hierarchy by describing an oppressive object order that mystifies and constrains the subject; but the individual subject is still presumed to be "already politically and morally competent."[20] Sartre's "radically free autonomous subject," at the heart of Critical Legal thought (at least, in Schlag's account), is "a stunningly liberal subject":[21] "Whereas the rule-of-law thinkers radically separate and distinguish subject and object, seeking to restrain and constrain the legal subject by means of 'objective law,' critical legal thinkers adopt the mirror image and strive to accomplish exactly the reverse."[22] If rule-of-law approaches fear the emancipation of the individual subject, Critical Legal thought celebrates it.[23] The same "competent intellectual and normative agent" who needs law in liberal legalism also needs freedom from law to emerge in Critical Legal thought.[24]

DIFFERENCE

The shared problem of the subject (hidden assumptions of relative autonomy) is not exactly the same problem in the diverse modes of contemporary legal thought discussed by Schlag. Critical Legal Studies, for example, typically approaches the object of law from the perspective of a structuralist critique, while exploring the subject phenomenologically. This dual analysis fails as a criticism of the presumed subject in conventional theory. That is, the structuralist critique of the *object*-forms privileged by traditional legal thought does not displace "conventional conceptual and social aesthetics,"[25] while the critical phenomenology describes a free subject who is constrained—"the subject is O.K. and all the problems are situated on the outside."[26]

Neopragmatism, on the other hand, has its own problem of the subject. While acknowledging "the subject as socially constructed," that image is *mediated* with the conflicting "image of the subject as in charge of his own thought and action."[27] In Schlag's assessment,

> the legal pragmatist stands outside his social construction as a kind of epistemic free agent who decides what to make ... of his own social constructedness. This understanding of the self—its agency and its situation—is, of course, utterly conventional—an instance of ... the "relatively autonomous self."[28]

The problem, for pragmatists, is that self-consciousness occurs according to conventional forms of self-reflection, and the socially constructed subject "initially contemplated by pragmatists" disappears.[29]

Finally, cultural conservatives, like Anthony Kronman in Schlag's account, presume a subject who is relatively free—"neither secured nor exhausted by culture"—but who is necessary to the preservation of culture.[30] The subject as "concierge," however, is not known on any basis to be trustworthy—the pregiven role is simply presupposed.[31]

All of these approaches, Schlag concludes, presume, and construct each of us as, a conventional liberal subject: "In his most educated moments, the liberal subject understands that he is socially and rhetorically constructed, but nonetheless retains his autonomy to decide just how constructed or autonomous he really is."[32] The danger of assuming the existence of such a subject is its "arresting" feature—critical reflection on law stops short of exploring "the space occupied by a presupposed competent individual subject."[33]

THE POLITICS OF FORM

> Only rarely ... will we find legal thought itself attempting to establish a radically different kind of subject in its very form, practice, or rhetoric.
> —Pierre Schlag, "The Problem of the Subject"

The Langdellian paradigm, Schlag explains, established an identity for legal academics as scientists, a role for judges as respectable rationalists who are informed by academics, an assumption of texts as transparent, and a repression of the problem of the subject. Although academics have lost their status as guides for the judiciary, the paradigm is still in place. Nevertheless, the problem of the subject *is* being recognized by some, within and outside the law, due to the tension between a presumed autonomy and the social and rhetorical constructions of theory and practice. Legal thinkers who ignore this tension

> may simply be rehearsing and reproducing the instrumentalist logic of bureaucratic practices.... [The supposition] that there is an epistemically and normatively competent subject.... is precisely what is being thrown in question [nowadays]: if the subject is constituted by its discourses and its context, who or what is in charge?[34]

Schlag refers to the unconscious replication of the Langdellian paradigm and its subject formation as *the politics of form*.[35] The politics of form cannot be recognized within conventional theory, because it is the very process that shapes our theorizing—we are "shaped" systematically to avoid recognizing the construction of our subject formations.[36]

In an earlier article on the politics of form,[37] Schlag begins with a popular inquiry in contemporary scholarship: "What is deconstruction?" The deconstructionist may reply that the question betrays an expectation that "deconstruction" will be a "something" that can be categorized within acceptable bounds of discourse—in short, the reply may annoy the inquirer and cause a dismissive reaction.[38] Such reactions are, for Schlag,

> a *rhetorical* confirmation of precisely what the deconstructionist said [in reply to the question]. Indeed, these dismissive reactions confirm that the question... is not just a question—but also an affirmative political act regulating the rhetorical paths that the intellectual traffic in questions and answers must take.[39]

That is, the linguistic *form* of legal thought is a matter of politics, but this feature of discourse is hidden or trivialized such that inquiry into form is repressed:[40] "What is interesting about this repression of form is that the repression is itself effectuated by means of form. What we have here is a *nested repression*: the repression of the repression."[41] For Schlag, traditional legal discourse is popularly conceived as a neutral vehicle for substantive thought, and having repressed its own form, it then forgets "that there has been any repression of form at all."[42]

Again, the effect of the politics of form is an unwillingness to interrogate the legal subject. The social, psychological, and rhetorical status of the legal thinker (judge, academic, lawyer) is exempt from inquiry.[43] On the bright side, deconstruction has the potential to undermine the privileged subject—rational, coherent—of traditional legal thought, but deconstruction can also be coopted or domesticated by traditional theory.[44]

PSYCHOANALYTIC TRACES

While Schlag attempts to sketch "the ways in which deconstruction might engage and resist the categorical regimes in force in the law's traditional discourse,"[45] which is not my focus here, an analogy with Lacanian psychoanalysis appears in Schlag's critique. Lacan, as explained in chapter 1, shares with Jacques Derrida a style of writing intended to subvert conventional understandings.[46] Thus the problematic *application* of Derridean deconstruction to law (identified by Schlag)[47] on the model on contemporary interdisciplinary work is similar to the problem of *using* Lacanian psychoanalysis in legal theory. In much "law and" scholarship, Schlag remarks,

> the foreign field is privileged as an instrument, a technique to resolve in an authoritarian manner a legally defined set of problems.... The foreign field is accorded great authority—but it is virtually always the role, the identity, the function of a *legal authority*.[48]

Potential challenges from foreign disciplines are then, in Schlag's account, "routinely neutralized because as soon as these foreign disciplines are 'applied' to law, they are subordinated to and transformed into the same old legal form."[49]

Returning to the subject, one aspect of the *form* of legal texts is the invariable establishment of "the self of the author [or] reader as autonomous, coherent," and "rational."[50] Schlag emphasizes that this characterization of the self is *not* accepted as a "conscious substantive proposition"—we *know* we are "situated in and constructed by various relations of culture, rhetoric, power."[51] Yet the *form* of legal texts denies that knowledge and "subconsciously reproduces [the autonomous] self as the constituting originating subject of law."[52] In this sense, the subject is partially constructed by the legal text—the subject of law acts as if it is autonomous, but "on some level" knows that it is not.[53]

There is some ambiguity in Schlag's use of the term "self." The rational, autonomous "self" is a rhetorical fiction in the form of American legal thought; the individual legal subject is a "relatively autonomous self," but this is also a fiction or construct of traditional legal thought; the actual "self of the legal thinker" is divided against itself, consciously recognizing its sociality and seeking refuge in texts that provide a picture or image of stability and a defense against its mere social or rhetorical existence. This *sounds* Lacanian, but in Schlag's treatment of these paradoxes, he is more philosophical than he is psychological,[54] more oriented to text as psyche than to psyche as text,[55] and more attuned to social than to psychoanalytic theory.[56]

Returning to *The Problem of the Subject*, we nevertheless find many elements of Schlag's argument expressed in psychoanalytic terms. Schlag identifies "nesting"—the reenvelopment of another's discourse into one's own—as an *unconscious* process.[57] Rule-of-law thinkers respond to the disappearance of the subject—a subject who can competently "discharge the rule-of-law mission"—with *denial*.[58] Critical legal scholars *project* their vision of self-determination into the space occupied by the legal subject.[59] The dominant form of legal thought is structured to *repress* the problem of the subject.[60] These psychoanalytic traces suggest that the reflections on the subject in Lacan's return to Freud may be helpful to legal theorists engaged in disclosing the problem (and trying to give an account) of the subject.

LACAN'S "SUBJECT" AND OURS

RETURNING TO FREUD

While I might hope to narrow the present discussion to Lacan's theory of the subject, all of Lacan's texts and the controversies he created, arguably, are about the subject—a subject of the unconscious, of psychoanalysis, of desire, of knowledge, of language, and of culture. There is no inside (e.g., psyche) and outside (e.g., culture) in Lacan's account of the subject, so everything—identities, desire, language, society, law—seems to be involved in the constitution of the subject.

Without attempting to capture the nuances in the hundreds of references to the "subject" in Lacan's texts, the themes of Lacanian theory identified in chapters 2 and 3 above are especially relevant to Schlag's critique of contemporary jurisprudence.

The Subject of the Other

In *Schema L*, discussed in chapter 2, Lacan illustrates the subject as a set of relations—relations within its self, and with others and the Other. Recall that there is no Freudian, unified ego in control, and there is no simple conscious/unconscious division. On the lefthand side of the scheme the self is split into a speaking subject (S) and an ego (or *moi*) that misrecognizes and misconstrues itself in fictional identities. On the righthand side are the others and the Other to which the split self responds—to create identities, to find structure. Internalized social conventions provide an example, as do misrecognitions of autonomy and freedom, of these relations.

While the Other is the *place* of desire, of parents, of the community, of social order, of internalized discourse, and of law, it is also unconscious, and therefore the term implies a sort of collective unconscious.[61] The subject, according to Lacan, "appears" in the Other, since the Other is the place of governing signifiers.[62] Yet again, there is no clean outside/inside distinction, as the subject is caught up in a network of language and law, of identifications and desire. Mapping those relations, for Lacan, is the project of psychoanalysis.

The Subject of Language

Lacan's notion of language (discussed in chapter 3) as determinative of the subject is multilayered, at times quite broad and general, and at times narrowly oriented to a revision of Saussurean linguistics. For example, the human subject is conceived as a "slave of language," and language is almost conterminous with culture in this conception.[63] Following Freud, the unconscious has a structure—affecting human thought and action—that is like language, thus language includes both conscious and unconscious meaning systems.[64] The symbolic order of language is primarily an unconscious order which envelops and shapes the destiny of the subject.[65] In another formulation, the subject is represented by or constituted by the symbolic order.[66]

The Subject of Law

Unlike Freud, Lacan does not turn in his later years from clinical psychoanalysis to social theory, in part because for Lacan the social aspect of psychical operations are "always already" present in the subject of analysis as a subject of language, of the Other, of law. In Ragland's formulation, Lacan claimed "that the subject is a network of identificatory and linguistic relations formed by the effects of the external world as they correspond to survival needs and demands for recognition."[67] Recalling Schlag's identification of an assumption in contemporary jurisprudence of a unified, rational subject,

> Lacan considers the twentieth-century subject to be that of empirical science.... [The] empirical subject believes in a transparency and objectivity of its own perceptions and has faith in a continuity between the perceiver and the perceived and between consciousness and reality.[68]

Lacan does not, however, simply denounce the pretensions of conscious rationality, but turns to alien and unconscious meanings, operations, and principles to describe subjectivity. Thus, for Lacan, a psychoanalytic account of the subject is necessary to all the human and social sciences, and will necessarily require a subversion of the presumed subject-in-control.

RETURNING TO LACAN

Lacan credits Freud with the revolutionary overthrow of the presumed conscious subject: "Since Freud the unconscious has been a chain of signifiers that somewhere (on another stage, in another scene, he wrote) is repeated, and insists on interfering in the breaks offered it by the effective discourse and the cognition that it informs."[69] Finding the structure of language in the unconscious, Lacan goes on to conceive the subject as a Speaking Subject (the subject of the enunciation) and as *spoken* (the subject of the statement).[70] In this account, the "traditional" or "classical" subject of self-knowledge begins to *fade*—the subject is represented (spoken) by a signifier and the speaking subject disappears (or does not know what he or she is saying, as in slips of the tongue). While the intricacies of Lacan's subversion of the subject—his account includes a critique of Hegel and a complicated graph exploring the dialectic of desire that characterizes the subject—are worthy of further study, I wish only to emphasize the role of psychoanalytic methodology in disciplinary reconceptions of the subject of language and its laws.

Paul Smith's *Discerning the Subject* (1988), informed in great part by Lacanian theory, in many ways parallels Schlag's *The Problem of the Subject*. John Mowitt, in his foreword to Smith's book, credits Smith not for *recovering* the subject but its problematization.[71] Smith exposes "the fact that the subject functions within the disciplinary structures of knowledge to provide their adherents with an alibi for the consistent inadequacy of disciplinary self-reflection."[72] The uncanny resemblance between Smith's and Schlag's critique of the failure to account for the subject (in the social sciences, for Smith, and in law, for Schlag) is intensified by their common concern with agency—with the subject as an agent of radical criticism. For both Smith and Schlag, the subject that is presumed to be free in conventional theory is not really free—the illusion of freedom allows an oppressive subject formation to go unnoticed—and genuine social or political agency is possible only in the recognition of one's constitution by social and discursive structures.

Smith, conceding that the "venerable opposition or dialectic between 'subject' and 'object,' between self and other, does not seem readily susceptible to being radically overturned; points out that "there has been a sustained effort to question the role of the 'subject' as the intending and knowing manipulator of the object, or as the conscious and coherent originator of meanings and actions."[73] The idea of *discerning* the subject is a play on the word "cern," meaning both to enclose *and* to accept an inheritance. In Smith's view, inquiry into the subject is limited ("cerned" or enclosed) by current theoretical discourse, *and* the subject is construed by its philosophical heritage "as the unified and coherent bearer of consciousness."[74] Hence the project to dis-*cern* or exceed the presumed subject. Like Schlag, Smith argues that privileging the subject from inquiry makes resistance both to "enclosure" and to our "heritage" almost impossible.[75]

Just as Schlag turns on Critical Legal Studies, with which he is often associated, Smith criticizes Marxism and neo-Marxism for alternatively superseding the subject by history and assuming the free subject of liberalism.[76] Recognizing this bind, Smith notes, the neo-Marxist Althusser turned to Lacan to supplement Marxian theory, but Althusser seemed to misread Lacanian theory and reduce it to a critique of ideology, to an account of a dominated subject.[77] Smith argues that

> In Lacan's re-reading of Freud's metapsychological theory, the "Subject" appears as a complicated articulation of different moments or instances and is conceived as a kind of process of production in the symbolic order.... Lacan leaves room for a consideration of subjectivity as contradictory, as structured in divisions and thus as never the solidified effect of discursive or ideological pressures.[78]

Smith also criticizes Pierre Macherey, an Althusserian literary critic, for failing to explore how the subject of ideology is dominated, and contrasts this failure with the more compelling approach of some Lacanian film critics:

> Within this more sophisticated and complex view of subjectivity, it would no longer be adequate to posit a social being as "always-already" a "subject," capable of recognizing itself as such. It would seem appropriate to talk instead of an overdetermination in the "subject's" process of construction [—] the effect of a continual and continuing series of overlapping subject-positions which may or may not be present to consciousness at any given moment.[79]

That is, social life is constituted by many discourses and texts, the effects of which vary, and some of which may enable agency and resistance.[80] Deconstruction, Smith notes, *seems* to offer a mode of resistance (it *does* for Schlag), but it "so totalizes the structure of discursive mechanisms as to allow no space for the subject/individual to take responsibility."[81] Indeed, Derrida's "reticence" toward using Freudian concepts reflects a concern that any "concept of a (conscious or unconscious) subject necessarily refers to a concept of substance—and thus of presence—out of which it is born."[82] For Smith, Derrida "tries to establish a kind of subjectless process which is in all essential ways given over to the force or forces of language."[83]

Smith's discussion is a replay (or preplay) of Schlag's reflections on the subject of law, but with a slightly different conclusion. Recall that Schlag finds in mainstream jurisprudence a failure to confront the problem of the subject, then ironically finds the same problem in Critical Legal Studies, then finds some hope in deconstruction for disclosing and even avoiding the politics of form that systematically hides the subject from inquiry. I use the term "avoiding" guardedly, but I notice that Schlag is combining his inquiry into the subject with his sense that *failure* to inquire into the subject results in "bureaucratic domination," in a "false aesthetic of social life," and in effective "institutions of instrumental control."[84] Smith's project in *Discerning the Subject* is similar, combining an inquiry into the subject (that is missing in mainstream disciplines *and*, ironically, in Marxian criticism) with a desire to restore the agent of resistance, of genuine political and social action. Unlike Schlag, Smith adds Derrida to his list of dead ends, and follows the neo-Marxian tradition—Adorno, Horkheimer, and Marcuse—in its turn to Freud. Even there, however, where the *goal* of resistance to ideology was most attractive, the unconscious was viewed merely as a reservoir of repressed content and not as a mediator of conscious life: "That is to say the unconscious ... must be seen as the site where social meanings and practices are negotiated *prior to* and *simultaneously with* any activity of the conscious agent."[85] Thus Smith turns to Lacan.

Lacanian theory, Smith argues, offers an account of the mediating function of the unconscious. The subject is produced or articulated by unconscious language, the discourse of the Other, yet in that moment is alienated from the Other by the "interference" of the unconscious. The subject, however, "discovers ... its construction in the field of the Other, and simultaneously erects itself in the garb of coherent 'subject.'. . . [The] subject deflects the effects of the unconscious."[86] This disavowal is interesting to Smith as it is reflected in an epistemological and discursive tradition (in the social sciences) that presupposes a knowledgeable subject. Even more interesting, epistemologies themselves

> are by and large hidden, while they yet remain as systems to which recourse is made for legitimation of particular social programs. For a simple example, [privileging] something like "human nature" can remain as a *post factum* device to explain the immutability of social formations.[87]

Notice how Smith uses the Lacanian subject—the subject constituted (or mediated) by an unconscious discourse—as the basis for a critique of the disciplines of social science. Like Schlag, Smith tries to demonstrate that traditional notions of a rational, conscious and autonomous subject, *as well as* the ideology critics who challenge such views, have neglected the question of the constitution of the subject. The subject of psychoanalysis is neither the knowing agent nor the dupe of ideology (or of a dominant discourse or social formation), which conceptions assume a certain stability and represent respectively the poles of individual freedom and social determinism. Rather, the subject is de-stabilized by the unconscious, rendering the "relation between the social and 'subject,' between epistemological and discursive force and the 'subject's' constitution," ragged and imbalanced.[88] For Smith, this account avoids both the illusion of autonomy by acknowledging the force of discursive or ideological formations, *and* the illusion of domination by acknowledging the failures of social formations in the contradictory, unpredictable subject of the unconscious.

Just as Schlag identifies a politics of form in legal discourse that arrests inquiry into the subject, Smith identifies a "metaparanoia" in, for example, the discipline of anthropology. Paranoia, typified by objectification or construction of a delusional "outside" world to stabilize contradictions "within," is here analogized with the discipline's construction of a fictional subject—unified, controlling—and a subsequent unwillingness to recognize it as a construct so as to secure the discipline from collapse.[89] "Here," Smith remarks, "I draw my analogy with the hermeneutic epistemologies of humanism where the observer's [fictional] wholesomeness prevents the recognition that the viewed world is actually its own product, a doubled image of itself."[90] From his vantage in literary criticism and cultural studies, Smith sees psychoanalysis and social theory flourishing in isolation from each other, with the former unable to problematize the subject of the latter.[91] From my viewpoint, psychoanalysis is hardly flourishing (outside the "literature and psychology" movement), but I agree with Smith that psychoanalysis is isolated, and certainly in legal theory the effect of psychoanalysis is minimal. To the extent, however, that the problem of the subject is confronted, legal theorists will either retreat into paranoic constructions of the previously assumed "knowing" subject or seek insights from a tradition—revitalized by Lacan—of critical *self*-reflection.

BACK TO SCHLAG

I noted, above, that Schlag's *Problem of the Subject* employs, at times, psychoanalytic terminology, but that no direct appeal to psychoanalytic methodology appears in the work. Significantly, in an earlier article entitled *Missing Pieces: A Cognitive Approach to Law*,[92] Schlag seemed (by his title) to be engaged in a psychological study of law. In his description of four "incommensurable cognitive frameworks," Schlag wanted "to break with the currently fashionable focus on epistemology and hermeneutics":[93] "Since cognition is a foreign territory for legal thinkers and one not obviously within the control of the individual thinker, describing the field in this way displaces (at least temporarily) the rationalist ego and resists (to some extent) the imperialism of rationalist form."[94]

While there are elements of a psychoanalytic approach in Schlag's descriptions of his four cognitive orientations—two privilege a rational ego (prerationalism, rationalism) and two de-center the self (modernism, postmodernism)—Schlag concedes that his cognitive frameworks are largely "ideational."[95] The four orientations are presented as conscious world views or belief systems—prerational consciousness, rational consciousness, and so on. When Schlag states that much "would no doubt be gained by broadening the inquiry," he has in mind a focus on professional practices or language (e.g., the metaphorical character of legal reasoning), not psychoanalytic inquiry into unconscious processes.[96] Freud is mentioned several times alongside Marx and Wittgenstein as disclosing a nonrational underside of conventional theory and discourse (in Freud's case, the field of the unconscious),[97] but Schlag basically ignores, or resists, the field of psychoanalytic inquiry into the subject. Even when remarking that prerational and rational orientations (with their privileged, unified "self") are dominant in legal theory, Schlag does not focus on psychoanalytic explanations of this dominance, which might explore the need to stabilize the split subject of the unconscious with an imaginary unity.

When Schlag does turn to various constructions of the subject (in *The Problem of the Subject*), and explains the resistance to inquiry into the presumption of a subject-in-control, a psychoanalytic turn is suggested (the politics of form is an *unconscious* structure) but bypassed to focus on the conscious ideational content of various subject-formations, not on the unconscious structures of the subject. This is not so much a criticism—Schlag's analyses are helpful—or an appeal to another overarching theoretical orientation, but rather a suggestion that if (in Schlag's words) "the problem of the subject and the politics of form are currently of concern (and possible to articulate),"[98] then that articulation should build upon psychoanalytic investigations (not all of which, of course, may prove helpful) of the subject.

That we have not yet turned to psychoanalysis, however, is hardly surprising. As Schlag makes clear, discourse over subjectivity is a threat to conventional legal thought, and many who traffic in psychoanalysis perceive its failure to be appropriated in law as a reflection of its challenge to current ideological presumptions.[99] Moreover, neo-Freudian ego psychology actually privileges the subject and provides no critical foundation for questioning the presumed subject of mainstream legal thought. Lacanian theory, which does provide a sophisticated account of the subject, is not yet a fixture in contemporary jurisprudence.

On the other hand, consider Patricia Williams's *Alchemy of Race and Rights* (1991), a work of special interest to law students and professors (she tells stories of law school teaching, exams, and faculty meetings) that betrays some influence by Lacan. Like Schlag, Williams believes that a shift from privileging "so-called objective, unmediated voices" in law to recognizing "hidden subjectivities and unexamined claims" will result in "a more nuanced sense of legal and social responsibility."[100] Reminiscent of Lacan's theory of imaginary identifications, Williams remarks that "blacks look into the mirror of frightened white faces for the reality of their [perceived] undesirability."[101] Such identities arise, Williams explains, in the context of a

> larger cultural picture. I know ... that the larger cultural picture is an illusion, albeit a powerful one, concocted by a perceptual consensus to which I am not a party [as a black female]; and that while these perceptions operate as dictators of truth, they are after all merely perceptions.[102]

Observing that the word "I" in Vietnamese means "your servant," which suggests a self-concept necessarily involving relationships, Williams suggests that in "our culture, seeing and feeling the dimension of harm done by separating self from other requires somewhat more work. Very little in our language or culture encourages looking at others as part of ourselves."[103] She then cites Lacan's attack on the objective "I" which Western culture confuses with the subject:

> This anomaly [is] manifested in its particular effects on every level of language, and first and foremost in the grammatical subject of the first person in our languages, ... [an] impossible mirage in linguistic forms ... in which the subject appears fundamentally in the position of being determinant or instrumental of action.[104]

The notion of the split subject—the subject of the Other and the subject of fictional identities—is also apparent in Williams's analysis of racism:

> [The] distancing does not stop with the separation of the white self from the black other. In addition, the cultural domination of blacks by whites means that the black self is placed at a distance even from itself.... [Blacks] are conditioned from infancy to see in themselves only what others, who despise them, see.[105]

Williams's concept of socialization is thus enriched by psychoanalytic inquiry—the efficacy of a dominant ideology is explained by reference to unconscious processes in the subject.

Williams's book is valuable for many reasons, but I mention it as another example (alongside Smith's nonlegal analysis) of inquiry into the subject by reference to Lacanian theory. Without claiming that Lacan offers a program for genuine social and legal responsibility, his work represents a sustained inquiry into the complexities of the self in its relations to the unconscious, to others, to language, and to law. If, as Schlag suggests, the subject formations of contemporary legal thought are "intellectually *exhausted*"; if the entire spectrum of legal theory exhibits a "prevailing and repetitive sameness,"[106] then Lacan's theory of the subject—which most certainly is neither exhausted nor guilty of "sameness"—is highly relevant, perhaps indispensable, to legal theoretical discourse.

Conclusion

> An interrogation of the very grounds of utterance, methodology, science, subjectivity, and so on, and an attempt to displace the epistemological certainty of the speaking "I," seem by now to have installed a critical force which is given over to, exactly and merely, interrogations and displacements.
> —Paul Smith, *Discerning the Subject*

The problem of the subject identified by Schlag (in legal theory) is, in Paul Smith's account, a problem throughout the humanities and social sciences. The problem is not so much that a "wrong" or "false" subject is presumed, but that the presumption of a subject at all, in abstraction (from a *known* object or from social and discursive formations), is a denial of the "agent whose knowledge and discourse—and thus whose activity—are no longer . . . the separate spheres which divide 'subject' from structure."[107] Once the *individual* subject is no longer presumed to exist, Lacan avoids the spiral into postmodernism by mapping out the subject as it appears in everyday language, in the misrecognitions and identities of the Ego in its everyday relations to others, and in its relation to the unconscious, to the determinative Other. Just at the point where Lacan tirelessly details the web of identificatory and linguistic relations in which the subject is caught, there is in psychoanalysis a hope—not a simplistic or romantic hope, but nevertheless a hope—that the subject can to some degree understand and navigate his or her way within the network. Lacan is first and foremost an analyst, not a critic of culture, and his description of our complex state of affairs provides the basis for some genuine, as opposed to illusionary, choices or selections as to whom or to what we will be subject.

If, or I should say "since," the foregoing aphorisms seem a bit too abstract, I focus in part 2 on particular legal phenomena—social hysteria in child abuse cases, the current takings controversy in land use law, Dickens's critique of lawyers, and the ethical dimension of the debate over religion in law and politics—to offer examples of specific Lacanian analyses of law.

PART II:

Legal Analysis in Lacanian Terms

5

Social Hysteria, Social Psychoanalysis, and Modern Witch-Hunts

> Psychoanalysis should aim to show us that we do not know those things we think we do; it therefore cannot assault our popular conceptions by using the very idiom it is intended to confront; a challenge to ideology cannot rest on a linguistic appeal to that same ideology.
> —Juliet Mitchell, "Introduction—1" to *Feminine Sexuality*

> For Lacan, ... Freud's most fundamental discovery [was] that the unconscious never ceases to challenge our apparent identity as [cohesive] subjects.
> —Jacqueline Rose, "Introduction—2" to *Femine Sexuality*

As the clinical category of "hysteria" disappears nowadays from official diagnostic usage,[1] the condition of the "hysteric" continues to intrigue many feminist critics, especially those theorists relying upon (or specifically rejecting) Lacanian psychoanalysis.[2] The hysteric in Lacan's account *fails* or *refuses* to fully surrender to the symbolic order, which account raises a serious ambiguity: if hysteria is a *failure* to submit, Lacanian theory appears phallocentric; if hysteria is a *refusal* to submit, Lacanian theory seems to offer a liberating model. In the next chapter, when I describe Lacan's associations of law with the father, and the Symbolic Order with maleness, I will reconsider the arguments concerning whether Lacan is locked, with Freud, in patriarchy. But first, in this chapter, the notion of hysteria as (feminine) refusal will be explored. (Significantly, I do not specifically address the characterization of hysteria, by Lacan and others, as a structure of Oedipal identifications or as a matter of reminiscences.)

Even before the debate among feminists over the place of women in Lacanian theory, the controversy in mainstream psychiatry leading to the demise of hysteria as a specific disease—hysteria now means a symptom in the *absence* of any disease—included a feminist charge that the traditional psychoanalytic category ("conversion hysteria") reflected a male-dominated institutional practice.[3] For such critics, sexist clinical assumptions led historically to diagnosis and treatment of healthy women as "hysterical."[4] The new wave of feminist interest in hysteria, however, takes the traditionally recognized symptoms more seriously: "Perhaps because they had no access to legitimate forms of political protest against their social and economic oppression, [Freud and Breuer's hysteric patients] waged a psychic one which expressed itself symbolically in hysterical symptoms."[5] In such formulations, the popular distinction between hysteria as a clinical category (whether a psychical disorder, a sexist mistake, or a "false" symptom) and as a social phenomenon ("mass" hysteria) begins to collapse. This collapse is initiated not merely because individual and social hysteria can be viewed roughly as two sides of the same coin (i.e., the psychiatric establishment responds hysterically to certain women by naming them mad—which conception retains the individual/social distinction), but because hysteria is a group (= women) symptom of a social, and not merely individual or even familial, disorder. Indeed, for Lacan, who restores hysteria to its central role in psychoanalytic theory, no clear boundary exists between the individual and the social—there is no unified self preceding social "influences," and gender differences are far more sociocultural than biological.

The purpose of this chapter is to reconsider, in light of psychoanalytic theory, Denis Brion's recent suggestion (in a law journal article)[6] that courts should recognize and employ a new category of "social hysteria" in child abuse cases. (Significantly, Brion is neither psychoanalytic nor Lacanian in his approach.) I conclude that Brion's notion of social hysteria, as an articulation of corresponding unconscious and social structures, represents an advance over current judicial responses to that phenomenon.

Modern Witchcraft

Brion identifies community hysteria as a disturbing feature, a sort of negative fringe effect, of the otherwise positive social and legal responses to actual, perhaps widespread, child abuse. Just as the hysteric is associated with symptoms masquerading as an organic disorder, community hysteria is (in Brion's formulation) linked to false accusations of child abuse. One might conclude that courts, like analysts, must recognize both the false and true aspects of hysteria—false as an indication of one type of disorder (organic, or in social terms, an empirical state of affairs), and true as an indication of another type of disorder (mental, or in social terms, a constructed or illusory state of affairs). That true/false distinction, however, is problematized by Brion in his historical and historiographical account of the Salem witchcraft trials. Even granting the falsehood of witchcraft accusations, hysteria as an unconscious reaction to social disorder is not exactly "false," and identifying such a reaction as an illusion is not exactly "true."

Reviewing the accusations of witchcraft as a reflection of social and political division, Brion attempts to disclose a hidden structure (in the Salem witchhunt) in which the occult is secondary to the establishment and breakdown of communal belief-systems—values, biases, and perceptions of reality. Thus the notion of hysteria, for Brion, has less to do with the accusers' imagining acts of witchcraft—that is, hysterical visions—than with the accusers' hysterical reactions to social disruption. The conscious identification of a threat to society, which happened to be witchcraft, had its roots in an unconscious fear of losing a way of life, not in a fear of witches.

This structure recurs, Brion argues, in cases involving mass false accusations of child abuse—Brion's primary examples are the childcare center controversies where large numbers of working parents and their children accused caretakers of engaging in monumental abuses including "sex rings," child pornography and satanic rituals. The conscious identification of a threat to society—child abusers—is sometimes an alibi for another threat—loss of family or community stability. Working parents likely resent someone who gets to spend all day with their respective children, and the caretaker may symbolize the loss of traditional family unity. Significantly, however, the identified threat is experienced as genuine, thus a reality is "constructed" which in retrospect can be challenged. On the other hand, the fear of family or community instability may remain unconscious.

While courts recognize the potential danger of communitywide child abuse accusations to those falsely accused, judicial recourse to conspiracy theories (for protecting the innocent) miss the point. As long as the accusers genuinely thought a threat existed, which Brion's notion of hysteria implies, then no conspiracy can be established. Brion thus argues both that courts should acknowledge the social constructions of reality in child abuse hysteria, and that accusers must assume responsibility for what they "see." More importantly, I think,

Brion reveals the complexity of social hysteria and challenges the popular notion of hysteria as a mere illusion based on irrational fear.

STRUCTURES OF HYSTERIA

Because the term "hysteria" is often presumed to have a clear meaning in popular discourse, and is defined variously in academic discourse, it is helpful initially to distinguish three "types" or "levels" of so-called hysterical behavior. First, an individual may be isolated and identified, in terms of classical psychoanalytic theory, *as* hysteric, or as exhibiting hysterical *behavior*, or as *having* a disorder classified as "hysteria."[7] On a second or intermediate level, a small group may be identified as becoming hysterical, which might imply a chain reaction of sorts among those who identify strongly with one member of the group or with each other, and each member may exhibit physical symptoms of hysteria. A third level, commonly understood as mass hysteria, exemplifies the chain-reaction phenomenon but is typically not associated with physical symptoms. (An obvious example of this latter type is the "Red scare" or communist hysteria in recent United States history; most accounts of that phenomenon use the term "hysteria" loosely, and in any event the term is ideational, not clinical.)[8] This three-level structure recurs, with slight or subversive modifications, in several historical and contemporary analyses of hysteria summarized below.

FREUD'S HYSTERIA

> Our first observations of repression and of the formulation of symptoms were made in connection with hysteria.
> —Sigmund Freud, "Inhibitions, Symptoms, and Anxiety"

While the notion of hysteria is ancient (in Egypt and Greece) and popular in medieval and modern Europe, its "heyday" occurs in the late nineteenth century.[9] Even though Freud's work with Breuer and Charcot is viewed less as the foundation for modern treatment of hysteria than as the starting point of psychoanalysis, their collective attention to hysteria as a psychological disorder was substantial.[10] Freud's early work was an investigation of a first-level (in my typology) disease involving abnormal emotional expression, a weakened (usually female) mind, dozens of physical symptoms (some less than genuine), repression of painful memories, and so forth.

Less well known is Freud's discussion of symptom formation in small groups, which appears in his analysis of the mechanism of "identification"—of one with another, in an "emotional tie":

> Supposing, for instance, that one of the girls in a boarding school has had a letter from [a secret love] which arouses her jealousy, and that she reacts to it with a fit of hysterics; then some of her friends who know about it will catch the fit, as we say, by mental infection. The mechanism is that of identification based upon the possibility or desire of putting oneself in the same situation.[11]

That process of identification, Freud explains, is not one of everyday sympathy—his example is not one where the ordinary sympathy among schoolmates should be assumed—but is a mark of "coincidence between two egos which has to be kept repressed."[12] Freud is describing, in my typology, a second level of hysterical symptoms.

The common quality shared by a small group through partial identification leads Freud to suspect that larger social group behavior—my third level of hysteria—may result from "an identification of this kind," particularly with respect to a leader.[13] While Freud's exploration of group (*Masse*) psychology is tentative and, in his own view, underdeveloped, it provided the basis for Adorno's psychoanalytic critique of fascism as a sort of collective hypnosis under the spell of a leader like Hitler.[14] Adorno observed (in the 1950s) that while the classical "neuroses such as conversion hysteria . . . now occur less frequently," a new disorder requires our attention. For Freud, Adorno explains, "the problem of mass psychology is closely related to the new type of psychological affliction so characteristic of the era which for socioeconomic reasons witnesses the decline of the individual and his subsequent weakness."[15] Just as Freud suspected dishonesty—dramatic exaggeration—on the part of hysterics,[16] Adorno finds a certain "phoniness" in the "act of identification on the part of the masses [with their leader] and [in] their supposed frenzy and hysteria":[17] "Just as little as people believe in the depths of their hearts that the Jews are the devil, do they completely believe in the leader. They do not really identify themselves with him but act this identification [and] perform their own enthusiasm."[18] In Adorno's sympathetic development of Freud's group psychology, a pejorative notion of mass hysteria is established which has very little to do with individual hysteria. Parallels exist with respect to phony and irrational behavior, but the two types are completely distinguishable except in those situations described by Freud's intermediate level (where identification with a schoolgirl "leader" coexists with hysteric fits).

LAW'S HYSTERIA

The three levels of hysteria identified with Freud (above) reappear in judicial opinions, but with a slight modification. First-level clinical hysteria remains completely distinct from third-level mass hysteria, but the second level is no longer intermediate; rather, hysteria in a small group is simply a minor version of mass hysteria (but a legally significant version if the small group is a jury or group of witnesses). Thus, in the law, first-level hysteria is a disease requiring medical attention, and second- and third-level hysteria are dangers to be avoided in the procedures of legal institutions. The greatest danger is not the small group or mass hysteria handled successfully by judges, but a social hysteria in which the courts participate.

Judicial recognition of hysteria as a neurotic disorder is simply an adoption of the clinical diagnostic term for a collection of symptoms and psychological functions. For example, conversion (as opposed to anxiety or phobia) hysteria—also called conversion disorder, conversion reaction, or conversion-type hysterical neurosis—is characterized by "an alteration or loss of physical functioning that suggests physical disorder, but that instead is apparently an expression of a psychological conflict or need."[19] With the support of psychiatric testimony, conversion hysteria is compensable in workers' compensation claims if the reaction is traceable to a work-related injury.[20]

Small group and mass hysteria, my second and third levels, are also discussed in hundreds of American judicial opinions, including child abuse cases. While a complete survey of such cases is beyond the scope of this study, the utility of a category of "social hysteria" in contemporary jurisprudence can easily be demonstrated, even though the notion is not particularly determinative.

For example, in *State v. Thill*,[21] a recent case involving a prosecution for child molestation, the defendant's attorney argued to the jury that his client was a victim of a witchhunt conducted by the prosecutor's office. After describing the history of "witch-mania" in England and the United States, the attorney suggested that those investigating and bringing charges in the case were also victims—of hysteria. The argument for recognition of small-group hysteria was unsuccessful but was discussed by the North Dakota Supreme Court (on appeal following conviction) as if it was an appropriate argument. The narrow issue on appeal, interestingly, was generally whether the defendant received effective assistance of counsel. Specifically, the court considered whether the prosecutor's jury argument in response to the witchhunt allegation—that the prosecutor's office was busy and did not bring charges without proof—should have been objected to by the defense attorney (or recognized by the trial judge) as unsupported by any evidence in the trial. Finding no obvious error, the court affirmed the conviction but noted its disapproval of the prosecutor's statement.

In other cases involving trial prejudice, attorneys have asked courts to recognize the community and jury hysteria that infected the proceedings. In *Darcy v. Handy*,[22] for example, a murder suspect (Darcy) was tried just after two of his companions in the alleged crime were convicted by a judge who (1) was present (but not presiding) at Darcy's trial, (2) made statements to the press (during Darcy's trial) about growing crime and praising the earlier convictions, and (3) participated in a sidebar conference in Darcy's trial. After conviction, Darcy brought a habeas corpus petition on the basis that an atmosphere of hysteria and prejudice prevailed at the murder trial. The court hearing the petition viewed the law as an antidote to such circumstances:

> Assuming arguendo there was some evidence of hysteria and prejudice before or at the trial, the law of Pennsylvania affords a number of methods of raising the question and spelling it out on the record.... Pre-trial, by challenging the array ... or by motion for continuance ... or change of venue.... At trial, by motion for withdrawal of juror.... Post-trial, by motion for a new trial.... Finally, [by] an appeal ... to the United States Supreme Court.[23]

Darcy lost in the U.S. Supreme Court, although three justices dissented.[24] Nevertheless, the danger of small and large group hysteria was recognized, and existing legal processes were characterized as guardians against that danger.

Grammer v. State,[25] another murder case, attracted extensive television, newspaper, and radio publicity before trial, resulting in a claim by defense counsel of "an existing 'hysteria' which, he felt, would prevent a fair and impartial jury trial 'anywhere in the country.'"[26] On appeal following conviction, the court doubted that hysteria was

> an accurate description of the apparent public state of mind. The newspaper accounts give no hint of anger, or of intense resentment in the community, such as exists when a child or woman is atrociously molested or raped, or there has been a series of such incidents or there is a racial element which has aroused abiding prejudice or passions in the public.[27]

As with *Darcy*, the appeal was unsuccessful, but again the possibility of a dangerous social hysteria was acknowledged, as was the role of the courts as mediators of public passion.

In the 1940s, some judges recognized (often dissenters) the anti-Japanese hysteria created by World War II;[28] in the 1950s, hysteria over communism, sometimes called "legislative" hysteria by reference to federal law, as well as hysteria over school integration were recognized by some courts;[29] in the 1960s, examples of hysteria over pornography, inner-city crime, and firearms were identified;[30] in the 1970s, judges observed "southern White" hysteria over civil rights reforms;[31] and in recent opinions, judges have identified or heard claims involving hysteria over homosexuality, AIDS, cancer, illegal drugs, product tampering/poisoning schemes, public library books, and even the *Dartmouth Review*.[32] Hysteria is, at least, part of the working vocabulary of judges.

Judges themselves have also been accused of being caught up in hysteria, not only by fellow dissenting judges but by legal scholars. For example, in a critique of *U.S. v. The Progressive, Inc.*, a case approving government censorship on the basis of an alleged danger to national security, Koffler and Gershman observed:

> Hysteria permeated the opinion and filled in the gaps of logic and deficiencies of evidence.... *The Progressive* suggests that whenever the administration can bring forth a claim sufficiently threatening to a frightened judiciary, publication of even readily available data may be censored.[33]

Another commentator, after noting that communists have, like witches, "inspired irrational fear and hysteria," argued that the U.S. Supreme Court was at times influenced by communist hysteria: "The Supreme Court has affirmed the convictions of some alleged communists... on the flimsiest of legal grounds."[34]

While no official meaning of the term hysteria, as a social phenomenon, arises from judicial and extrajudicial legal literature, "hysteria" is popularly understood in law as an irrational, unjustified, overly "emotional" reaction to a perceived (but imaginary) threat. The term is pejorative but sometimes forgiving, since its victims are seen to be caught up in something. Most significantly for the present study, social hysteria is viewed as having nothing to do with clinical hysteria.

WITCHCRAFT HYSTERIA

> The delusions from which the witches, their victims, and their judges suffered [in 17th-century New England] found social, institutionalized expression, and drew on beliefs generally held and rarely questioned. Yet the mental conflicts that gave rise to suspicions, accusations, and confessions... were experiences of individuals.
>
> —Peter Gay, *Freud for Historians*

The strong distinction between hysteria as an individual disorder and as a group phenomenon, in Freudian theory and in judicial decision making, is weakened when one turns to the history of witchcraft phobia.

The three "levels" of hysteria are identifiable—the witch as hysteric, the hysterical victims and accusers (with physical symptoms), and the public frenzy—but are interdependent.

For example, Brian Levack, in his study of witchhunts in early modern Europe, notes that witches were often thought to be hysterics, although most were probably mythomaniacs or simply senile.[35] Second-level behavior, on the other hand, involving those who suffered maladies allegedly inflicted by witches, probably was "some form of what we would call hysteria."[36] Finally, Levack observes that large witchhunts were characterized by

> a mood of profound fear or panic [or "mania" or "craze"] while the hunt was going on.... Appearances suggest that communities involved in witch-hunting sometimes experienced a form of mass hysteria [,but] this psychic development [must be distinguished] from the pathological hysteria that groups of demoniacs contracted.[37]

The "signs of clinical hysteria" were absent in the large community, which exhibited a type of collective obsessional behavior arising out of a general anxiety.[38] Like

> the people who experienced the Red Scares of 1919–20 and 1947–54, these villagers ... became terrified—terrified that their closest friends and neighbors were witches, ... perhaps even terrified that they themselves might be falsely accused. This terror led them to support the trials ... and even to imagine that they witnessed people flying through the air.[39]

Again, however, Levack distinguishes such mass hysteria from the abnormal behavior of the "occasional sadistic judge or hangman, the compulsive witch-finder, the insane or 'melancholic' witch."[40]

Although the clinical and social forms of hysteria coexist and are interdependent in the history of witchcraft, the distinction remains quite strong. However, in some recent feminist reflections on hysteria, the clinical *is* the social.

FRENCH FEMINIST HYSTERIA

> Dora ... is simply a little witch. Speaking in tongues, hallucinating, gagging, accusing Breuer of illicit paternity. Anna O. is another witchy women.
> —Sandra Gilbert, "Introduction: A Tarantella of Theory"

Freud saw a connection between his hysterical patients and those possessed by the devil in fifteenth-century Europe,[41] and certain contemporary feminists see in the roles of sorceress and of hysteric "exemplary tropes for the female condition."[42] "These women, to escape the misfortune of their economic and familial exploitation, chose to suffer spectacularly before an audience of men; it is an attack of spectacle, a crisis of suffering."[43] The link between hysteria and repressive cultural structures highlights women as outsiders—those deprived of power and voice, those to be feared and distrusted.[44] Most women—historically, impliedly—submit to culture. But the hysteric, in this narrative, refuses to integrate; she rejects and escapes the symbolic order; she "unties familiar bonds, introduces disorder into the well-regulated unfolding of everyday life, gives rise to magic in ostensible reason":[45]

> [What] is hysteria if not precisely the effect and testimony of a failed interpellation; what is the hysterical question if not an articulation of the incapacity of the subject to fulfill the symbolic identification, to assume fully and without restraint the symbolic mandate?[46]

We reach in such formulations a notion of hysteria as a mark of repressive social structures. In terms of my typology, the first- and second-level conceptions of hysteria—as an individual pathology and as a small group phenomenon (with physical symptoms)—seem to merge because the dis-ease is a cultural affair. Yet the hysterics are not "ill." Rather, hysterics share a common reaction to a common feature of social life (common to all women). The third-level phenomenon—mass hysteria—is almost expendable, except in the suggestion that a first-level psychological disorder (illusions), without its physical symptoms, is now located in patriarchal society. Like Victor Hugo's Quasimodo, who in Cixous's reading is the "bearer of the justice that surpasses the unjust justice of human institutions,"[47] the hysteric as a "revolting" (in both senses) outsider highlights the madness of those in control. Repressive cultural structures reflect a hysterical fear not just of the sorceress and hysteric but of women generally.

Theoretical difficulties with such a third-level account—society as hysterical—are evident. Some have argued, for example, that the postmodern age has shattered illusions of control (especially patriarchal control), that we regularly masquerade in media-created images, and that gender roles have become confused, all leaving society hystericized.[48] However, by "asserting that hysteria is omnipresent, specialists evade both its present precise locus and their own failure to master and control its manifestations."[49] We might, then, leave aside the implication that a notion of mass hysteria is useful to the feminist account that identifies with the hysteric as the symbol of women's suppression.

Theorizing hysteria as theorizing the feminine, however, is also controversial for some feminist critics. Beret Strong, for example, argues that

> the contemporary French feminists [Clément, Cixous, Irigaray, Montrelay], though celebrating woman's plurality and freedom in her body, have not moved beyond the vocabulary of a stagnant tradition.... [T]hough we can say that the hysteric speaks the truth of her difference by refusing the so-called "health" of a sick system, refusal is not everything.[50]

Strong, agreeing that hysteria "has functioned to serve masculine ideology and repression," argues for a new lexicon that will help feminists break the "theoretical habit complicitous with a diseased typology of sexual difference."[51] The point is well taken, given the reversal of meanings in the terminology retained in new accounts of hysteria.

Without detailing further the significance of feminist solidarity with the hysteric, the influence of Lacan upon contemporary reconsiderations of hysteria is clear. Lacan's notion of the subject, as constituted by (and splintered into) both language and relationships of identity, challenges the distinction between first-level "individual" hysteria and third-level "social" hysteria. Indeed, for Lacan, sexual difference itself is primarily a cultural construct; thus hysteria is not viewed by Lacan as an individual property.[52]

LACAN'S HYSTERIA

> As is true for all women, and for reasons that are at the very basis of the most elementary forms of social exchange (the very reasons Dora gives as a ground for her revolt), the problem of her condition is fundamentally that of accepting herself as an object of desire for man.
> —Jacques Lacan, "Intervention on Transference"

Martha Evans confirms, in her genealogy of hysteria in modern France, that Lacan's reflections on hysteria are scattered and do not constitute a coherent study.[53] For example, Lacan views the hysteric in terms of her lack, her unsatisfied desire, her language (which constitutes her desire), her Oedipal conflicts, and so forth. However, Lacan's characterization (in one "phase" of his thought) of hysteria as a type of discourse is a recognition of a recurrent structure of refusal, protest, and complaint in analysis and in everyday relations. Thus while Lacan usually characterized the hysteric as feminine, at times "hysteria" referred to

> the process that, in his view, had to occur at the beginning of every analysis. The analysand, no matter what the presenting neurosis,

had to put the unconscious in action, had to allow his or her symptoms to take on a symbolic meaning.... According to Lacan, until this hystericization occurred, the real analytic dialogue could not commence.[54]

The parallel between hysteria and analysis generally was particularly clear to Freud when he became interested in sorcery and read the inquisitors' manual, *Malleus Maleficarum* ("The Witches' Hammer"). Freud wrote to Fliess asking,

> Do you remember how I always said that the mediaeval theory of possession ... was identical with our theory of a foreign body and a splitting of consciousness? ... Why are their confessions under torture so like the communications made by my [hysterical] patients in psychical treatment?[55]

Cixous answers that the sorceress and hysteric share a life of exclusion, repression, and exploitation. In a similar formulation:

> Although women's move from the stake to the analytic couch looks like progress, French feminists [like Cixous] assert that the progress is only apparent. If women are no longer burned alive, it is not because political and social repression has ceased; it has only become more hidden, more insidious.[56]

Significantly, the "hysteric is in ignorance, perhaps in innocence; but it is a matter of a *refusal*, an escape, a *rejection*, and this innocence will soon be denounced [by the analyst or inquisitor] as guilt, except that it is unconscious."[57] In the field of the unconscious, the personal and the social seem to merge. Thus Lacan, in a linguistic reformulation of unconscious relations, observed that the constituting "symbolic order [of language] literally subdues [woman], transcends her."[58] Hysteria can then be characterized by "refusal or failure of the subject to enter the symbolic system of language as it shapes gender markings."[59]

Even a brief consideration of this one feature of Lacanian theory puts the three-level typology of hysteria in question. Not only has the line between illness and normalcy virtually disappeared, which is a legacy even of Freud, and not only have links been established between culture and hysteria, which is a legacy even of mainstream psychiatry, but the locus of first- and second-level hysteria is now social. The "individual" hysteric *is* the "small-group" hysteric, since the hysteric is never alone—she is a prisoner of a family *system*, of a gender ideology, not merely of her own mind or family. As for the rest of us—we need not use the term "mass hysteria"—we are perhaps more imprisoned than the hysteric. Our own symbolic constitution, our own identification with society, is more complete. The "normal" ego, for Lacan, is clearly not the unified self or control center of Western humanism, but rather a fragmenting series of unconscious identifications (with others, with language).[60]

In his reflections on the mechanism of identification in group psychology, Freud wrote that each "individual is a component part of numerous groups, he is bound by ties of identification in many directions, and he has built up his ego ideal upon the most various models. Each individual therefore has a share in numerous group minds."[61] For Lacan, Freud's insight is not limited to the questions of group psychology, as if individual psychology is a different matter, but is rather a description of the subject of the unconscious—all of us:

> At first this seems to us like an abolition, a destruction of the subject as such. The subject transformed into this polycephalic image seems to be somewhat acephalic. If there is an image which could represent for us the Freudian notion of the unconscious, it is indeed that of the acephalic subject, of a subject who no longer has an *ego*, who doesn't belong to the *ego*.[62]

Returning to Brion's analysis, the community hysteria in Salem and in cases involving mass false accusations of child abuse can be viewed either as a matter of illusions and irrationality with respect to witches and child molesters, or as a matter of unacknowledged social and political disorder. By emphasizing the latter, Brion goes beyond the traditional Freudian's, the jurist's, and the historian's version of hysteria. Social hysteria is not only a real problem (false accusations) with an illusory cause (fear of a "psychical" reality), but an illusory problem (witches, child abusers) with a real cause (fear of social disruption). This is not to say that false accusations of child abuse are to be taken any less seriously, but rather to recognize unconscious structures of language and social identity. Brion is thus allied with those recent accounts of hysteria as a refusal of culture.

Recall that Freud saw parallels between hysterical symptoms based on illusion ("born of an unfulfilled wish") or fantasy ("psychological reality," not "ordinary objective reality"), on the one hand, and the irrationality (at least sometimes) of the group mind, on the other.[63] For Lacan, however, and certainly for the feminists who see the hysteric as heroine, clinical and small group hysteria is not a sign of individual or infectious illusion, but is rather a recurrent marker of almost inevitable social illusions. Brion is adopting, it seems, the latter approach even as he reserves a pejorative connotation—*false* accusations of child abuse—in his conception of social hysteria.

Hysteria as the Backroad to the Unconscious

> The interpretation of dreams is in fact the royal road to the unconscious.
> —Sigmund Freud, *Five Lectures on Psychoanalysis*

> In fact, however, the dream work is only the first to be discovered of a whole series of psychical processes, responsible for the generation of hysterical symptoms, of phobias, obsessions and delusions.
> —Sigmund Freud, *On Dreams*

Lacan found Freud's Dora case especially important for understanding analysis—"since it involves a hysteric, the screen of the *ego* is fairly transparent." Lacan thus agrees with Freud that in hysteria "the threshold is [lowest] between the unconscious and the conscious, or rather, between the analytic discourse and the *word* of the symptom."[64] In a broader formulation—beyond the clinic—of this transparency, hysteria seems to evince "a particular responsiveness to social conditions and ideology."[65] In terms of feminist cultural criticism, hysteria is therefore "a kind of bellwether for both the acknowledged and unacknowledged expectations that shape women's lives."[66] Even Freud acknowledged one cause of hysteria in socially prescribed roles, such as sick-nursing, wherein some women "were obliged to suppress their own feelings, needs and ambitions in order to care for someone else."[67] In feminist rereadings of Freud, however, he is criticized for failing to see that the hysterics' powerlessness was "*not* simply characteristic of [their respective] personal histories, but [was] the *sine qua non* social experience in turn-of-the-century Vienna."[68] For Lacan, things are not quite so simple—social "experience" includes Oedipal identifications and insertion of the subject into language—but he is no less critical of Freud. Lacan concedes that discovery of the relations between desire and language and of the mechanisms of the unconscious—features of Freud's "genius"—remained undeveloped. Indeed, Lacan points out, Freud's own desire to analyze and understand women was never analyzed, so "hysteria places us . . . on the track of some kind of original sin in analysis."[69]

The repression of experiences of sexual child abuse was, for Freud, another cause of hysteria.[70] He is thus credited for acknowledging the shocking fact of child abuse and the psychological consequences of the child abuse victim's powerlessness.[71] (Of course, Freud has also been accused of engineering a coverup of child abuse,[72] and even for causing, through his disciples in the psychoanalytic establishment, the phenomenon of false accusations of child abuse.)[73] Freud identified his temporary error, however, in believing his patients' stories of child abuse, and was "at last obliged to recognize that these scenes of seduction had never taken place."[74] In this analysis, hysteria is a reaction to a fantasy of child abuse, and is revealed to Freud in a false accusation.

Freud's distinction between material and psychical reality was a clarification of his earlier "impression of the possibility that there could be powerful mental processes which nevertheless remained hidden from ... consciousness."[75] In contemporary legal theory, this general insight is at the basis of Charles Lawrence's critique of legislative and judicial responses to racism, discussed in chapter 2, which responses often ignore the possibility of unconscious racism.[76] Brion's analysis of false accusations of child abuse is, however, not just an appeal for lawmakers and courts to acknowledge unconscious illusions, but to recognize hysteria as an unconscious structure of refusal of social reality. The "social" aspect of social hysteria is not a mere reference to a deluded group without physical symptoms, but its essence.

Conclusion

In terms of my three-level typology, Brion is concerned with the possible false accusation made by a child, or by several children who claim to have witnessed abuse, or by a community in fear of child abuse. Without denying the reality of child abuse, and while acknowledging the danger of second-level "suggestive" reactions of child witnesses, Brion shifts our attention away from the recognized fear of widespread child abuse to the possibility of an unconscious fear and refusal of social upheaval.[77] Unconscious refusal—of social boundaries, or of a symbolic order of law and language—is characteristic of hysteria in contemporary rereadings of Freud.

Brion's formulation of mass hysteria at Salem and in contemporary child abuse cases reflects such an unconscious refusal of the loss of community or control, or the loss of the American Dream or the traditional family. Despite the perceived role of courts as controllers of hysteria, Brion's analysis reveals that legal processes and institutions may be functioning in various ways to initiate and maintain social hysteria.[78] First, the courts in child abuse cases have provided an official discourse—concerning conspiracy as consciously acting in concert—that presumes conscious autonomy and thus represses even the concept of an unconscious. Second, courts provide a forum for the social hysteria surrounding child abuse in their lack of evidentiary control. Finally, courts provide a myth of resolution, an image of a cure, in the final judgment in the proceedings.

As the above discussion indicates, there is no "working definition" of social hysteria, and I do not view Brion's argument as formulating a new psychoanalytic category for the social sciences. Nevertheless, existing judicial recourse to hysteria as either a clinical diagnosis or an emotionally charged jury or community (to which a form of procedural "riot control" is applied) appears reductionistic in today's child abuse cases. Brion enriches the current framework for legal analysis by introducing a psychoanalytic inquiry of the unconscious structures underlying the surface fears of contemporary communities.

6

"Name-of-the-Father," the Logic of Psychosis, and Real Estate

> The truth [says Lacan] . . . is that which runs after truth—and that is where I am running, where I am taking you, like Actaeon's hounds, after me. When I find the goddess's hiding place, I will no doubt be changed into a stag, and you can devour me.
> —Jacques Lacan, *The Four Fundamental Concepts of Psychoanalysis*

> "My friends," says [Mr. Chadband], "what is this which we now behold as being spread before us? Refreshment. Do we need refreshment, then, my friends? We do. And why do we need refreshment, my friends? Because we are but mortal, . . . because we are but of the earth, because we are not of the air. Can we fly, my friends? We cannot. Why can we not fly, my friends?"
> —Charles Dickens, *Bleak House*

To critics and first-time readers of Jacques Lacan and his discipled commentators, Lacan at times surely must appear like the "Reverend" Chadband in Dickens's caricature, and his followers like Mrs. Snagsby.[1] Pretentiousness and even an audience appear, but nothing of substance appears to remain after the performance.[2] The difference, of course, is that Lacan in his sermonic moments is joking, while the comical Chadband is not. On the other hand, even when Lacan is joking, he is not only joking—the master "character" he assumes is not *merely* a comedy routine, but a lecture style. Therefore, to the extent that the lesson being taught is that lessons are not so easily taught, that "words fail,"[3] the analogy returns.

I return to the characters of *Bleak House* in the next chapter, because that text provides another opportunity to demonstrate the relevance of Lacan for legal theory and practice. In the present chapter, I consider Lacan's "figure" of law, the so-called Name-of-the-Father, because it is by no means clear how that conception serves my presentation of Lacan as useful in critical legal theory. Like theologians who are curious to see the word "God" used now and then in Lacan's texts, legal theorists see the word "Law" but wonder whether Lacan thought much about legal processes and institutions. Our wonderment is perhaps greatest when, at the outset of his discussion of Judge Schreber's famous delusion, Lacan declares:

> The attribution of procreation to the father can only be the effect of a pure signifier, of a recognition, not of a real father, but of what religion has taught us to refer to as the Name-of-the-Father.
> ... Freud [was led] to link the appearance of the signifier of the Father, as author of Law, with death, even to the murder of the Father—thus showing that if this murder is the fruitful moment of debt through which the subject binds himself for life to the Law, the symbolic Father is, in so far as he signifies this Law, the dead Father.[4]

Obviously, Lacan is here in a summary mode—the passage is an inventory list of interrelated themes about law: patriarchy, religion, the Name-of-the-Father as a pure signifier (that is, an anchor to all significations), the distinction between the symbolic and a real father, Freud's mythical father murdered by the primal horde, and the network of law and culture that binds all subjects. Lacan's psychoanalytic ethnology of law, which seems to ignore lawyers and clients as well as judicial opinions and statutes,[5] culminates in an account of the function of law *as*, and not simply *in*, culture and language.

Just as Lacan's use of the term "law" betrays an unfamiliar focus and theoretical framework, so too the ordinary terms used (by Lacan and his commentators) to elucidate that framework carry unfamiliar meanings and nuances. For example, the function of law is clearest in the so-called Symbolic Order (or plane, or register) of human experience and cognition, which is for Lacan the order of language—language not as a tool for communication between relatively autonomous subjects but as a structure of governing signifiers, often unconscious in their operation and effects. At the most obvious level, legal processes and institutions function within the symbolic order, structuring our lives and stabilizing our self-images and our relationships. On a deeper level, the logic and law of language is a feature of the symbolic order generally, so that specifically legal structures and other social codes and conventions share in the constitution of the subject by language, again including conscious and unconscious "discourse." At an even more foundational level, the Law is associated by Lacan with the Name-of-the-Father, a master signifier upon which the entire signifying network of culture and language relies—the fundamental Law of the Name-of-the-Father divides and differentiates, thereby supporting the unconscious representations and grammatical structures in thought and speech. The place (or locus or field) of the chain of determinative signifiers, as well as the Name-of-the-Father metaphor, is the Other—Lacan's ambiguous term for the paradoxically exterior field in which the subject appears and on which the subject is dependent for its very constitution.[6]

In contemporary academic discourse, I have seen the term "Other" used to designate those persons or groups who are marginalized, those identified as different from "us" and who are thereby disempowered by a ruling ideology or mainstream discourse. Lacan's notion of the Other, discussed in chapter 2, is quite distinct from the idea of an excluded minority. The Other in Lacanian theory is as much internalized as it is exterior, and (in various formulations and contexts) refers to the place from which language is received, thus the place of parents and later the community, but also the place of unconscious discourse, which suggests a "collective" unconscious that mediates intersubjective language.[7] On the other hand, to the extent that popular notions of otherness imply that construction of a self is based on identifications with certain but not all other persons, Lacanian theory includes a comparable conception. Thus, while the above description of the symbolic order of determinative signifiers may sound like linguistic reductionism, Lacan acknowledges a second order, the identificatory or imaginary, which coexists with the symbolic order. The ego, in Lacan's revision of Freud, is split off from the Speaking Subject and constructs a mythical self-identity in response to the images of others. A third order, the real, designates for Lacan the unknowable "outside" of the reality experienced by the subject, who is caught in the symbolic network and in imaginary identifications, both of which are mediated by "real" effects and events.[8] The "distance" between the three orders is only theoretical, however, since the subject is constituted by interactions—the symbolic order stabilizes the imaginary, the imaginary disrupts the symbolic, and so forth. Moreover, Freudian distinctions between conscious and unconscious, and between reality and fantasy, are problematized since the symbolic and imaginary orders each include conscious and unconscious functions, and the subject's reality is constructed both by language and in relationships to others and to the Other.

Beginnings

Since the summary or inventory passage quoted above appears at the gateway to Lacan's return to the Schreber case, which concerns a trained lawyer and distinguished jurist gone mad, the case provides an inviting entry point to Lacan's conception of Law.

JUDGE SCHREBER'S PSYCHOSIS

> The patient's delusional system amounts to this: he is called to redeem the world.... The most essential part of his mission of redemption is that it is necessary for him [against his own preferences] first of all to be transformed into a woman.
> —Physician's report for Judge Schreber

At the age of forty-two, Daniel Paul Schreber (1842–1911) was admitted to a Leipzig clinic for eight months, but afterward he returned to the bench for eight years.[9] However, just months after a promotion to chief judge of the Court of Appeals in Dresden, he suffered an anxiety attack, attempted suicide, and reentered the clinic in Leipzig. In less than a year, he was legally committed to the Sonnenstein Clinic for almost nine years. Schreber's writings late in that period, published (in 1903) as a book, were merely an attempt to explain to his wife and friends why, for example, he wore feminine ornaments several hours each day. Eventually, he contested his legal commitment and won.[10]

Schreber's *Memoirs of My Nervous Illness*, translated into English in 1955, sets forth a complicated explanation of the immortal human soul, located in the nerves of the body, and of God as essentially an infinite number of nerves. In his hallucinatory moments, the stars were living beings who spoke to Schreber in human language about God, and at times Schreber used special terminology attributed to a divine language. He became convinced that the destruction of the world was at hand, but also that by his own transformation into a female he could become God's mate and redeem the world to its lost state of bliss.

Freud's analysis of Judge Schreber is a close reading and interpretation of these deluded autobiographical writings that might appear only to be rambling and nonsensical.[11] The *Memoirs*, obviously the work of an intellectual, were widely discussed by psychiatrists even before Freud declared the book invaluable. Following Freud's own analysis, the case attracted the attention of many, including Lacan who takes Freud's advice and reexamines the case.

Freud identified the gender transformation fantasy as primary—the wishful object being his doctor—and Freud explained that Schreber's resistance led to a delusion of persecution by his doctor and then God. His personal disaster was projected as a sense of worldwide catastrophe; the break with reality led to delusions and hallucinations, including the Redeemer fantasy and the related belief that he was (or must become) God's wife (to give birth to a better human race). The case demonstrated for Freud the mechanism of paranoia (rooted in this case is an infantile conflict between Schreber and his father as well as a fear of castration) and the roles of projection and repression in paranoia symptom formation.

Breaking with the psychoanalytic establishment, Lacan remarks that Freud's analysis reveals the relation between the signifier and the subject, the manner in which the subject is structured by the signifier.[12] Observing that Ernest Jones "refused to admit that any collectivity of men could fail to recognize the fact of experience" that coitus and a noticeable lapse of time precede childbirth, Lacan replies that if "the symbolic context requires it, paternity will nonetheless be attributed to the fact that the woman met a spirit at some fountain or some rock in which he is supposed to live"[13] Then, Lacan makes the statement I quoted above "that the attribution of procreation to the father can only be the effect of a pure signifier." There can be a *father* without a signifier, but not knowledge of the father's "state of being."[14]

In briefest terms, Schreber's "condition" was for Lacan triggered by the *foreclosure* of the Name-of-the-Father—in terms of real property, the symbolic father was forfeited, and there was nothing in his place.[15] The signifier was not merely repressed, but its metaphoric effect had become inadequate.

> It is the lack of the Name-of-the-Father [in the Other] which, by the hole that it opens up in the signified, sets off the cascade of reshapings of the signifier from which the increasing disaster of the imaginary proceeds, to the point at which the level is reached at which signifier and signified are stabilized in the delusional metaphor.[16]

Schreber's hallucination of miraculously created birds speaking to him appears to Lacan as the trace or fringe effect indicating that "the signifier that remained silent in the subject projects from its darkness a gleam of signification on to the surface of the real, then illuminates the real with a flash projected from below its basement of nothingness."[17] The "defect of symbolic metaphor" opened a gap in the field of the imaginary that could only be resolved by emasculation, a prospect that first appeared horrible to Schreber, then acceptable, then necessary for human redemption.[18]

This is no simple story of paternal inadequacy, or the absence of a real father, but a structural account of psychosis as a defect in the law of the signifier. (Jeffrey Mehlman's observation that French readings of Freud involve a "displacement of meaning normally brought to bear on clinical data"[19] seems to apply here.) The promulgator of law is missing—Lacan is careful to explain that the Name-of-the-Father can "succeed" without a real father,[20] and even that a real father who is actually a legislator can exclude "the Name-of-the-Father from its position in the signifier."[21]

Willy Apollan, a Lacanian analyst, remarks that the psychotic does not lose touch with reality, but loses "the social tie to the Other." Most of us neutralize the lack of foundation or guarantee in language by "myths and beliefs of all kinds, on which are grounded the value of our social relationships."[22] We repress well; we submit to socialization and symbolization processes, to law and language.[23] But the psychotic is "destitute and empty-handed" in the face of the lack in language.[24] Deprived of the "phallic or primary signifier for separation that is identified with language and forms an unconscious," that "imposes culture or order on nature," that is "synonymous with Law,"[25] the psychotic is unable to build

> a fictitious ground in his relation to the Other. . . . [H]e won't accept the myths and beliefs that sustain the social ties. . . .
>
> Thus the psychotic arises from the collapse of the world, constructing a delusional foundation for a new and incipient world of his own.[26]

Normalcy, in this account, is just another structure, alongside psychosis, of human subjectivity.[27]

LACAN'S SERMON, TO "SEMINARIANS," ON THE NAMES-OF-THE-FATHER

> [Lacan's] value lies less in his availability to appropriation as an orthodoxy and more in the openness of the questions he raises: if he valued such openness in the text of Freud, then we should [look] beyond the dictae and formulae for what remains radical and provocative.
>
> —Michael Walsh, *Reading the Real*

If the term "sermon" is associated with a certain solemnity or heaviness, then Lacan's "Introduction to the Names-of-the-Father Seminar" fits— on the night before Lacan would begin his yearlong seminar on the topic, he discovered that the "introductory" lecture would be his last under the auspices of the Société Française de Psychanalyse. Instead of engaging in a "theatrical ploy" and waiting until the end of the lecture to announce the news, Lacan apologized at the outset for the fact that no sequel would follow, and requested that absolute silence be maintained during the session.[28] All of this was not Lacan's usual style.

While the session was rich in its thematic diversity, Lacan particularly wanted to begin a further inquiry into the matters concerning Schreber, namely, the paternal metaphor and the determination of the subject as an effect of the signifier. Lacan suggests that the myth of the father in *Totem and Taboo*—briefly that the primordial father, who is the head of a precultural hoard (before the incest taboo, before law), is murdered—is central to Freud's teaching. Lacan here identifies the foundation of the Western ecclesiastical tradition, traceable in contemporary priests as fathers, in the history of the church fathers, and in the God of Moses who reveals Himself by names (Shem, Elohim, El Shadday).[29] Abraham's sacrifice, so vividly depicted in Caravaggio's painting,[30] confirms "the role of the father in bringing the child into culture and making him a member of society."[31] An angel appears in the *name* of God to interrupt the sacrifice; the covenant with God, transmissible only through the paternal blessing, is for Lacan a *passing through* His Name.[32] The Name-of-the-Father brings the Law of the Father, which structures the symbolic order of civilization itself.

The Name-of-the-Father as a passage or point of entry into cultural subjectivity recurs throughout Lacan's seminars. The name (*nom*) or "No" (*non*) of the Father allows access to the symbolic order by providing a dividing principle or structure of law. The place of the symbolic father

> marks the impossibility of [the subject's] union with [the] mother or with the [imaginary] mirror-self. The phallus is the original signifier of this impossibility, and is thus the foundation of the whole scene of metonymic displacement and metaphoric substitution.... The decisive passage to post-infant existence is the submission to the law of substitution and displacement, to the unattainability of primary desire.[33]

Thus *Desire*—primary and unattainable desire—is created by the phallic division or law of the Father. When Lacan says that the Name-of-the-Father "sustains the structure of desire with the structure of law,"[34] recall that for Lacan the bond between a mother and child

> is broken by the intrusion of Language, the symbolic structure of relations that makes individual articulation possible.... Language is the inevitability of distance, of the presence and absence of the signifier in the signified, in which the [unbroken bond] can be no more than a memory of desire.[35]

The concept of an intrusive Law-as-Father here distills for some commentators an "essential dimension of all language: the rock-like permance that language aims at imposing upon a chaotic, ephemeral world."[36] But the function of the symbolic father is not as a mere linguistic structure in any traditional sense of the term "linguistic." While one may accuse Lacan of reducing everything to language, the notion of language is at the same time expanded to include, or become, structure itself.[37]

If the function of the symbolic father as the originator of desire is clearest in the Oedipal conflict between mother, child, and father, the function of the symbolic father as the originator of law is clearest in the myth of Freud's *Totem and Taboo*—while the dead father is gone, or in the exterior Other, the Other remains determinative in culture and speech. Lacan says of Schreber that the Name-of-the-Father did *not* attain the place of the Other.[38] The implication is that, for most of us, the paternal metaphor provides an anchor, albeit silent and invisible, in the process of signification. But for Schreber, the Other has become oppositional, beyond speech, where it functions as a tyrant instead of a lawmaker. In terms of Lacan's three orders of being (imaginary, real, symbolic), we might say that the "imaginary becomes real ... by passing through the symbolic dimension without being submitted to its exactions."[39]

THE LACAN CONTROVERSY IN FEMINIST STUDIES

The paternal metaphor, the law of the father, the phallic structuration of the symbolic—it is easy to understand why Lacanian theory troubles many feminist scholars. Rejecting Lacan, however, is only one of three responses among feminists to his apparently "patriarchal" framework. *First*, one could argue that Lacan's analysis of the foreclosure of the Name-of-the-Father is all a neutral and harmless metaphor to describe the operation of law and language.[40] The phallic signifier, in this response, has nothing to do with actual men and much to do with the function of division in language—it "does not denote any sexual gender of superiority."[41] *Second*, one could base a feminist critique of culture on Lacan's analysis, since Lacan demonstrates that sexual identity is a masking process learned through the dynamics of identity and language; the priority of changeable culture over unchangeable biological conditions is here emphasized. In Ragland's formulation,

> Feminists who reject Lacan's argumentation have construed his concepts of Phallus and Castration in a literal sense and therefore view his thought erroneously as prescriptive and finalistic. In my read-

ing of Lacan I find quite the reverse: a theoretical basis for a continued feminist rewriting of Other (A) messages that can promise some change in the light of more profound understanding of psychoanalytic causality.[42]

Third, one could criticize Lacan for hiding (and reproducing) male dominance in his equation of Western culture with culture itself, that is, by displacing his focus from social relations to seemingly universal relations of language; for these critics, the Name-of-the-Father does not initiate culture and language, but rather patriarchal culture and language.[43] Psychoanalytic discourse, with its *phallic* model, "shares the values promulgated by patriarchal society and culture."[44]

I view Lacan's work as descriptive, not prescriptive, and while I agree that "we assimilate society's gender myths within our own psychic structure," I also acknowledge both "the need to restructure" those myths[45] and the possibility of resistance by the subject to the symbolic order (see chapter 4). At the same time, I appreciate the warnings of Lacan's feminist critics, as well as their insistence that sexist implications of Lacan be condemned for what they are.

A TURNING POINT

Lacan's reanalysis of Schreber's case helps to clarify numerous ambiguities, discussed in previous chapters, concerning Lacan's clinical conceptions of the signifier as constitutive of the subject, of the Other as the *place* of speech (or desire, or truth), and so forth. Schreber's psychosis, however, also provides a point of inquiry concerning the function of law in the subject and in culture.

A turning point or crossroads is reached over and over again in Lacanian theory, and is exemplified in Lacan's Name-of-the-Father invention. On the one hand, Lacan is concerned about psychosis as madness, about its structure and "logic" and possible "treatment." Some practicing psychoanalysts take this turn and explore Lacan's suggestive scheme in their own work. For example, Gerard Pommier accepts Lacan's Name-of-the-Father as "the condition for access to ordinary speech," and sees psychosis as foreclosure, but Pommier also sees an evolution in and potential revision of Lacan's work. Three "agents of paternity" appear to Pommier: the real (in the Lacanian sense of the undefinable) father of myth (Freud's primal father); the imaginary (or "living") father; and the symbolic (or "dead") father who gives the name. Foreclosure, in Pommier's revision, does not involve *absence* of any one of these agents—the psychotic can "have" all three—but rather of their interrelationship, "the knot which holds them together."⁴⁶ Schreber's delirium is thus an "unknotting" of the imaginary function which typically fills in the vacancy in the Other with, and reserved for, the Law-as-Father.

On the other hand, the nature of Lacanian theory expands Lacan's audience beyond the clinicians. Thus, while Lacan was himself a practicing analyst, the clinical data of Schreber's case is often handled as would a philosopher, anthropologist, or linguist. The focus is displaced away from Freud's categories to the operation of language (which Lacan would hold was latent in Freud in any event), and language is here conceived as determinative, as culture, as law. Thus Lacanian theory elicits interest from those in literary theory and cultural studies as an analytical framework of our state of affairs generally—of the effects of language and its structures on human thought and action. We all live in accordance with (typically unconscious) imaginary identifications, within a (typically unconscious) symbolic *order* of law and language, and up against an unmovable and unknowable *real*.

Endings

> My analogy, of course, is meant to be nothing more than suggestive—one wouldn't wish to certify anyone in particular as clinically psychotic.
> —Paul Smith, *Discerning the Subject*

Paul Smith, discussed in chapter 4, notes that "paranoia has often been used—and often very loosely—as a point of reference for explanation of particular social forms and practices." Smith then proceeds to identify a "metaparanoia" in humanist anthropology in its unwillingness "to recognize the condition of its own interpretations as constructs, fictions, imaginary narratives." Paranoia here "is a kind of archetypal objectifying device, an arrangement by which the 'subject' produces and interprets its world and then reconciles its own putative and defensive coherence with what is established *a priori* to be an objective formation."⁴⁷ The paranoia in the discipline of anthropology, Smith continues, appears typical of traditional epistemology in all disciplines that presume an unimpeachable "subject" who resides in a correspondence between discourse and the objective world.⁴⁸

Smith's psychoanalytic category thus describes a normalcy in modern epistemology, but one subject to critique as ideological: "In stressing the paranoid aspect of this ideologically sanctioned arrangement I am hoping merely to find some leverage by which to remove, or even just budge, the pretensions to ... general knowledge ... [to some holistic sense of the order of things]."⁴⁹ In the remainder of this chapter, I too seek leverage—from Lacan's analysis of Schreber—against the pretensions of order in law.

REGULATORY TAKINGS

If the function of law is to name, to divide, or to prohibit, both "sides" in the current takings controversy (in constitutional law) look for a division between what is to be called a compensable regulatory taking and what is to be called a justifiable exercise of police power to protect the environment and thus our health, safety, and welfare. The U.S. Supreme Court, in *Lucas v. South Carolina Coastal Council*,[50] placed the controversy on center stage five years ago (1992), and much has been written by law students and scholars about what was clarified in the Court's decision and what remains in confusion. My own focus, quite narrow, is on the psychotic structure of the plaintiff's— David Lucas's—legal arguments.

Lucas bought two residential beachfront lots for $975,000 in 1986, but in 1988 the South Carolina Beachfront Management Act prohibited construction of habitable structures on the lots. A regulatory takings suit for compensation was filed, and a $1.2 million judgment was awarded by the trial court. The South Carolina Supreme Court reversed, finding no "taking" because the challenged regulation prevented a serious public harm, similar to a nuisance, and nuisance regulation does not require compensation. The U.S. Supreme Court reversed and remanded, confirming that loss of "all economically beneficial uses in the name of the common good" constitutes a taking requiring compensation, *unless* the proscribed use was not part of the landowner's title under clearly existing background principles of state nuisance and property law.[51]

Focusing on the parties' briefs (to the U.S. Supreme Court), the legal significance of which is now eclipsed by the Court's opinion, a striking contrast appears as to their mood, style, and content. The responsive brief of the Coastal Council is confident and repressive— no mention is made of a serious line-drawing problem in takings jurisprudence. The case is re-presented to the Court as unworthy of Certiorari (under Rule 10), as lacking in federal questions (under Rule 14[H]), as unripe (because Lucas had not exhausted state remedies), and finally as not really presenting a takings claim (because Lucas did not challenge the ordinance as going beyond nuisance regulation, which type of regulation is not a taking). In short, the law (mostly procedural) is the law, and the coastal protection act is law at its best.

The petitioner's brief, on the other hand, is written in the voice of destitution and disorientation—on Lucas's way to the U.S. Supreme

Court, the law failed to function, to provide lines and distinctions. Regulatory takings law, an already "nettlesome field" of split decisions and complicated balancing acts, was "utterly" subverted, indeed "jettisoned," in South Carolina. No line appears between the rights of "wild-eyed tree huggers"—Lucas's words[52]—and property owners. Nuisance regulation has collapsed into the police power, even though the case graphically illustrates the need for a distinction. Lucas needs to have the function of law returned to him.

The strategies of argument adopted by counsel in *Lucas* are probably not unique. I suspect there are numerous cases where the structure of one (or both) parties' argument is—while not so expressed—that the law is not functioning to order the symbolic. I am not referring to the mere absence of *clear* lines—as in Ronald Dworkin's "hard" cases—but to the situation where the lines, for whatever reason, disappear.

Because trial and appellate procedures provide judgments that fix the world of litigating parties in stages leading up the highest court's final judgment, the moment of Lucas's "anxiety attack" is clear. Prior to the enactment of the coastal protection act, Lucas as developer knew the rules—property use is not unlimited, reasonable regulations are valid—and they made sense. Impliedly, Lucas could submit to them and work with them. In Lacanian terms, the imaginary order of objects and experiences was submitted to the symbolic order. Lucas perceived his property as his own, but he also knew of local zoning boards and state environmental protection agencies; he perceived successful developments in South Carolina but also pollution and persistent beachfront degradation. These images were named and stabilized in the symbolic order of land-use development law: regulations that go too far are takings.[53] That stability is, of course, a bit fictional, since no one is quite sure what "too far" means, but the takings clause (in the Fifth Amendment) promises that there is a line, somewhere, between a valid regulation and government confiscation. Even when the new regulation threatened to disrupt the symbolic, the trial court's judgment confirmed Lucas's understanding of the legal order. Then, suddenly, a majority of justices on the South Carolina Supreme Court held that no compensation is warranted for governmental protection against "a serious public harm."[54] Two dissenting justices predicted disaster—the majority's characterization of the challenged regulation as nuisance prevention "would totally eviscerate the takings clause."[55]

The disaster initiated by the lack of Law proceeds, Lacan suggests, in a cascade of reshapings of the signifier until the imaginary order is stabilized in a delusional metaphor. Soon after the loss in the highest court of South Carolina, Lucas realized that the missing line between valid and invalid regulation was ... him—he was *the* line, the point at which government had gone too far. Therefore, *he* must go to the U.S. Supreme Court because his case could redeem the regulatory takings doctrine.

From the "environmentalist" side in the takings controversy, one fully expected the charge that Lucas's world (in which his "right" to develop was taken) is delusional. Less predictable was the argument in the amicus curiae brief in support of Lucas from the Institute of Justice. Richard Epstein, the author of that brief, gave new meaning to the term "amicus" when he criticized the legal argument in Lucas's brief. Counsel for Lucas had taken the position that compensation is required whenever a regulation "effects a total wipeout of the use value" of property, irrespective of the government's justification.[56] Such an "extreme" position, Epstein observes, "reflects a preoccupation with the individual case without regard to the overall structure of takings law."[57] In essence, Lucas remained disoriented.

LAW AND PROPERTY

In Lacan's analysis of Schreber, a logical sequence of symptoms follows the foreclosure of the originary signifier. Those symptoms appear, by analogy, in the brief history of the *Lucas* case. Just as the paternal metaphor failed to function to initiate the symbolic in Schreber's own world, the law concerning regulatory takings did not function to protect the expectations of a beachfront property owner. Just as the Name-of-the-Father was not merely repressed but missing in Schreber's world, only to return in the voices that spoke to him in a new language, Lucas heard, I'm certain, the extraordinary voices of attorneys—particularly attorneys representing organizations concerned with property rights—telling him he had the perfect case with the perfect facts, that his suffering was a symbol of what goes wrong when the takings doctrine fails. The prospect of transformation from developer to plaintiff, like Schreber's gender transformation, probably appeared to Lucas first as horrible, but then bearable and finally necessary. Just as Schreber's world became apocalyptic, Lucas became an animated spokesman for those who are being deprived of their dearest right—to property—by professional environmental activists. And finally, just as Schreber resolved the crisis in his world by assuming the role of Redeemer, Lucas stands confidently on his property in the *Newsweek* photograph,[58] like a giant, with a stern look on his face, as if holding the key to getting the country back on track. He was, in his Warholian moment of fame, the very symbol of property rights. All of this unfolded when the dead fathers of our country, the drafters of the Fifth Amendment, were foreclosed in South Carolina.

This use of clinical data—the symptoms of psychosis—beyond the clinic is suggested in Lacan's own analysis, that is, in the turn to the structure and unconscious operation of language in the lives of those bound as subjects to law. Like Freudians who see homosexuality, not a missing signifier, in Schreber's case, we tend in law to focus on authoritative doctrines and institutions instead of the semiotic processes in our specialized discourse. Lacan shifts our attention not only to the structures of language, the scene of semiotics, but to unconscious structures, the scene of psychoanalysis. By highlighting our identification with and dependency on law—our desire—and by locating the mediation of that desire in the symbolic order, Lacan provides a framework for analysis of doctrinal controversies *as* social rather than *in* a social "context." That is, the subject of law is *the* subject. Moreover, Lacan's account of the subject is, I think, intended to be neither politically conservative nor radical, but foundational and prepolitical. Whatever one's assessment of that possibility, any implied conservatism—outside the law is tyranny—or perceived outline for a radical critique of law—as ideological socialization—are important but secondary to Lacan's attempt to map out the structures of subjectivity.

Lucas's ultimate victory returned the function of law to his world. Whether the environmentalist movement was sent reeling into social psychosis by Justice Scalia's opinion is not clear—the analysis was narrow enough to return the function of line drawing without clearly drawing the lines.[59]

What does a Lacanian analysis of *Lucas* add to the substantial body of legal scholarship that appeared following the U.S. Supreme Court's opinion? In one sense, every possible legal argument was offered in criticism and support of *Lucas*. Symposia were held at numerous law schools to debate the status of takings law, and the organizers never thought to add a psychoanalytic perspective to their menu of responses. The resulting debates often proceeded in what might be termed a discourse of shock or disbelief. That is, property rights advocates were shocked that environmental protectionists thought they could win this one—the idea that those in power could simply identify a serious social harm and charge a landowner for its prevention renders property ownership meaningless. Critics of *Lucas* were just as surprised that anyone could view property rights as anything other than a governmental matter—property ownership is a set of legal categories just like nuisance law, environmental regulations, and constitutional interpretation. A similar division between scholars is seen in the discussion of whether a clear rule is even possible; on both the environmentalist and property rights sides of the takings debate, there are scholars who cannot believe that clear rules are just a pipe dream, alongside those who are surprised that anyone still believes in clear rules after seventy years of cases leaving the controversy unsettled. A Lacanian approach mediates these two divisions: the first is a reflection of the fact that lawlike structures exceed governmental legalities, while the second reveals how those structures require a faithful and submissive subject or collectivity of subjects for their support.

Conclusion

> Storms and shifting sands could literally wash away David H. Lucas' beachfront property in South Carolina. Over the [past forty-odd] years the shoreline has moved back and forth more than 200 feet.
> —*St. Louis Past Dispatch*, July 13, 1992

Some losses do not occur merely in the symbolic order. And even in that order, gaps and discontinuities appear that do not call into question the symbolic itself. The structuring images and texts of culture, including legal culture, sometimes fail or miss. But the failure of the function of law leaves the language and logic of everyday life in disorder. Thus, Lacan reserves for the figure of law a key position in his philosophical anthropology: the Name-of-the-Father initiates the symbolic order that is constitutive of the subject—the subject of psychoanalysis, of language, and of law. Moreover, Lacan's investigation of the structure of psychosis complements a general theory of the subject constituted in the symbolic, caught up in imaginary identifications that provide a fiction of a unified self, and living up against the unknowable real. Significantly, it is the contrast with normalcy, provided by psychosis, that demonstrates for Lacan the *ordinary* operations of the symbolic order.

Paradoxically, the significance of legal theory is both reduced and magnified in Lacan's account of the subject: reduced, because legal processes and institutions are just another set of images and texts alongside others in social life; magnified, however, because the symbolic order of language is lawlike. The discourse of the Other provides names, sets boundaries, grants identities, and mediates desire like a court or legislature. Just as the field of "law and ..." subdisciplines is growing, the recent popularity of Lacan in literary and cultural studies invites our participation in "and law" enterprises. In a fundamental sense, though not at all immediately apparent, Lacan's law is ours.

7

Two Ideological Monsters: The Subject of the Bar and the Object of Desire in *Bleak House*

> "It won't do to have truth and justice on his side, he must have law and lawyers," exclaims the old girl, apparently persuaded that the latter form a separate establishment, and have dissolved partnership with truth and justice for ever and a day.
> —Charles Dickens, *Bleak House*

The famous images of sluggish legal processes and decayed legal institutions in Dickens's *Bleak House* strikes many as capturing some truths about Western law generally, even in its current forms. Of course *Bleak House* is a fictional construct—a detective story or mystery full of exaggerated characters and situations—and not an historical account, but that distinction fades in light of the narrativity of (and devices of emplotment that appear in) historiography. Moreover, cases like *Jarndyce v. Jarndyce* did[1] and do[2] arise; and while such cases are rare, some of their features are not. Lawyers recognize in *Bleak House* certain characteristics of contemporary law practice, client relationships, judicial processes, and so forth. To the extent that Dickens predicted a cataclysmic collapse of the English legal system (and even society), he was (so far) wrong,[3] but his literary descriptions of people and society are generally viewed as compelling and insightful.[4]

The use of literature as a source of understanding about law, as well as the use of law to understand literature, are growing enterprises in legal scholarship.[5] This chapter falls in the former category insofar as my concern is not with interpreting the intended meaning of, or identifying Dickens's well-placed themes in, *Bleak House*. Just as Jacques Lacan used Poe's *Purloined Letter*,[6] or Slavoj Zizek uses popular culture (i.e., jokes, films, science fiction)[7] to illustrate some of the counterintuitive and controversial features of contemporary psychoanalytic theory, I treat certain representations in *Bleak House* as allegories. If that practice seems reductionistic, I make no claim to have captured the essence of the novel.[8] On the other hand, in terms of postmodern consciousness, the meaning of *Bleak House* is not severely limited by the text or by Dickens,[9] thus I may accidentally "use law to understand literature."

The purpose of this chapter is to explore two forms of the critique of legal ideology, the first being relatively well understood and the second—based on Zizek's reading of Lacan—quite complicated and perhaps unfamiliar. I conclude that the critique of legal ideology can be enriched by Lacanian psychoanalytic theory, and in the next chapter I offer an example of how such an enriched critique of legal ideology might be used nowadays.

LAW'S SUBJECTS AND OBJECTS OF DESIRE

> "Kenge," said my guardian, . . . "do you ask *me* to believe that any good is to come of Jarndyce and Jarndyce?"
> "Oh, really, Mr. Jarndyce! Prejudice, Prejudice. My dear sir, this is a very great country. Its system of equity is a very great system, a very great system. Really, really!" (576)

John Jarndyce, firmly within the network of law, maintains (in his "animosity") a psychical distance from its promises. When attorney Kenge says of a will that it is a perfect document, that it could not "have been stated more plainly and to the purpose if it had been a case at law," Jarndyce asks, "Did you ever know English Law, or equity either, plain and to the purpose?" (576).

Even those characters less experienced in legal matters—especially those characters—have little faith in the possibilities of justice in law. Law is an impossibility, thus any "honorable" Chancery Court lawyer would give the warning: "Suffer any wrong that can be done to you rather than come here" (2). Mr. George, for example, as a subject of law generally and specifically (in his business debts), will trust no lawyer even when he is wrongly accused of murdering attorney Tulkinghorn. Trooper George proposes to tell the truth as his defense:

> "But the mere truth won't do," rejoined [John Jarndyce].
> "Won't it indeed, sir? Rather a bad look-out for me!," Mr. George good-humoredly observed.

> "You must have a lawyer," ...
> "I ask your pardon, sir," said Mr. George.... "But I must decidedly beg to be excused from anything of the sort.... No lawyer! I don't take kindly to the breed." (482)

In fact, Mr. George opines, if he had kept clearer of law and lawyers, he wouldn't be in "this place"; moreover, even if he was guilty, and a lawyer could "get him off" by keeping him quiet, by chopping "the evidence small" and by quibbling, he "would rather be hanged in [his] own way.... What I say is I must come off clear and full or not at all.... If they can't make me innocent out of whole truth, they are not likely to do it out of anything less.... And if they are, it's worth nothing to me" (484).

However, Mr. George's mother "impresses upon" him that he needs "the best advice obtainable by money and influence." Only for her, to alleviate her suffering, is he willing to "yield up his case to the greatest lawyers that can be got; [he] must not be self-willed, however right" (515).[10] Nevertheless, as with John Jarndyce, the belief in law's possibilities are absent—Mr. George remains self-willed and suspicious, in contrast to the subjects of the bar and those who desire law's objects.

LAWYERS

> "I [Lady Dedlock] dread one person very much.... He is Sir Leicester Dedlock's lawyer, mechanically faithful without attachment.... I may keep him at a standstill, but I can never shake him off.... He is indifferent to everything but his calling." (347–48)

Tulkinghorn, one of Dickens's major lawyer-figures, is known by John Jarndyce "both by sight and by reputation, and it was certain that he was a dangerous man" (406). Dedlock's lawyer is impenetrable—he "melts" in and out of rooms; he dwells "among mankind," but without consortion, nesting in the "holes and corners of human nature," not in "its broader and better range" (396). One knows Tulkinghorn to one's sorrow: "He is a confoundedly bad kind of man. He is a slow-torturing kind of man. He is no more like flesh and blood than a rusty old carbine is" (434). Trooper George's "rusty carbine" comparison is confirmed as a metaphor in Dickens's description of the late-night assassination of Tulkinghorn: "What's that? Who fired a gun or pistol? ... Has Mr. Tulkinghorn been disturbed? ... It must be something unusual indeed to bring him out of his shell.... What power of cannon might it take to shake that rusty old man out of his immovable composure?" (450–51).

While Tulkinghorn is exceptional, a "high priest of [his] noble [clients'] mysteries" (396), his death does not even wound the law generally, as plenty of lesser "priests" (with lesser clients) populate the world of the novel, each of whom share to some degree the ideals embodied in Tulkinghorn. I consider only Vholes, since I will in the next section consider his client Richard Carstone as one who does not keep his psychical distance from the law—Richard in his delusion believes in law's possibilities, in law as the place of truth and justice.

Vholes, with his less-glamorous practice, is not unlike Tulkinghorn in reputation among the lower classes of litigants in Chancery: "You don't like Vholes, I hope? *Don't* like Vholes. Dan-gerous man!" (560). But in society at large,

> Mr. Vholes is a very respectable man. He has not a large business, but ... is allowed by the greater attorneys ... to be a most respectable man. He never misses a chance in his practice, ... never takes any pleasure, ... is reserved and serious, [and his] digestion is impaired, [all of] which is highly respectable. (371)

Vholes follows the "one great principle of English law"—"to make business for itself" at the expense of others[11]—thus his fidelity to his client Richard is always limited by respectability, by business interests:

> I wish to say no more of any third party than is necessary. I wish to leave my good name unsullied. I also desire to live in amity with my professional brethren.... [Your] interests are now paramount in his office. I shall not rest ... and when I ultimately congratulate you ... on your accession to fortune, ... all between us is ended. (374–75)

Such wordiness and proprieties make Richard angry and impatient, but Vholes always offers some immediate relief to the dejected litigant, some rekindling of hope in the suit. Thereafter, Richard neither blames himself nor his lawyer, neither the suit nor Chancery, as he is slowly consumed; but this

> fighting with shadows and being defeated by them necessitates the setting up of substances to combat; from the impalpable suit which no man alive can understand, the time for that being long gone by, it has become a gloomy relief to turn to the palpable figure of [John Jarndyce] and make *him* his enemy. (375–76)

Richard, fully aware that John Jarndyce now embodies for him the abstractions of the lawsuit, nevertheless believes in the accuracy, the truth, of that symbolism—Jarndyce really is, for Richard, his antagonist and oppressor.[12] This inability to see the gaping flaws in legal processes and institutions—including law practice—is a carefully analyzed form of delusion in Dickens's account of law.

LAWSUITS

> Take what is known as passional psychosis, which seems so much closer to what is called normal. If in this case the prevalence of litigiousness is stressed, it's because the subject can't come to terms with a certain loss or injury because his entire life appears to be centered around compensation for the injury suffered and the claim it entails.
>
> —Jacques Lacan, *Seminar, Book 3*

Richard's delusion is on the surface identical to that of the mad Miss Flite, but due to her years of experience there is a difference. Miss Flite keeps her place in Chancery long after she recognizes the futility of her (and Richard's) cause:

> "I expect a judgment. Shortly. My father expected a judgment," said Miss Flite. "My brother. My sister. They all expected a judgment...."
> "Would it not be wiser," said I, "to expect this judgment no more?"
> "Why... of course it would.... But... there's a dreadful attraction in that place.... You *can't* leave it. And you *must* expect." (337–38)

Chancery *draws* people, and draws out of them their sense, good looks, good qualities, nightly rest—"I went to look at the Monster... and I was drawn to stay there" (338). She knows all the signs, and she sees them "beginning" in Richard—"Let someone hold him back. Or, he'll be drawn to ruin" (339).

Richard, "young and handsome, and in all respects so perfectly" Miss Flite's opposite, is "so dreadfully like her" in his "clouded, eager, seeking look" (335). And he knows that he, like Miss Flite, appears deluded; but if his friends only knew the accumulated papers in the case, if they would apply themselves, they would see what he sees.

> "But do you think that among those many papers there is much truth and justice, Richard?"
> "There is truth and justice somewhere in the case, Esther."
> "Or was once, long ago," said I.
> "Is—is—must be somewhere," pursued Richard impetuously, "and must be brought out." (358)

Yes, the suit has changed him, yes, others have failed to bring it to an end, but "I devote myself to it. I make it the object of my life" (358).

Much later, when he looks "worn and haggard," he explains: "Call it madness.... But it is no such thing; it is the one object I have to pursue" (415, 417). Even later, Richard's pursuit in Chancery is almost seen as a mistake, but then as destiny: "To make short of a long story, I am afraid I have wanted an object; but I have an object now—or it has me—and it is too late to discuss it. Take me as I am, and make the best of me" (472). Miss Flite will discuss "it"; Richard will not (and he dies on the eve of his worthless victory in Chancery).

DICKENS AS PSYCHOLOGIST

> Nothing can obscure the illusions and the greeds and disputes that drive people to place their reliance on Chancery and help to sustain it. Richard is the classical case in point.... A goodnatured, improvident man places his faith in riches and in the Court's capacity to satisfy this desire.
> —Joseph Gold, *Charles Dickens: Radical Moralist*

Joseph Gold argues that "one of Dickens' principal concerns and talents was the exploration of the psychology of behavior," and notes the fascination of psychiatrists with Dickens's novels.[13] In the opening chapter of *Bleak House*, to be "In Chancery" is a state of mind, a condition of perception, "as though one were to speak of being... 'in a trance.'"[14] Gordon Hirsch's explicitly psychoanalytic approach to *Bleak House* (which novel is "concerned primarily with mystery, curiosity, and investigation—with making connections and finding links") uses Freudian categories to explore the effects of Chancery: "The mysteries of *Bleak House* are connected at root with the child's curiosity about parental sexuality and his struggle to manage his own complex and ambivalent feelings about that sexuality."[15] Hence Richard is a self-destructive obsessional neurotic, his major symptom being his inability to choose a profession; his uncertainty and procrastination mirror Chancery, into which he was born and where his Oedipal conflicts are re-constituted—"Chancery becomes the institutional symbol for the parents."[16]

More recent studies of *Bleak House* also include recourse to psychoanalytic and even Lacanian theory. For example, Pam Morris's *Dickens's Class Consciousness: A Marginal View* (1991)[17] utilizes Lacan and Althusser to "reposition" Dickens's novels outside his authorial intentions; the representation of law in *Bleak House* as an ultimate structure of mystification is justified, since

> law is the ... guarantor of the existing "providential" dispensations of property, privilege, and power. Moreover, law is the formal institution for defining ... what is legitimate.... [Law] is unveiled

as the mechanism of submission, constructing subjects who "willingly" subject themselves to subjections.[18]

In this reading, the social orders of discourse, including law's "mystifying systems of meaning which sustain" power structures, become examples of Lacan's symbolic order and Althusser's ideological structures of interpellation.[19]

Audrey Jaffe's *Vanishing Points* (1991) focuses on Esther's narrative in *Bleak House*:

> Esther comes into existence for herself already structured by what Lacan calls the symbolic: by language, morality, and the law. Feeling herself both guilty and innocent, she fashions her narrative to confirm her as the latter but not the former [—she denies her "unpleasurable self"].[20]

In the end, she constructs the imaginary "world which reflects only the self she wishes to see":[21] "Esther's narrative thus reflects the conflict necessitated by the taking of a place within the social world, for, empowered as narrator to construct an identity for herself, she can only do so by choosing one identity and rejecting another."[22] This "almost allegorical enactment of [Lacan's] mirror stage" recurs, Jaffe demonstrates, at various moments in Dickens's novels.[23]

Without challenging the careful reading of *Bleak House* by Jaffe, her work (unlike Morris's) betrays the tendency to appropriate Lacan's seemingly quite accessible notions of the symbolic and imaginary "registers" in cultural studies, at the expense of Lacan's conception of desire. In her focus on Esther and not on those lawyers and litigants caught up in Chancery, the cost is negligible. For critics of legal ideology, however, the terms "symbolic" and "imaginary" can function to reduce Lacanian theory to the commonplace. As Slavoj Zizek has demonstrated, the failure to take desire and its object into account in ideology-critiques can render such critiques ineffective. It is not so much that the terms "symbolic" and "imaginary" are not useful markers in social theory, but rather that such terms alone tend to support an ideology of subjects as being *determined*, as if the desire and enjoyment of the subject are beside the point.

ZIZEK'S FANTASY

> Belief, far from being an "intimate," purely mental state, is always *materialized* in our effective social activity: belief supports the fantasy which regulates social reality.
> —Slavoj Zizek, *The Sublime Object of Ideology*

The place of Lacan in the critique of ideology, including legal ideology, is not clear. Conceiving ideology as "false consciousness" is now out of fashion, giving way to a conception of ideology as a human condition. Lacan's notion of the subject constituted in imaginary and symbolic relations seems to fill that bill, as Althusser's appropriation of Lacan for neo-Marxism demonstrated,[24] but aficionados of Lacan are less than comfortable with such syntheses—either because the hope for liberation (through an active, historical subject) seems unjustified or, almost conversely, because psychoanalytic categories are somehow reduced to the terms of sociohistorical determinism.[25] However, the suggestion of postmodernism that we live in a post-ideological era—because the beliefs that support ideologies have been called into question—is also not compelling to Lacanians, because, in Marxian and Lacanian terms, people's "beliefs, superstitions and metaphysical mystifications, supposedly surmounted by the rational, utilitarian personality, are embodied in the 'social relations between things.' They no longer believe, *but the things themselves believe for them.*"[26] That is, rather than people having interior beliefs and exterior knowledge, "it is belief which is radically exterior, embodied in the practical, effective procedure of people."[27] A place for Lacan in ideology theory therefore remains, but only in a reconsideration of Lacan and in a new definition of ideology.

Zizek—in a series of contrasts involving Freud and Marx, Lacan and Althusser—identifies two types of ideology-critique. With respect to Freud's dream theory, for example, one can characterize the latent text as containing the hidden meaning of the manifest text (which appears meaningless); interpretation of a dream is then a translation of the latent text into everyday language. Such an approach, however, identifies unconscious desire as the latent thought, the dream's signification, rather than recognizing the latent text as an articulation of something else. Zizek therefore argues that the

> structure [of the dream] is always triple; there are always three elements at work: the *manifest dream-text*, the latent *dream-content* or thought and the *unconscious desire* articulated in a dream. This desire attaches itself to the dream, it intercalates itself in the interspace between the latent thought and the manifest text; it is therefore not " ... deeper" in relation to the latent thought, it is decidedly more "on the surface" ... its only place is in the *form* of the "dream."[28]

Just as we must get rid of our fascination with the "hidden meaning" of the dream—"the content concealed behind the form"—and focus on the form itself, so in ideology critique we must examine the process by which an ideology installs itself as effective.[29]

To clarify this distinction between form- and content-based analyses, Zizek contrasts two views of the ideological "dream." If one conceives "of ideology as a dreamlike construction hindering us from seeing the real state of things," then the critique of ideology consists of "throwing away the ideological spectacles," just as we awaken from a dream into reality and realize we were confused. In psychoanalytic theory, however, one is much closer during the dream to the "fantasy framework which determines our activity" in reality; the ideological dream is not "an illusion masking the real state of things, but ... an (unconscious) fantasy structuring our social reality itself.... The only way to break the power of our ideological dream is to confront the real of our desire which announces itself in this dream."[30] We might say, paraphrasing Zizek on Freud on dreams,[31] that the structure of ideology is always triple: (1) *unconscious desire* attaches itself to the form of ideology, intercalating itself in the interspace between (2) *ideological "thought" content* and (3) *manifest reality*. The "illusion is not on the side of knowledge, it is already on the side of reality itself, of what people are doing.... What they overlook, what they misrecognize, is not the reality but the illusion which is structuring their reality, their real social activity."[32] The significance of ideology is not that it hides reality from us, but rather that it announces our reality. Fantasy, in Lacan's sense of an answer to unconscious desire, is on the side of reality, not the dream.[33]

Anti-Semitism, for Zizek, exemplifies the operation of fantasy in ideology:

> It is not enough to say that we must liberate ourselves of so-called "anti-Semitic prejudices." ... We must confront ... how the ideological figure of the "Jew" is invested with our unconscious desire, with how we have constructed this figure to escape a certain deadlock of our desire.[34]

That is, the remedy for ideological anti-Semitism is not simply production of evidence that "Jews are really not like that," as if ideology is opposed to reality, because ideological anti-Semitism has nothing to do with Jews—it "is a way to stitch up the inconsistency of our own ideological system."[35] Thus in Germany in the 1930s, the experience of having a Jewish neighbor who was *not* unclean, scheming, or exploitative could actually be turned into an argument for anti-Semitism:

> "You see how dangerous they really are? It is difficult to recognize their real nature. They hide behind the mask of everyday appearance...." An ideology really succeeds when even the facts which at first sight contradict it start to function as arguments in its favour.[36]

The paranoid construction of anti-Semitism is not a matter of misapprehended facts—each new experience of reality can be redetermined or structured by ideology. Thus in *Bleak House*, the evidence that Chancery is *not* bringing relief to its litigants tends to demonstrate, for Richard, how much more he needs it and how much harder he must work within its processes; John Jarndyce's apparent kindness to Richard demonstrates as well how bad Jarndyce really is.

Some critics of ideology emphasize the discursive field or symbolic order that operates to determine subjects in their language. Thus a discourse analysis of anti-Semitism might identify the association of Jews with financial dealings, and show how social antagonism is (linguistically) displaced into antagonism between a sound society and the Jew, or how various features (profiteer, schemer, corruptor) are (linguistically) condensed into a coded message. But this logic, Zizek notes, "is not sufficient to explain how the figure of the Jew captures our desire; to penetrate its fascinating force, we must take into account the way 'Jew' enters the framework of fantasy structuring our enjoyment."[37] Fantasy, in Zizek's account, is a "scenario filling out the empty space of a fundamental impossibility, a screen masking a void."[38] The fantasy at work in fascist anti-Semitism is that of a social Whole, without antagonism, and the "Jew"—an external element that causes antagonism—is a "fetish which simultaneously denies and embodies the structural impossibility of 'Society.'"[39] Society without antagonism does not exist, yet a social fantasy operates to mask this "nothing" and give its "internal negativity" a "positive existence."[40] In working through the fantasy, we can recognize that the excesses attributed to the Jew reveals the ideological subject's—society's—character.

Two Ideologies in *Bleak House*

> Custom is the whole of equity for the sole reason that it is accepted. That is the mystic basis of its authority. Anyone who tries to bring it back to its first principle destroys it.
> —Blaise Pascal, *Pensées*

> For the law to function "normally" ... the dependence of the law on its own process of enunciation ... must be repressed into the unconscious, through the ideological, imaginary experience of the "meaning" of the law, of its foundation in Justice, Truth (or, in a more modern way, functionality).
> —Slavoj Zizek, *The Sublime Object of Ideology*

The ideological system in which Dickens's lawyers operate in *Bleak House* can be viewed as primarily discursive, as a symbolic order.

To be named a lawyer is to hold a position of power; legal documents determine the existence of property and wealth; and judges create order with their words. Lawyers know how, and are the only people allowed, to make the system "work." Dickens's lawyers avoid feelings, including any notions of truth and justice that do not serve the symbolic conventions. If one is accused of breaking the law, one needs a lawyer to present a workable defense—otherwise, the innocent can be prosecuted, and the guilty will never get off. The system is ideological in the most obvious sense: the pronouncement of guilt or innocence does not necessarily match reality. In Chancery as well, a victorious litigant may lose everything to legal fees, or die before victory is won, which reveals an ideological, not real, benefit of law.

Such a critique, however, does not explain Richard's unique attachment to the law. Indeed, the ideological features of law are transparent for many characters in *Bleak House*, from the wealthiest like John Jarndyce to the poorest like Miss Flite. Both will have recourse to the law, but not with any confidence in its truth or justice. For Richard, however, the impossibility (or lack) of truth and justice is covered over by a fantasy of victory—the justice due him—in the lawsuit.

One might simply view Richard as lazy or greedy, as someone who is willing to set aside a normal life to gamble on a lottery, but Dickens clearly constructs a deluded subject in Richard. Richard believes he is going after justice, *and* that law is in that business. His subjection to the symbolic order of law is surely complete, but there is more to his delusion than confidence in law—his foolhardy belief in legal processes is not the fantasy but its "support." Recall the triple structure of Zizek's dream-based ideology theory; in Richard's case, there is the promise of law (ideological content), the miserable actualities of Chancery (manifest reality), and his more than active pursuit of his case which announces his (unconscious) desire to patch up the cracks in law so visible to those around him. Obviously, in the world of Dickens's *Bleak House*, the ideological promise of law is not by itself effective—as each year passes, the "coded message" of the symbolic order is fooling fewer and fewer Londoners.

Richard's fantasy, the justice due him in Chancery, is like the fantasy of the "social Whole" in fascist anti-Semitism—there is nothing *behind* the fantasy except the impossibility or lack, which must be filled to support the fantasy. Richard's lawsuit, together with his lawyer's representation of his interests therein, provides an object of his unconscious desire—unconscious not because Richard is not aware of his anxiety for justice, but unconscious insofar as he desires to fill a void with a fantasy. Richard is decidedly *not* aware of the impossibility of justice in Chancery, an impossibility constructed by Dickens and disclosed to the omniscient narrator in and readers of *Bleak House*. While the spell of legal ideology can explain Richard's delusion, the fantasy of justice in Chancery supported by an object of desire—his lawsuit—can explain why the ideology affects Richard and not all others.[41]

CONCLUSION

> Like the author, the fictive character has [in recent literary theory] been deconstructed into an effect of textual codes, a kind of thematic mirage, and the psychoanalytic study of the putative unconscious of characters has also fallen into disrepute.
> —Peter Brooks, "The Idea of a Psychoanalytic Literary Criticism"

It would not be enough to say that Richard should have worked through his fantasy, and seen in the excesses of his projection of evil upon John Jarndyce a truth about himself. Richard's delusion is, among other things,[42] an illustration of how ideology can work. My recourse to the field of psychoanalysis—via Freud, Lacan, and Zizek—is an attempt to avoid the extremes of mainstream legal theory, associated with scholars who fear that acknowledging the ideological foundation of law will result in nihilism, and also the extremes of critical legal scholarship, with which the critique of ideology is most often associated. Contemporary critiques of ideology that focus on the blinders created by social and linguistic conventions tend to be either deterministic, which calls into question critics' presumed position outside ideology, or rationalistic, insofar as ideology is viewed as a temporary condition affecting an otherwise free-thinking subject. Both tendencies, as any mainstream scholar who is suspicious of Critical Legal Studies knows, undermine the critique of ideology—the Critical Legal scholar either fails to be self-critical of his or her own ideology, or such scholars presume a rational, autonomous subject. The recourse to the psychoanalytic, exemplified in Zizek's Lacanian analysis, offers an explanation of the effectiveness of ideology without lapsing into symbolic order determinism or post-ideological optimism. In *Bleak House*, it is true that most of the lawyers, in their lifelessness, have become dupes of the symbolic order; moreover, Esther and John Jarndyce, in their wisdom, seem to have "rationally" avoided the traps of Chancery; but Richard is trapped in the extreme, not merely because the law structures his experience, but because his fantasy materializes the law that structures his experience. All three character types exist nowadays, but the third "type," least likely to be recognized in current categories—whether mainstream or critical—of legal analysis, is brought into focus by Lacanian theory.

8

Lacanian Ethics and the Debate over Religion in Politics

> Wouldn't it be interesting to wonder about the significance of our absence [as psychoanalysts] from the field of what might be called a science of virtues, a practical reason, the sphere of common sense? For in truth one cannot say that we ever intervene in the field of any virtue. We clear paths and ways, and we hope that what is called virtue will take root.
> —Jacques Lacan, *Seminar, Book 7*

American Critical Legal Studies has its own antinomies, its own indeterminancies, such that it is difficult to talk as though it is a unified position or movement, or even a single methodology or strategy. Generally, however, Critical Legal Studies is a multifaceted critique of mainstream legal ideology. Predictably, those who are suspicious of Critical Legal Studies have, from the beginning, asked how the critical theorist explains or escapes his or her own ideology,[1] and the answer is often that ideology is inescapable. Thus the critical project is about disclosure of ideology, not about the claim to know the truth outside ideology.[2]

Psychoanalysis is, of course, the model for this disclosure-without-judgment ideal, even though critical theorists are often attacked for failing to be self-critical concerning their own (leftist, feminist, sixties-style, multicultural, or postcolonial) moral judgments. In a similar attack, analysts are often accused of imposing their culture's ethics-of-the-moment in their practice.[3] Aaron Green, the unnamed exemplary New York analyst in Janet Malcolm's *Impossible Profession*,[4] follows Freud's directive to avoid engaging in moral influence, the ideal being only to assist the patient in making automatic behavior less automatic, to acquaint the patient with himself or herself.[5] And even for Jacques Lacan, with whom Aaron Green is unimpressed,[6] analysis involves a form of love that does not suppose the analyst knows what is good for another.[7] I think that the two projects—self-conscious ideology-critique and nonjudgmental analysis—merge in Lacanian social psychoanalysis, but it is fair to ask how the hidden materials of culture and law are like the hidden conflicts of personality disclosed by Freud.

LACAN'S SEMINAR ON ETHICS

The book jacket for the 1992 English translation of Lacan's 1959-60 Seminar on the ethics of psychoanalysis[8] includes two promises—the first, a quotation from Lacan's introduction, assures the purchaser-reader that the topic of ethics provided Lacan the opportunity to clarify the matters raised by him in his seminar throughout the late 1950s;[9] the second promise, from the editor Jacques-Alain Miller, confirms that the book does indeed capture many of Lacan's central ideas,[10] such as the languagelike structure of the unconscious, the determinative power of the signifier, the law of desire, and so forth.

Having struggled with Lacan's texts for years, I saw these words and became excited enough to purchase a cloth-bound edition, knowing full well it would appear soon in paper, in reliance on these representations. I am now convinced that those who will read the volume several times, outline it, and perhaps consult a few contradictory commentaries on Lacanian ethics,[11] will find the two promises to be truth-in-advertising, though such readers will always wonder whether it was Lacan's or their own efforts that supported the promises.

The 1959-60 Seminar on the ethics of psychoanalysis is decidedly *not* a uniquely accessible summary of Lacanian theory; it is rather *just another seminar*[12] which leaves the reader with the responsibility to do his or her own summation. For to explain Lacan, even to oneself, is a gap-filling interpretive exercise, so that when you arrive at page 251 you fully believe Lacan when he says he never intended

> to leave behind ... any of those handles which will enable [readers] to append a suffix in the form of an "-ism" ... [;Lacan claimed to be pleased that] *none* of [his] terms [manages] to impress itself ... as the essential term. ... None of the [confusing terms like the Symbolic and "the signifier" and "desire"] will in the end enable [a reader] to turn into an intellectual cricket on [Lacan's] account.[13]

Unfortunately, when I read these words, I had already decided to write about the now-offensive topic of Lacanianism. There is a challenge here, however, to *do* something with Lacan, to view his texts as suggestive and open-ended,[14] even as valuable in the projects of Critical Legal theory.

The use of psychoanalytic terminology and conceptions is common enough in Critical Legal theory,[15] so Lacan fits in (or can be fitted in) to any rethinking of the Freudo-Marxian synthesis, even if Lacan does not revive that synthesis.[16] Moreover, the questions of ethics, of agency and responsibility, are central in postmodern discourse about law, and since Lacan's decentered, split and perhaps splintered subject[17] is a mark of postmodern theory, we ought to wonder about his notion of the ethical.

I am not forgetting here the debate over whether Lacan *is* a postmodern,[18] and I am aware of the criticism by Borch-Jacobson and others that Lacan's terminology, his talk of the subject of desire, reinstates the problem of the subject, though Borch-Jacobson concedes that excluding the subject of desire because it is impossible to represent is "difficult to think."[19] Given Lacan's intentional evasiveness and ambiguity in discussing the subject of desire, I view Borch-Jacobson's remarks not so much as a critique of Lacan but as a critique of anyone who tries to describe Lacan's ethics in a brief chapter of a book on Lacan.

On first reading of the Seminar on the ethics of psychoanalysis, a topic that might seem to be susceptible to clarity and organization, Lacan *is* evasive and ambiguous—the text is a wide-ranging and disjointed account of the analytic situation,[20] and of moral philosophy with reference to Plato and Aristotle, to Hegel and Bentham, and to Kant and the Marquis de Sade;[21] along the way, Lacan explicates six or eight Freudian categories,[22] a few episodes from art history,[23] the text of *Antigone*,[24] and the nature of beauty[25] and even religion[26]—it is easy to believe that the project is unfinished, and that twelve years after the seminar Lacan said that while he didn't write books, he wanted to write one on ethics.[27] (He did not.)

"THE GOOD" AS BAD

In briefest terms, the Seminar is a sustained critique of any ethical theorizing that begins with an attempt to define the good, or the sovereign or supreme good.[28] For Lacan, the appropriate starting point for ethical reflection is the desire of the subject,[29] thus his critique of various notions of the good is constructive. Several times in the Seminar,

Lacan refers to the good as a *barrier* to desire.[30] There are at least four senses in which the barrier metaphor is employed, and by describing each I hope to highlight one theme of the seminar of interest to legal theorists. Significantly, Lacan does *not* speak of the good as an appropriate ethical barrier to our unethical desires—his emphasis is quite the contrary, insofar as human desire is far better than any "social" good.

First, the notion of the good, whether described in terms of a natural order or in terms of pleasure or happiness or wealth, is a barrier to theoretical discourse, because it functions to support ethical reflection that does not attend to a preliminary or foundational matter: to give an account of desire.[31] Of course, Lacan does not say that any old account of desire will do—he is critical of both the view that desire is bad and must be controlled in the name of Law, *and* the view that desire must be liberated in the name of pleasure. The first view fails to recognize the mutual bond between desire and law, that is, the manner in which law makes transgression possible *as well as* the manner in which the law of desire is prior to and beyond morality.[32] The second view, toward liberation, fails historically: the more the theory, the more social criticism, and the more duties we can imagine with which to burden the liberated subject.[33] Freud's pleasure principle, at least, revealed a system that tends toward deception, toward a hallucinating satisfaction that requires a reality principle to correct and restrain the instincts.[34]

The second sense in which the good is a barrier to desire is in the analytic situation—against the view that psychoanalysis is a moralizing discourse, Lacan confirms that the analyst does not deliver virtue, but rather clears pathways and then, perhaps, hopes for virtue.[35] Surely an ethical judgment is here in play, but the goal is to reveal, or to let the subject reveal, his or her desire, *not* to help the subject colonize his or her lack with mirages of other happy people, or with his or her "own good," or even society's good.[36] The analytic "cure," if that's even the right word, is to know and experience the absolute disarray into which our desire leads us, to know the human condition.[37]

If that sounds pessimistic, Lacan anticipates the criticism that a gathering of leftist intellectuals might have. Calling upon the images of the fool and the scoundrel in Elizabethan drama, Lacan concedes that right-wing intellectuals *are* scoundrels in their appeal to the *reality* of the human condition, but he also notes that a gathering of right-wing intellectuals leads to collective foolery.[38] Leftist intellectuals, on the other hand, are innocent fools in their optimism, but gathered together they trick each other (as do scoundrels) into believing that progress does not require enormous costs.[39]

The third sense given to the good as a barrier to desire is not so different from the first two senses (that the good is misleading in (1) theoretical and (2) analytical discourse), and it is the third sense that allows the editor Miller to promise that the seminar on ethics clarifies many of Lacan's key concepts: the good is a signifying construction, and is structured by rather than giving structure to the symbolic order.[40] Just as psychical functions are revealed, after some effort, in symbolic processes, the desire of the subject is revealed, though never completely, in the subject's relationship with language.[41] Moral law is an after effect, a trace or oversimplification, of desire.[42]

My fourth and final sense in which the good is a barrier to desire is as a description of the structure or law of the desiring subject. Lacan remarks that the "sphere of the good erects a strong wall across the path of our desire," and then Lacan suggests that the field of ethics is beyond, rather than exemplified by, that wall.[43]

Before exploring that point, I should probably attempt a half-page summary of the seminar on ethics, in the style of a junior high book report: Lacan explains his notion of fundamental desire by reference to the subject's orientation to, and impulse to find, a lost object or *Das Ding*, which Thing is characterized by its absence but is not *nothing*—it regulates its representations and it confers a law or order on the desiring subject, which desire is never fully satisfied.[44] A substitute for satisfaction of primary desire is available, through sublimation, in objects with collective social value, but such satisfaction is a delusion, an imaginary scheme.[45] Works of art and literature, given enough collective education as to their value, sometimes avoid and sometimes represent the Thing to satisfy our empty desire.[46] Religion, as well, provides a substitute to avoid that emptiness, and even scientific *un*belief is a repudiation of *Das Ding*.[47] Lacan then explores in some detail the relationship of desire to love, to erotic instincts, to the Death Drive, to *jouissance*, to transgression, and to beauty.[48] I realize that my aphorisms do not do justice to his ethical inquiry; I can, however, highlight a move that Lacan makes toward the end of the seminar that should be of interest to those in law.[49] Lacan offers a reading of *Antigone* that he hopes can derail our imaginary preoccupations with the "Good" as the starting point for ethical reflection.[50] The obvious conflict between Antigone's law and the law that the community thinks is just can help us see and define desire—the catharsis of the tragedy can be our own purging.[51]

If Creon seeks the good, the good of all, Antigone's desire aims beyond the good.[52] And when she is caught, and stopped, the law of Creon brings tragedy all around.[53] For Lacan, Antigone is not in the legal community, but in the field of the Other—she leaves written law behind and appeals to the law at the limit; she goes back to the point where language enters the subject, to the kingdom of the dead, where she exemplifies desire before it is articulated in the symbolic.[54]

After his commentary on *Antigone*, Lacan returns, at the very end of the seminar on ethics, to the analytic situation—which is not intended to put the subject in a position where everything works out for the good.[55] To terminate an analysis with comfort, to guarantee a cultural dream-of-the-moment, is a fraud.[56]

By the way, there's another book on psychoanalysis and ethics, by Ernest Wallwork,[57] which is much clearer and far better organized than Lacan's seminar. Like Lacan, Wallwork comes to terms with the tragic sense of life implied by uncontrollable desire, but Wallwork goes on to conclude that Freud *also* gave us a liberal notion of the rule of law, and a set of moral values grounded in happiness, social necessity, and rationality.[58] This seems to me to be precisely not Lacan's reading of Freud. Lacan concedes that the very notion of ethics involves a measure or standard, and he also confirms that Freudian instincts provide no such measure; the measure that Lacan proposes is a return to the meaning of action, of human action that cannot keep up with desire, since desire slips beyond the barriers of our good deeds.[59] Desire will not be controlled by a dominant political order, because it is our destiny, and it will keep returning as the law that we never completely know.[60]

LAW AND DESIRE

Mark Bracher's recent book, entitled *Lacan, Discourse, and Social Change*,[61] is an attempt to employ Lacanian ethics in the service of cultural studies. Bracher's strategy for analyzing a particular discursive cultural artifact, like a novel or a political debate, is to avoid interpreting the *artifact*—instead he proposes to interpret the dominant interpretations of the artifact.[62] His three-step methodology involves, first, identifying the manifest, collective *effect* produced by an artifact;[63] then, second, identifying the elements of the manifest discourse that are responsible for that effect, including its images and the subject's identities that are determined by the discourse;[64] third, Bracher tries to identify the nonmanifest factors, the particular desires and ideals that are appealed to by the elements producing the manifest effect.[65] Bracher tests his method with several examples, starting with discourse concerning pornography, where the images are easy;[66] he then turns to the abortion controversy,[67] then to political campaign rhetoric,[68] then to the debates over ideological literature, such as Conrad's novels that engender ideological critiques,[69] and finally he treats the supposedly non-ideological poetry of the romantics.[70] In each case, the goal is to withhold moralizing in order to map the paths of desire.

Following Bracher, I think that legal processes and institutions are cultural artifacts that produce manifest effects in our discourse, according to the nonmanifest elements of desire. For example, in the great, ongoing, unresolved debates over the constitutional status of abortion, religiously motivated political activism, pornography, or hate speech, Bracher's Lacanian analysis would identify the manifest, collective effect of each debate on a large number of people—in my examples, the two sides in each debate who respond passionately but differently. (Of course, more than two positions may be identifiable; Bracher's "only claim about the scope of the responses [that he investigates] is that in each case the particular type of response ... is widespread enough to be of potential social significance.")[71] Next, Bracher would identify the elements of discourse responsible for each identified effect—"specific configurations of images, signifiers, and fantasies" that must have produced these effects.[72] Finally, if "the specificity is great enough [with respect to both the images and the response], one should be able to pinpoint with considerable certainty precisely what textual elements are operating on what psychological structures."[73] Such structures include, for example, the desire for recognition that can be gratified or frustrated in discourse, the desires and fantasies associated with subjective identifications, and enjoyment or lack thereof:

> What must be done, essentially, is to reveal to subjects that what they are asking for (and perhaps think they are getting) in their values, ideals, conscious wishes, and identifications is not the only expression or even the most truthful embodiment of what they really desire or find gratification in.[74]

As in analysis, the "audience [is referred to] its own desire—embodied in the fantasies imbricated in its own response—as the basis upon which" change is possible.[75]

The discourses of legal controversies—as Bracher's analyses of anti-abortionist discourse and political rhetoric demonstrate—appeal alternatively to our lack of and desires for, as well as our fantasies concerning, identity, recognition, community, "goods," and power. Indeed, law is a major repository of our demands, and a major producer of gratification and frustration with respect to social desires. To paraphrase Lacan,[76] wouldn't it be interesting to wonder about our *absence* as legal theorists from what might be called an ethics of the good? Perhaps we should be, in a less violent and authoritative manner, clearing paths and ways in the hope that what is called virtue will take root.

In the remainder of this chapter, I focus on the discourse concerning pluralism among legal and political scholars, wherein the fantasy of rationality confronts the overt beliefs of the religious, and where both "sides" appeal to terms like freedom, tolerance, and liberty for rhetorical support.

Reason and Religion in Law and Politics

In a recent essay on the relevance of Jacques Lacan's work for theological discourse, William James Earle raises the question of "reason and religion since Freud":

> How can we, this far into the discussion, find anything that does not have the form of ever more insistent repetition, like the interminable rehashing of frozen positions in a family quarrel? Put the problem... another way: What would make the disagreement between religious and nonreligious people tractable if it isn't tractable already?[77]

In the fields of law and politics, the disagreement isn't tractable, now as ever. Religious activists claim to be marginalized by an increasingly secular culture, while the nonreligious point to the enormous potential—and historical reality—of religion as an exemplar of marginalization.

As Earle explains, religion was suspect in psychoanalysis from the very beginning—Freud was "Enlightened" regarding the historical tension between faith and reason.[78] From that perspective, from "the outside, faith may seem like a reaction formation to... established knowledge [such that] the nondisappearance of religion... occasions surprise."[79] Yet religion remains, and social scientists, observing the phenomena of the religious Right as well as religiously inspired ideals of economic justice that each nowadays affect politics (perhaps differently), have apparently renewed their interest in religion.[80] Among legal scholars, the controversy over the propriety of religious influence in law and politics—including public discourse, voting, lobbying, law making, and judicial decision making—has become an industry.

The debate is complicated because of the diverse contexts of religious influence in legal processes and institutions (e.g., a religious citizen's vote for a congressional candidate seems less controversial than a vote by a religious Supreme Court justice concerning a case on appeal). Moreover, one's position in the debate has everything to do with one's view of religion (an illusion, or a system of morals like any other?), influence (an appeal to church or scriptural authority, or an "indirect" reliance on cultural conventions?), and law (a relatively neutral affair, or an ideological superstructure?). The variety of perspectives in the debate makes summary of the issues difficult, but two interesting (and opposing) positions are clearly identifiable, which I call the liberal (or Rawlsian, or public reason) approach and the religious pluralist position. Proponents of the former approach privatize religion and appeal to shared values (like tolerance or liberty) that allegedly transcend religious and moral differences. Proponents of the latter view likewise appeal to values (like tolerance or liberty), but not on secular, neutral, or rationalist grounds; rather, such values are *part of* their religious perspective, which perspective is as suspicious of public rationality as the liberals are of public religion. In briefest terms, the liberal believes that judicial and legislative decisions should be justified by public reasons, while the religious pluralist questions the public/private distinction as well as the possibility of avoiding faithlike commitments in either law making or theories of justice.

My focus in the remainder of this chapter is on the conflict between these two positions, though the current legal debate also includes (1) scholars who are hostile toward religion either because of its epistemological inferiority or because of its historical intolerance, and (2) scholars who believe that biblical morality should be imposed by law. I mention these other two perspectives only as contrasts to the two on which I focus: liberal theories of justice are not typically hostile toward religion (since religion is a source of private values that can sometimes become public reasons), and religious pluralism is not typically an appeal to scriptural authority in law. Religious pluralism is, like the liberal account of public reason, a theory of justice, albeit a theory grounded in overt religious beliefs (concerning, e.g., human dignity, freedom, and dependence upon some "god").[81] Thus the confrontation I discuss is centered on the notion of pluralism as either a reason-based limit on religious imposition or a religiously based limit on the impositions of public reason.

The disagreement between theorists of pluralism may seem trivial, and in easy cases it is. But hard cases—the current controversies concerning abortion, environmental ethics, animal rights, welfare assistance, punishment, and military policy,[82] and I would add school choice voucher systems and voting rights—highlight the underdeterminacy of notions like pluralism. That is, the ideals of tolerance and recourse to shared values and forms of reasoning fail as standards by which to judge conflicting moral claims—both "sides" in these controversies offer reasonable *interpretations* of our shared values. The liberal in such hard cases often appeals to individual freedom as a "trump" to avoid imposition of privately held religious and moral values. From the religious pluralist perspective, however, the liberal solution is a veiled imposition—not only is moral imposition unavoidable in law and politics, but privileging individual freedom over other values is not, in hard cases, a pluralistic move. The timing and context of the liberal appeal to individual freedom reveal a particular interpretation of pluralism.

At first glance, the debate between liberal and religious pluralists is a dead end—an "interminable rehashing of frozen positions" on faith and reason. On closer examination, however, the pluralism debate is located between those extremes, and might be better characterized as a practical argument over the best theoretical orientation concerning common ideals like liberty, diversity, and freedom. The liberals respect religion, but seek to limit its political influence; the religious pluralists respect public reason, but likewise seek to limit its political influence. Both sides claim the high ground of toleration and accuse the other of unwittingly imposing private morality.

What can psychoanalytic understanding offer to the impasse over pluralism? Traditionally, discussions concerning Freud and religion resulted in a similar impasse. The rhetorical strategies of orthodox psychoanalysts and of orthodox religionists each

> has now proved its usefulness and its limits. These limits are now clear to everyone except those religionists who cannot help finding religion anywhere a serious concern (that is, everywhere [in Freud]) and those psychoanalysts incapable of noticing anything in religion except neurosis. For both these ... analyses, everything is finally the same thing.[83]

On the other hand, Lacanian psychoanalytic understanding, in at least some of its variants, provides an opportunity to rethink the clash of reason and religion. In the next section, I revisit the possibilities of a Lacanian contribution to the critique of legal ideology—which ideology includes the belief in rational grounds for law. When I later compare the communitarian critique of Rawlsian public reason with the response of religious pluralists to liberal notions of pluralism, I discuss some recent celebrations of otherness, both among Rawls's critics and among psychoanalytic theorists, especially those inspired by Lacan's accounts of the subject (of desire, of law, of the Other), of analysis, and of ethics. I conclude that the respect for and responsibility toward others that theories of pluralism purport to offer is exemplified by Lacanian ethics, *and* that the religious pluralists, not the pluralists of public reason, find support in psychoanalytic understandings of the relationships between subjects of law and politics.

Significantly, the emphasis on "otherness" (that I associate variously with Rawls's critics, postmodern psychoanalytic theorists, Lacan, and religious pluralists) has two aspects or moments that must be distinguished. First, according to theories of the social construction of the subject, we depend on others—their images and language—for our very "selves"; this, of course, is a critique of any individualism based on notions of independent, rational subjects. Second, to the extent that we desire or demand to be desired or recognized by others, a tendency toward mastery or domination persists together with a failure to recognize the other qua other; this analysis of subjectivity is a critique of "rational" appeals to our sameness or to our shared heritage of values, which appeals either to reduce subjectivity to an abstract formality or identify rationality with a dominant discourse—in both cases denying social diversity. This oscillation of perspectives on otherness as a marker of our sociality *and* of our singularity seems odd, but both are in play in critical (or postmodern, or "relational") accounts of the subject of law and politics.

> It is not the world as it is that necessitates our callings but the relationships in which we participate.... [The] claim to "objective knowledge" ... denigrates ... views ... of sundry religions, political action groups, ethnicities.... In terms of its relational implications, "science talk" is thus as totalizing as that of the demagogy that science has sought to replace. [Much] the same conclusions follow in the case of the language of morality and ethics. The claim to Foundational or first moral principles has much the same relational effect.[84]

LACAN AND THE CRITIQUE OF LEGAL IDEOLOGY

In the Frankfurt School (i.e., neo-Marxian critical theory) critique of ideology, which in part attempted to disclose the inevitable effects of unconscious belief-structures, the utility of Freudian psychoanalytic conceptions was immediately recognized (e.g., by Horkheimer, Adorno, Fromm and Marcuse).[85] Critical Legal Studies, associated with the effort to demonstrate the indeterminacy (and political tilt) of legal doctrine, has roots in neo-Marxism and thus shares an affinity with psychoanalysis.[86] To date, however, many of the appropriations of psychoanalysis into the critique of legal institutions and processes have been simplistic (e.g., law as a father figure; law reflecting repression of uncomfortable prejudices, etc.). The work of Jacques Lacan, on the other hand, invites a reconsideration of the role of social structures, including law, in constituting the subject of psychoanalysis. While traditional psychoanalytic social theory focuses on our collective projection of law as stable, our collective repression of desires through law, and our collective alienation from legal institutions, each of which is a valid inquiry, Lacan shifts the attention of critics of legal ideology to the construction of the subject of law in the symbolic and imaginary orders, that is, by language and identificatory images.

The strength of the critique of ideology has always been the ability to identify hidden structures of power; its weakness has always been the failure of the critic to remain self-critical. That is, critical discourse often proceeds as if the critic is beyond or above ideology. Psychoanalytic understanding is here helpful in providing a role for the social critic as analyst—as one who merely exposes and allows subjects to work through otherwise hidden beliefs, desires, and fantasies with respect to social institutions. Lacanian psychoanalysis, however, is particularly attentive to the cultural constitution of that subject—the distance between "self" and "influential" power structures is collapsed.

The language and images produced by legal institutions and processes provide an example of the social constitution of the subject. Lacan's notion of the Other—the unconscious, the place of parents, culture, and language—includes legal processes and institutions which we internalize and to which we submit. Law provides images and a language by which we understand our family structures, our relation to property, our sense of being wronged or harmed, and the enforceability of our promises. Thus our beliefs, desires, and fantasies regarding such matters are not just mediated by law, but constructed in legal terms. The relationship between law and its subjects is not an instance of social influence on an independent self, nor an instance of a social institution within the control of collective selves, but rather is a typical instance of self-constitution—the outside is *within*, the self is *social*, and law is effective because it is internalized. Thus in "Lacanian analysis of politics, neither the psychic nor the social acquires the status of first cause, because neither one wholly or unidirectionally determines the other."[87]

In addition to illustrating Lacanian categories, psychoanalytic reflection on law also demonstrates the tentative and changeable character of law. Judicial opinions and legal-doctrinal treatises, which often exemplify a discourse of stability, rationality, and neutrality, are challenged by psychoanalytic methods that reveal law to be a structure supported by the beliefs, desires, and fantasies of its subjects. One might then conclude that law is hopelessly ideological, but that would miss the point (of psychoanalysis) that the structures of belief, desire, and fantasy are not forever hidden. Some degree of control, and therefore change, is within the reach of the subject. Similarly, a degree of control over and change within law is possible precisely because the law is dependent upon, not outside, its subjects' knowledge.

Yet the promise of control—even a "degree of control," is problematical in Lacan's and any theory of a radically situated subject. Indeed, proponents of public reason consider the concession of any degree of autonomy as the foil of their communitarian critics.

The Communitarian Critique of Rawls

The details of the Rawlsian commentary-canon, comprising over two decades of apologetic, revisionist, and critical scholarship in response to *A Theory of Justice* (Harvard: 1971)—which industry is now reinvigorated by Rawls's *Political Liberalism* (Columbia: 1993)—are obviously beyond the scope of my remarks. A few features of the Rawls phenomenon, however, are significant for debates over religion in law, and significant as well for debates over the identity of the "self" or subject in various disciplines.

Rawls and his disciples attempt to construct a framework of public reason that might justify and set limits on political and legal power over free and rational subjects. Significantly, the notion of public reason is, in many respects, antifoundationalist, postmodern, and friendly toward religion. Public reason is created by an overlapping consensus on the facts and values of our culture at this point in time, thus the values of all philosophical or religious tradition are welcome to the extent that they overlap with one another.[88] While the Rawlsian appeal, in the construction of public reason, to common sense and uncontroversial scientific facts sounds to me traditional and uncritical, the sensitivity to cultural imbeddedness does not. Moreover, while the liberal emphasis on the sovereign individual seems to deny any celebration of otherness, maybe celebrating individuality comes close to a pluralistic respect for the other.[89] And finally, while the appeal to the "fact" of pluralism seems to deny the contestability of the term pluralism, Rawls is perhaps only offering an orientation that he believes would be acceptable to people from diverse value systems.

Michael Sandel, on the other hand, early on pointed out the limits of Rawls's account of the subject;[90] the response of some Rawlsian apologists to Sandel's communitarian critique is telling, particularly with respect to psychoanalytic understandings of the political subject. The Rawlsian subject is one who carefully reflects, in light of relevant facts, on his or her desires, and then chooses rational principles and courses of political action.[91] Sandel questions the possibility of such detachment, since the subject is radically situated in a community—our identities and loyalties are preestablished.[92] In terms of the critique of ideology described above, the Rawlsian subject's "choice" "amounts to no more than identifying existing wants and matching them with the means of their satisfaction, [such that] prevailing desires and conceptions of the good will be thoroughly implicated in the selection of principle."[93] The Rawlsian response to this aspect of the communitarian critique is twofold. First, Rawls is not in the business of supplying universal standards of justice, and he concedes that his principles serve a particular society at a particular time.[94] Second, when Sandel concedes that a subject has *some* role, some "choice," in the constitution of its identity, the Rawlsian fails to see any significant grounds for the communitarian critique.[95] Sandel, that is,

> may be right to suggest... that people [do not] exist with fully formed preferences and motives in some pre-social environment. But this does not mean that the self must be the product of *political* experience. To the extent that character is formed by the social environment, it is the family, the neighborhood, and the local community that usually matter.[96]

The point is that "in political *argument*, such commitments and attachments [must] be left behind."[97]

Rather than demonstrating the similarity between Rawls and Sandel, however, the reference to the family and the local community as the "social environment" demonstrates a Rawlsian failure to take the social aspect of subjectivity seriously. From the Rawlsian perspective, the subject is merely influenced by an environment, *not* radically situated in a pregiven language and a series of imaginary identifications.

According to C. Fred Alford, Sandel also fails to take the social aspect of subjectivity seriously:

> While the concept of the socially constituted self is central to Sandel's project, [*Liberalism and the Limits of Justice*, 1982] contains virtually no analysis of what this term might mean.... Sandel treats the concept... as if it were a strictly formal assumption.[98]

This gap in Sandel's analysis is, of course, the "concern of most psychoanalytic social theory today,"[99] and Alford builds his own account on Kleinian theory (finding in Rawls a paranoid-schizoid position for which Rawls's theory of justice—justice as fear of others—is a defense).[100] Whether one hopes (like Alford) to save Rawlsian theory from Sandel by a psychoanalytically informed revisionism, or to assist Sandel by filling in the gap with a psychoanalytic account of the subject (my own preference), the need to explore the notion of social constitution is clear.

I highlight this seemingly minor scuffle between Sandel and certain defenders of Rawls because it exemplifies a debate concerning postmodern challenges (to traditional ideals of truth, rationality, and freedom) in almost every discipline—in the natural sciences with respect to contemporary philosophy of science (science as textual, cultural, and so forth), and in the social sciences and humanities with respect to critical reflection on their received notions of the subject, their disciplinary texts, and the real-world events they purport to describe. The genuine disagreements in the debate over postmodernism are not between believers in pure science and universal values, on the one hand, and those who doubt everything, on the other. Proponents of either extreme are usually straw people constructed by critics, but the critics view themselves as *between* the extremes. Thus a theorist of public reason like Rawls is willing to concede social and historical contingency, and his critics are willing to concede the possibility (with some effort) of an active subject. Outside the debate over Rawls, this situation is best illustrated in current discussions of Derrida, who is regularly but unfairly "accused of subscribing to a Nietzschean-style philosophical irrationalism."[101]

> Derrida [often] makes it clear that he is not endorsing a philosophical irrationalism or unlimited relativism of interpretive discourse.... A correct reading of his writings ... would understand that the value of truth is never contested or destroyed, but only reinscribed in a more powerful, larger and more stable context.[102]

Indeed, discussions of Derrida are perhaps not so far from the debate over Rawls, since many (including Derrida) believe that "deconstruction was not, nor had it ever been, nihilistic, opposed to justice, or even (God forbid) unconcerned with justice, but ... was, quite the contrary, fully committed to the critique of injustice."[103] Of course, such a reminder that postmodern critiques are reconcilable with ethical commitments is just an introduction, and not a solution, to the problem of agency for theories of socially constructed subjects: "Since discussions about justice implicitly or explicitly assume and generate assumptions about who 'we' are and why we are living together, discourse about justice cannot do without concepts of subjectivity."[104]

The significant differences between theories of justice will be in the details of each's image of, or failure to imagine, who we are.

Proponents of psychoanalytic theory, I think, are uniquely positioned to participate in all of these extrapsychological debates about the subject—about its construction and its potential as an agent. Yet the matter of subjectivity is not settled in the field of psychoanalysis, which has its own version of the postmodern debate. At one extreme are those who dwell among analysts *only* as critics, that is, who read the literature as historians, all the while believing exaggeratedly that "psychoanalysis is surely one of the most thoroughly refuted theories existing."[105] Less extreme are those like Thomas Nagel, who recently reviewed Paul Robinson's *Freud and His Critics* (1993):

> [According] to the facile subjectivism which now blights many of the humanities and social sciences[,] anyone who thinks that some questions have right and wrong answers, which can be confirmed or refuted by evidence and argument, is an epistemological cave man.
> Robinson incorrectly attributes such a view to Freud.... It is of no service to Freud to defend him by appealing to this slothful outlook—let alone to ascribe it to him.[106]

Modernistic debates over the scientific status of psychoanalysis continue, but many feel that abandonment of the obsession with science is the key to the survival of psychoanalysis.[107] Echoing Foucault, Jane Flax remarks that psychoanalysis "will have to generate discourse-specific epistemologies. It must become more conscious of and self-reflective about the politics of its theories, clinical practices, and its relation to other forms of power and knowledge."[108] Flax thus heralds the postmodern phase of analytic theory—critical of empiricism, attentive to linguistic circuits of power, yet retaining local productions of truth.[109] If the subject was thought to have disappeared completely in postmodern theory, there is a return of the subject through

> the partial recognition of new and ignored subjectivities in identity politics and multicultural models [,which recognition] reveals that the subject pronounced dead in the 1960s was a very particular one, not to be mourned by all: white, bourgeois, humanist, male, heterosexual, a subject who only pretended to be universal.[110]

In Flax's terminology, postmodernism calls into question the natural, transcendental, or ahistorical "traits" traditionally associated with individuals. The "constitution of this individual and our belief in its existence... is not 'true' in some ontological or essentialist sense. It is an effect of a subjectivity constituted in and through certain discourses, including psychoanalysis."[111] The last phrase, "including psychoanalysis," signals the division within that discourse concerning truth and subjectivity.

With respect to Lacan, commentators remain divided over the status of his return to Freud. When Earle remarked that the "picture of the psyche offered by Freud and subscribed to by Lacan is an improvement on Enlightenment psychology because it is objectively more correct,"[112] David Crownfield balked: "It seems to me that the whole *philosophical* issue raised by the Freud-Lacan critique is precisely how rationality, intelligibility, and truth function after such ideas of 'objectively correct' views of the psyche have proven illusory."[113] Notwithstanding these ongoing disagreements within the field of psychoanalysis, the potential for its contribution to legal and political discourse is evident—the debates over theories of justice come down to pictures of how (much) the subject is constituted. Before concluding that certain Lacanian variations on psychoanalytic understanding are exemplary of such opportunities, I return to the theory of religious pluralism.

The Religious Pluralist's Critique of Rawls

Much of the debate over religion in law concerns the fear of majoritorian impositions of religious values (through legislation or court decisions) upon those who do not share those values. (Recall Alford's analysis of Rawls's "original position" thesis—that we should adopt political principles behind a veil of ignorance regarding our status in society—as a paranoid-schizoid position involving fear of what others would do to us.) Indeed, the standard example of religious influence on law is the legislator's or judge's recourse to a sacred text as legal authority. While I agree that such a model offends popular notions of pluralism, the far more interesting question is what to do with a religious theory of pluralism when it is offered, alongside Rawlsian theories, as another orientation for political and legal processes and institutions.

Consider that the Rawlsian notion of overlapping consensus excludes values from a particular religious or moral tradition until they become public reasons by virtue of the overlap with values from other traditions. Since pluralism is a shared value in our own political system, it would seem that a religiously based theory of pluralism would be welcome in law and politics. (By "religiously based theory," I refer not to a political theory that is present in a sacred text, if such a thing exists, but to one which is based on notions from a sacred text, e.g., that people should be free—from others or from state interference—

to choose whether to obey admonitions like "love thy neighbor" or "help the poor.")[114] It turns out, however, that the introduction of religious ideals of pluralism—which might give religion more play in law and politics—ruins the usefulness of pluralism as a way to distinguish reasonable from religious principles. Pluralism for the Rawlsian was not supposed to be a contested value, but a fact of our cultural diversity.

Pluralism, however,

> is also a fact about our different understandings of the meaning of that public political culture itself, about the meaning, for instance, of such ideas and principles of freedom and equality. Indeed, even if we possess [a shared fund of ideas], we may nonetheless ... understand the fund ... within different contexts of interpretation.[115]

Because the specific interpretations or understandings of our shared "fund" of principles and ideas are so diverse, the fund becomes ineffective in particular legal cases and controversies. In other words, as soon as a particularized sense of freedom or pluralism is adopted, it loses its certification as "public reason." And that is the religious pluralist's response to Rawls—there is no theory of public reason (based on common sense, science, or shared values) that is significantly different, in terms of faithlike commitments, from theories based on religious principles. The project of liberal individualism—advocating neutrality toward all values as a way of promoting certain values of liberty and tolerance—leads to a question: what "is to prevent that principled neutrality ... from extending to those basic values of liberty and human dignity as well ...?"[116] The answer is faith. This is not, however, merely an epistemological critique—it is also a vision of the subject of law as a subject of language, of cultural identities, and of desire.

The liberal ideal of rational deliberation between people who set aside "their individual personalities, relationships, and histories" is bolstered by a rhetoric of self-indifference and respect for others.[117] Explaining how such a political appeal to rational thought, with its tendency to emphasize "sameness," does not respect others is the project of critical social theory.

> [We] often think that people fail to agree because they are too wedded to their own interests and viewpoints, too distracted by their attachments and weaknesses, and therefore too partial....
>
> But it is precisely in discussions of policy matters that particularities cannot be overlooked [—] the particular interests, histories, loyalties, capacities, fears, and aspirations of the group in question.[118]

The emphasis on recognizing particularity as a feature of respect for others is familiar in postmodern reflections on politics and justice. For example, Derrida's ethics of Otherness in his recent work on justice[119] requires "that we see a situation in all of its singularity [and] that we attempt to see things from the Other's point of view, using her vocabulary and her way of understanding the world."[120] Steven Hendley, in his recent account of the pluralism debate between liberalism (including Rawls) and communitarianism (including Charles Taylor and Michael Walzer), draws upon Lyotard and Levinas to show that pluralism demands "that we acknowledge the limits of our own social understanding of the world and its value in the understanding of another, that we recognize, in other words, not merely what we share with others but the limits of what we share."[121] Hendley's identifications of conflicts between incommensurable traditions (Lyotard), of an obligation to recognize others in their alterity (Levinas), and of the need to avoid claims based on domination of others each highlight a feature of contemporary psychoanalytic theory, especially in its Lacanian formulations.

OTHERNESS AND SINGULARITY IN PSYCHOANALYSIS

Slavoj Zizek recently proposed, as an intersubjective supplement to Lacan's counsel to never renounce your desire,[122] the following maxim of psychoanalytic ethics: "Avoid as much as possible any violation of the fantasy space of the other, i.e., respect . . . the other's 'particular absolute,' the way he organizes his universe of meaning in a way absolutely particular to him."[123] That is, we should respect the other *not* because the other resembles our imaginary selves, and *not* because we share in the symbolic order, but because the other's dignity is in his particularity—"that part of him that we can be sure we can never share."[124] Lacan's "discourse" of the analyst "accounts for the particularity of each person's desire"—the "truth" outside the universal and general.[125] Thus "there is no common sense in psychoanalysis . . . only particular, peculiar sense."[126] The opposite of analytic "discourse" is that of the master, which is "the discursive structure of politics [in its] hegemonic ideological formation."[127] Significantly, psychoanalysis "is political precisely to the extent that the discursive position of the analyst diametrically opposes that of the master discourse, for the latter of which all division is repressed by the uniticity of certainty."[128]

Democracy as a "formal link of abstract individuals," Zizek points out, is a denial of—an attempt to elude or level—concrete human needs, interests, and beliefs"; contemporary democratic theory is characterized by a failure to assume the antagonism of diversity.[129] Western law, as well, in its "anxiety to avoid mythology,... denies the figure of the Other [or more precisely] certain 'myth-ridden' others."[130] Jane Flax, from a psychoanalytic feminist perspective, argues that "the universal sameness posited within liberalism has a distinctly masculine character."[131] Without questioning Flax's identification of women as Other in public life, since that notion is central to Lacanian theory,[132] I would suggest that religious communities often occupy the place of the feminine Other; for example, the feminine is often associated with the relational, which like a religious emphasis on interpersonal relationships (e.g., love of and sacrifice for others) is deemed to be irrational. Indeed, Zizek's definition of "new social movements," like feminism, ecology, and the peace movement, might include religious pluralists:

> Their aim is much more radical than that of the ordinary political parties: what they are striving after is a fundamental transformation of the entire mode of action and belief... what is at stake... is not just a political belief but an entire life attitude. And such a project..., once formulated as a political program, necessarily undermines the very foundations of formal democracy.[133]

The basis on which religion is suspect in law and politics is its difference, its otherness, its irrationality, its particularity, its failure to be the same as other voices in the public square.

LACAN IN THE SERVICE OF RELIGION

Interest is growing in the relevance of Lacanian theory for religious studies, and numerous "points of contact" have been identified.[134] I limit my remarks to Lacan's notions of otherness and psychoanalytic ethics, insofar as they illuminate certain features of the debates over pluralism in law and religion discourse.

CELEBRATING OTHERNESS

Stephen K. White's critique of liberal (e.g., Rawlsian) notions of justice calls for fostering, not merely tolerating, otherness:

> Here the contrast with traditional views of justice can be described as one between approaches that are more strongly attuned to a sense of responsibility to otherness versus ones attuned primarily to a responsibility to act, or more specifically... a responsibility to author determinate and unambiguous principles for judgment and action.[135]

Drawing on the work of Walzer, Lyotard, Foucault, and Habermas, White argues for a "new" pluralism that recognizes how "dominant discourses and institutions ... so structure public meanings and social relationships that alternate discourses and forms of life find critical footholds difficult to secure."[136]

White does not mention religious pluralism, but the response of religious scholars to liberal ideals of public reason is an accusation that the latter is not *really* pluralistic—does *not* really respect the other. Religious socialization is viewed by the liberal as a bias to be set aside in law and politics, rather than as an instance of inescapable socialization. The liberal subject allegedly stands outside discourse and symbolization, identities and culturation, even as these are conceded as facts to be interpreted. The very self-description of the religious subject, on the other hand, is a confession of dependence on belief-structures as the only available foundations. Not only is it faith all the way down, but all the way up as political theorizing is built upon beliefs (whether conscious or hidden).

Nor does White mention Lacan, whose work suggests that the

> modes of our subjectivity and the modes of our being-with-others are mutually determinative. Because of the intermeshing of self and other that appears in the function of culture, language, and individual others in the formation of the subject, the problem of self-development becomes one of the relational modes. That is, there is a necessary ethical dimension to Lacan's model of self-development.[137]

Religion, when ethically oriented to pluralism, describes a mode of being-with-others even as it provides identities and symbolic cultural structures in the formation of the subject.[138] Though this aspect of religion receives little attention by Lacan, the pluralistic orientation toward respect of others—in their singularity, not in their sameness—is at the heart of his psychoanalytic ethics.

LACANIAN ETHICS REVISITED

In his persistent critique of American ego psychology, Lacan challenged the tendencies toward master discourses in psychoanalysis. For Lacan, the model of analysis is not unlike the self-critical styles of ideology-critique, wherein the goal is disclosure and understanding, not domination in accordance with pretensions of truth and reason. At first glance, therefore, any analogy between Lacanian ethics and religious pluralism appears strained because of the association of religion with master discourses. A religiously based notion of pluralism is not, of course, a proposal to legislate biblical norms; nevertheless, political theories are typically offered as the best orientation in the marketplace of ideas, so even theories of pluralism seem to exceed mere disclosure and understanding. I think, however, that advancing ethical responsibility toward others on the basis of a religious tradition is less than impositional, since the religious political theorist concedes his or her own sociality. The religious theorist, that is, concedes—and this is a major reason for religious interest in Lacan—that the subject is constructed by imaginary (in Lacan's sense) and symbolic structures. No claim is made that we may stand outside those structures—only that we can disclose and confess our dependence upon them.

As to the question of agency and resistance, it is interesting that a transparent religious commitment—not simply religious experience or an inherited religious unconscious—roughly provides a picture of the "liberated" Lacanian subject. Without escaping the imaginary and symbolic orders, the believer chooses the images and language to which he or she will be subjected. In this picture, however, unbelief is out of the question—the only choice that is not a commitment to some belief system is the option of ignorance. That is why the ethics of psychoanalysis are about disclosure, not rules for good living. Some degree of freedom and control is available, but it depends on what you know about yourself and about what you want. If you know a lot, Lacan teaches, you will know how much you take (and will continue to take) from language, from others, and from the Other.

Religious communities, at the same time, provide a picture of the manner in which the symbolic and imaginary orders envelop the self-critical subject. The idea of separation from and resistance to a dominant culture implies not an escape from the imaginary or the symbolic, but an overt communal belief that they are inescapable.

Conclusion

> For Lacan, as for Kojève, human appetite is oriented more toward the subjectivity of others (in a struggle for recognition between "self" and "other") than toward pleasure or a release of physical tensions. The religious dimension is closely associated with the theme of a possible relation to the other as other and the question of whether recognition is something to be coerced through domination or given in the mode of love.
> —Eugene Webb, *The New Social Psychology of France*

In academic circles, proponents of psychoanalytic theory learn to be guarded in their scholarly discussions—one needs to develop a standard set of responses regarding embarrassing episodes in the history of psychoanalysis, the impact of neurobiological and cognitive scientific advances, the theoretical and clinical diversity among analysts, and so forth. Even in psychoanalytic circles, however, arguing in favor of *either* Lacanian theory *or* religion is risky, and I have done both.

As to Lacan, I think that the criticisms that his work is unreadable or that it can be read to say anything one wants—the two criticisms are related—are misplaced; Lacan was both aware of and pleased with the confusion over the essence or central theme in his seminars.[139] In my own appropriation of Lacan, above, I have perhaps too casually identified some of his ethical themes, but I think the ever-unfolding details of his and his disciples' theory of the subject support the analogy to certain religious conceptions of dependence on and respect for others. Just one example, from a survey of religious developments of Lacanian theory,[140] is René Girard, whose notions of mimesis (e.g., imitation of Christ) and sacrifice (e.g., ritual reenactments in religious symbolism) betray Lacan's influence: "Man is the creature who does not know what to desire, and he turns to others in order to make up his mind."[141]

As to religion, which term is no less ambiguous than "political theory" or "psychology," I obviously intend only to identify one particular type of religious political activism, namely those who believe their own perspective provides "a more solid foundation than does pragmatic liberalism" for a pluralist and nonconfessional state.[142] The relevance here of Lacanian accounts of the subject and its "others" is twofold: first, the theory of the social construction of the subject in relation to others presents a philosophical challenge to the vision of a pragmatic liberal subject; second, the theory of the singularity of subjects provides a basis for the respect of others as others. Both are implied in Lacanian ethics and are essential to the religious critique of liberal pluralism.

Psychoanalytic theory provides, in the context of the impasse over religion in law and politics, both an explanation of what is going on— what the debate is about—*and* an orientation, I believe, that turns the advantage—a rare gift in the history of psychoanalysis—toward some religious thinkers.

9

Concluding Remarks

In my opening chapter, I identified several contradictory criticisms of Lacan—too Freudian, not Freudian; too postmodern, not postmodern—and I suggested that our inability to categorize Lacanian theory is primarily a sign of its critical potential, not its lack of clarity. There is, surely, a lack of clarity in Lacan's style and method, but I have tried to demonstrate that the source of much of the confusion surrounding Lacan is the complexity and unfamiliarity of Lacanian theory. That complexity is justified, I believe, because the objects of inquiry—desire, law, language—are complex; in my own field of inquiry, legal processes and institutions, things are never clear, obvious, or uncomplicated. As to the numerous identifiable schools and approaches in legal scholarship that each try to explain the nature and operation of law, I think that Lacan's unfamiliarity is also a strength. The value of Lacanian theory for law will be its delivery of new insights, which might take the form of highlighting or prioritizing an aspect of law that has been missed, downplayed, or left undeveloped. Indeed, the very notion of psychoanalysis implies attending to that which is effective but hidden, or perhaps revealed in mistakes, accidents, slips of the tongue, or dreams, all of which might appear as insignificant for our conscious, rational, undertakings.

By subtitling this book *Toward a Psychoanalytic Critical Theory*, I intend to ally Lacan's approach to critical movements in legal theory, such as critical legal studies, feminism, and critical race studies, each of which represents a challenge to mainstream legal theory. In these alternative perspectives, legal processes and institutions are characterized as political, not neutral; as interpretive, not scientific; as marginalizing, not inclusive, of certain classes or communities; and so forth. I think that Lacan's attention to the internalization of cultural (including legal) images, the power of language (including legal language), and the subject of the Other (including law alongside desire and other unconscious functions) are useful not only in the critique of established legal theory and practice, but also for the internal debates among progressive scholars about human agency and the possibility of resistance and reform.

Lacan is neither Freudian nor anti-Freudian, neither traditional nor postmodern, and I would add that the "subject" in Lacan's account is neither autonomous nor incapacitated, neither rational nor surrealistic. All of these are false dualisms. In Lacan, the unconscious, language, other people, ideology, and law are strikingly powerful, but not all-powerful. Their operations are strikingly hidden, but not completely unknowable. Lacan offers a method of inquiry in such circumstances that is not easily accessible or simplistic—that is its weakness, and its strength, in terms of contemporary legal theory.

NOTES

CHAPTER 1

1. Compare Ellie Ragland-Sullivan, *Jacques Lacan and the Philosophy of Psychoanalysis* (Chicago: University of Illinois Press, 1987), ix ("Lacan's revolutionary theories in psychoanalysis have immediate and indisputable relevance for philosophy, linguistics, literary theory, and the wider disciplines in the human sciences") with Norman Holland, *The Critical I* (New York: Columbia University Press, 1992), 208 ("What can [Lacan] contribute to literature, philosophy, or quite simply, our understanding of the world around and within us? . . . I have to conclude, not much.").
2. *See* Brian Leiter, "Intellectual Voyeurism in Legal Scholarship," *Yale J. L. & Humanities* 4 (1992): 79, 91 (focusing on misreadings of Nietsche).
3. Ragland-Sullivan, supra note 1, at x.
4. Jacques Lacan, "The Agency of the Letter in the Unconscious or Reason since Freud," in *Écrits: A Selection*, trans. A. Sheridan (New York: W. W. Norton, 1977), 146.
5. Samuel Weber, *Return to Freud: Jacques Lacan's Dislocation of Psychoanalysis*, trans. M. Levine (Cambridge: Cambridge University Press, 1991), 1.
6. Id. at xiii.
7. *See* Patrick Colm Hogan, "Structure and Ambiguity in the Symbolic Order: Some Prolegomena to the Understanding and Criticism of Lacan," in *Criticism & Lacan: Essays and Dialogue on Language, Structure and the Unconscious*, ed. P. Hogan and L. Pandit (Athens: University of Georgia Press, 1990), at 7: "In Lacan's writings, any given term might bear not only its ordinary French meaning, but another, technical meaning, derived from its function as transnational substitute for a further, usually German term. Thus readers of English translations are often confused by evidently hazy passages, the originals of which are clear and precise."
8. Malcolm Bowie, *Lacan* (Cambridge: Harvard University Press, 1991), 3–4.
9. *See* Eugen Bär, "Understanding Lacan," in *Psychoanalysis and Contemporary Science* 3 (1974): 473–99, ed. L. Goldberger and V. Rosen.
10. *See* Richard Chessick, *Psychology of the Self and the Treatment of Narcissism* (Northvale, N.J.: Aronson, 1985), 292.
11. Ragland-Sullivan, supra note 1, at 220.
12. Bowie, supra note 8, at 14 (for example, "Lacan's theory of the unconscious as a signifying chain is presented as a necessary outgrowth of an earlier phase of his thinking in which the unconscious had scarcely existed." Id. at 15 [footnote omitted]).
13. Ragland-Sullivan, supra note 1, at xxii.
14. Jacques-Alain Miller, "How Psychoanalysis Cures According to Lacan," *Newsletter of the Freudian Field* 1, no. 2 (1987): 4, 5–6.

15. Jacques-Alain Miller, "Classified Index of the Major Concepts," in *Écrits*, supra note 4, at 327.
16. Lacan, "The Function and Field of Speech and Language in Psychoanalysis," in *Écrits*, supra note 4, at 64.
17. Id. at 65.
18. *See*, for example, "The Agency of the Letter," supra note 4, at 146–78.
19. Slavoj Zizek, "The Real in Ideology," *PsychCritique* 2 (1987): 255.
20. *See* Ragland-Sullivan, supra note 1, at 192–95.
21. Bowie, supra note 8, at 111.
22. *See* Bowie, supra note 8, at 3: "Many other analysts have of course written unclearly.... But Lacan is quite alone in placing a continuous positive valuation upon ambiguity, and in suggesting that students of the unconscious mind, when they become writers, are somehow morally obliged to be difficult."
23. Weber, supra note 5, at xi–xii. The writings of Lacan and Derrida are, Weber argues, "two of the most powerful forces working to keep the alterity of language from being isolated and foreclosed." Id. at xii.
24. Id. at xiii.
25. Miller, supra note 14, at 26–27.
26. Jacques Lacan, *Television*, ed. J. Copjec and trans. D. Hollier, R. Krauss, and A. Michelson (New York: W. W. Norton, 1990), 45.
27. *See* Wilden's extended posttranslation commentary in Jacques Lacan, *Speech and Language in Psychoanalysis*, ed. and trans. A. Wilden (Baltimore: Johns Hopkins University Press, 1968).
28. *See* Wilden, "Translator's Introduction," in Lacan, supra note 27, at ix: "It is almost impossible to write any sort of substantial introduction to Lacan unless the reader has first been introduced to him."
29. Louis Althusser, *Lenin and Philosophy and Other Essays* (New York: Monthly Review Press, 1971), 209.
30. Paul Smith, *Discerning the Subject* (Minnesota: University of Minnesota Press, 1988), 20. For an attempt to correct and redeem Althusser's critique of ideology along Lacanian lines, *see* Henry Krips, "Interpellation, Antagonisms, Repetition," *Rethinking Marxism* 7, no. 4 (1994): 59.
31. *See* Althusser, supra note 29 at 162.
32. J. Henriques, W. Hollway, C. Urwin, C. Venn, and V. Walkerdine, *Changing the Subject* (New York: Methuen, 1984), 217. A similar evaluation of Lacan is made by Anthony Elliot in his *Psychoanalytic Theory* (Oxford: Blackwell, 1994), at 99–102.
33. *See* John Brenkman, *Culture and Domination* (Ithaca: Cornell University Press, 1987), 157. Briefly, the impasses Brenkman identifies result from the premises of hermeneutics, Marxism, and Freudian psychoanalysis—each of which inform and ultimately problematize contemporary socially critical interpretations of cultural practices.
34. Peter Gabel, "The Phenomenology of Rights-Consciousness and the Pact of the Withdrawn Selves," *Tex. L. Rev.* 62 1563, 1565 n. 3; *see also* "Dukakis's Defeat and the Transformative Possibilities of Legal Culture," *Tikkun* 4 (March/April 1989): 14 (revisionistic-Lacanian analysis of social desire in politics).
35. Dragan Milovanovic, *Postmodern Law and Disorder: Psychoanalytic Semiotics, Chaos, and Juridic Exegeses* (Liverpool: Deb. Charles, 1992), reviewed

in David Caudill, "Coming to Terms with Lacan: Legal Discourse as Analysand," *Int'l J. for the Semiotics of Law* 6 (1993): 203.
36. Ragland-Sullivan, supra note 1, at 273.
37. Id. at 299.
38. Smith, supra note 30, at 22.
39. *See* Stephen Frosh, *The Politics of Psychoanalysis: An Introduction to Freudian and Post-Freudian Theory* (London: Macmillan Educ., 1987), 137: "[It] can be argued that Lacan's insistence on the constructive primacy of language leads to a form of pessimistic determinism (the subject is fully determined by culture) and can also be used to legitimize oppressive practices (the Symbolic is structured by the Law of the Father, and one cannot escape that)."
40. Id. at 138.
41. *See* Lacan, *Television*, supra note 26, at 18, 20.
42. Lacan, "The Freudian Thing, or the Meaning of the Return to Freud in Psychoanalysis," in *Écrits*, supra note 4, at 116.
43. *See* Barry Richards, *Images of Freud: Cultural Responses to Psychoanalysis* (London: J. M. Dent & Sons, 1989), 74.
44. *See* generally Frosh, supra note 39, at 5–10.
45. *See* Peter Brooks, "The Idea of a Psychoanalytic Literary Criticism," *Critical Inquiry* 13 (1987): 334.
46. *See* generally Frosh, supra note 39, at 10–15.
47. Leonard Kaplan and Vincent Rinella, "Jurisprudence and the Appropriation of the Psychoanalytic: A Study in Ideology and Form," *Int'l J. L. & Psychiatry* 11 (1988): 215, 216.
48. Id. at 248.
49. *See* Holland, supra note 1, at 193; in defense of Lacan, see my review essay entitled "Post-Postmodern Redemptions of Self, Text, and Event," *Cardozo Studies in Law and Literature* 5 (1993): 137, 147–58.
50. Id. at 197.
51. Id. at 208.
52. Ragland-Sullivan, supra note 1, at 170.
53. William Kerrigan, "Terminating Lacan," *S. Atl. Q* 88 (1989): 993, 1007.
54. Id. at 998 ("Psychoanalysis does not belong to ... the uncontroversial"). Lacan, however, does look "worse from a positivist perspective because ... [he] seems committed to indispensable laws ... however obscure they may actually be in his oblique but always self-important expositions." Id.
55. Id.
56. Id. at 1000.
57. Id. at 1003.
58. Id. at 1007.
59. James Boyle, "A Process of Denial: Bork and Post-Modern Conservatism," *Yale J. L. & Humanities* 3, 267 n. 5.
60. Kerrigan, supra note 53, at 1007.
61. J. M. Balkin, "What Is a Postmodern Constitutionalism?" *Mich. L. Rev.* 90 (1992): 1966, 1972.
62. Id. at 1967–72.
63. *See* Nathaniel Berman, "Modernism, Nationalism, and the Rhetoric of Reconstruction," *Yale J. L. & Humanities* 4 (1992): 351, 380.
64. Sanford Levinson and J. M. Balkin, "Law, Music, and Other Performing Arts," *U. PA. L. Rev.* 139 (1991): 1597, 1629.

65. Stanley Fish's antifoundationalism, for example, roughly fits my (and probably some others') definition of postmodern tendencies. *See generally Doing What Comes Naturally: Change, Rhetoric, and the Practice of Theory in Literary and Legal Studies* (Durham: Duke University Press, 1989). Richard Weisberg's recent *Poethics* (New York: Columbia University Press, 1992) challenges postmodern tendencies, including Fish's, on grounds of their ethical bankruptcy; note, however, that Weisberg is hardly "traditional," confirming my point that the extremes of either traditional and postmodern approaches are equally unattractive; Fish, perhaps, represents an anomaly in my paradigm.
66. Henry Sussman, "Psychoanalysis Modern and Post-Modern," in *Psychoanalysis and...*, ed. R. Feldstein and H. Sussman (New York: Routledge, 1990), 131, 136.
67. Id. at 137. "From early on in Freud's work,... the unconscious functions as a mental repository in which the incommensurate [and] the inconsistent... prevail. Lending coherence to the disorderly mass of associations and tracing the origins of a trauma at least partially involve an interpretative quest for structure." Id. at 139.
68. Id. at 143, citing Jacques Lacan, *The Four Fundamental Concepts of Psychoanalysis*, ed. J. A. Miller and trans. A. Sheridan (New York: W. W. Norton, 1978), 85–87, 130–31, 156.
69. Sussman, supra note 66, at 144.
70. Id. at 146.
71. Id. at 148.
72. Id. at 142.
73. *See* Miller, supra note 14, at 5–6.
74. *See* Jacques-Alain Miller, "Introductory Remarks before the Screening of Television," *Newsletter of the Freudian Field* 2, no. 1 (1988): 6, 9.
75. Id. at 14.
76. *Newsletter of the Freudian Field* 1, no. 2 (1987): 31.
77. Id. at 32–33; *see also* Lacan, "The Subversion of the Subject and the Dialectic of Desire in the Freudian Unconscious," in *Écrits*, supra note 4, at 310–11 ("no metalanguage can be spoken").
78. Zizek, supra note 76, at 36.
79. Id.
80. Ragland-Sullivan, supra note 1, at 181; *see also* Lacan, *Écrits*, supra note 4, at 150 ("no signification can be sustained other than by reference to another signification").
81. Holland, supra note 1, at 107–18.
82. Id. at 111.
83. Id. at 143, 194, 198.
84. *See*, for example, Ragland-Sullivan, supra note 1, at 203: "Lacan's marriage of the concepts of subject, structure, and signifier creates... an entirely different meaning to that of the static Saussurean structuralism with which he is thoughtlessly associated. Lacanian theory... also throws doubt on Noam Chomsky's claim to have supplanted the usefulness of any structuralism in linguistics."
85. Kerrigan, supra note 53, at 1001–2.
86. *See* Jacques Derrida, *The Post Card: From Socrates to Freud and Beyond*, trans. A. Bass (Chicago: University of Chicago Press, 1987); *see also* Derrida, "For the Love of Lacan," *Cardozo L. Rev.* 16 (1995): 699.

87. Kerrigan, supra note 53, at 1003.
88. Colin MacCabe, "On Discourse," in *The Talking Cure: Essays in Psychoanalysis and Language*, ed. C. MacCabe (London: Macmillan Press, 1981), 213.
89. Ragland-Sullivan, supra note 1, at 272; the terms "Other," "je," and "moi" are discussed in chapter 2.
90. Miller, supra note 14, at 7.
91. *See* Peter Brooks, "Bouillabaisse" (book review), *Yale L. J.* 99 (1990): 1147, 1154: "But wherever you seek the source of the notion of law, you must recognize it as a fundamental category of thought of all known human societies. Thus to identify it simply as a product of ideology, as that gun at one's head that is one's head, is to fail to analyze the head and how what's there got there."
92. *See* Michael S. Moore, "The Interpretive Turn in Modern Theory: A Turn for the Worse?" *Stan. L. Rev.* 41 (1989): 871.
93. Refer to chapter 4 of this book.
94. *See* Pierre Schlag, "The Problem of the Subject," *Tex. L. Rev.* 69 (1991): 1627, 1630.
95. Hogan, supra note 7, at 8-9.
96. *See*, for example Jane Flax, *Thinking Fragments: Psychoanalysis, Feminism, and Postmodernism in the Contemporary West* (Berkeley and Los Angeles: University of California Press, 1990): "I [do not] consider [Lacan's] work to be a very promising supplement or contribution to the development of feminist theorizing . . . his work is . . . even more pervaded by masculinist assumptions than Freud."

CHAPTER 2

This chapter is a substantially modified version of a paper delivered to the Fifth International Round Table on Law and Semiotics, Reading, Pennsylvania, April 18-21, 1991; *see* David S. Caudill, "Jacques Lacan and Our State of Affairs: Preliminary Remarks on Law as Other," in *Law and the Human Sciences*, vol. 3 of the series *Semiotics and the Human Sciences*, ed. R. Kevelson (New York: Peter Lang, 1992), and "Lacan and Law: Networking with the Big O(ther)," *Stud. in Psychoan. Theory* 1 (1992): 25.
1. *But see* Peter Goodrich, *Languages of Law: From Logics of Memory to Nomadic Masks* (London: Weidenfeld and Nicolson, 1990), 282: "The entry of the individual into the symbolic, the transition . . . from lack to identity, is the condition of institutional existence, the capture of the subject by law." Fine, but I was only captured in the sense that everyone is.
2. *See* id. at 274, quoting and translating Pierre Legendre, *L'Inestimable Object de la Transmission: Étude sur le Principle Généalogique en Occident* (Paris: Fayard, 1985), 75: "The awful fate of the lawyer is that he can speak only the truth. In Legendre's formulation, 'The speaking being is spoken, it is spoken by the discourse of institutions, dogmatic discourse.'" *See also* Goodrich, supra note 1, at 273-74: "Dogmatics here connotes a reason that has turned away from the world, a cult of innocence in the face of life: the law loses itself in its function, decadently and aimlessly staggering from case to case, from distinction to distinction, innocently and ignorantly applying grammatical rules to subjugate questions of meaning. [The medieval jurists of civil and canon Law] were sleepwalk-

ers.... Their discourse was a borrowed speech.... The jurist['s]... life was a surrogate one."

For Jacques Lacan, the big (or capital) "O" Other (*Autre*)—termed the "big Other" in translations of Lacan's early seminars—has multiple meanings, but generally refers to that which is exterior to and determinative of the subject, variously designated as the place of the parents and later the law (which is internalized), and as an unconscious discourse analogous to the discourse of dreams—the place of truth in Freudian terms. Refer to note 49 infra; *see also* Slavoj Zizek, *The Sublime Object of Ideology* (London: Verso, 1989), 46 ("the big Other, the alienating symbolic network"); *see generally* Lacan, "The Function and Field of Speech and Language in Psychoanalysis, in *Écrits: A Selection*, trans. A. Sheridan (New York: W. W. Norton, 1977), 55 ("the unconscious of the subject is the discourse of the Other"); Lacan, "On a Question Preliminary to Any Possible Treatment of Psychosis," in *Écrits*, 193 ("the condition of the [neurotic or psychotic] subject... is dependent on what is being unfolded in the Other."); Lacan, "The Subversion of the Subject and the Dialectic of Desire in the Freudian Unconscious," in *Écrits*, 311 (the Mother, sometimes, as "Other").

3. *See* Peter Goodrich, "Psychoanalysis in Legal Education: Notes on the Violence of the Sign," in *Law and Semiotics*, ed. R. Kevelson (New York: Peter Lang, 1987), at 205: "In Kafka's all too appropriate parable of the law, the metaphor for law is that of a jealously guarded yet fictive citadel, a gate beyond which there is nothing to learn. The ideological function of the gatekeeper is to prevent the student from addressing the question of authority and of law... which would lead to the discovery that nothing is protected, that the law does not exist except as a secret that is exhausted in the very form of its transmission."

4. *See* Zizek, supra note 2, at 68.

5. Although much has been made of Lacan's incomprehensibility (by Lacan himself and others), the same could be said—quite arbitrarily, I think—of Kant, Hegel, Husserl, and Heidegger, or nowadays, Derrida, Gadamer, and Ricoeur.

6. *See* Jacques Lacan, *Television*, ed. J. Copjec and trans. D. Hollier, R. Krauss, and A. Michelson (New York: W. W. Norton, 1990): "Psychoanalysis would allow you... the hope of refining and clarifying the unconscious, of which you're the subject." *See also* Jacques-Alain Miller, "How Psychoanalysis Cures According to Lacan," *Newsletter of the Freudian Field* 1, no. 2 (1987): 4, 25: "[By focusing on linguistics, you] may gain understanding of how analysis cures.... How come speech has such an effect on the ego, the self, or the subject? Lacan's position is a most radical one. If speech has such an effect on the subject, you have to suppose that this subject is, I would say, completely speech; that the subject of your 'operation' as analyst is completely speech."

See generally James Glogowski, "The Therapeutic Effect of Psychoanalysis: The Intervention of Lacan," in *Criticism and Lacan: Essays and Dialogue on Language, Structure, and the Unconscious*, ed. P. Hogan and L. Pandit (Athens: University Georgia Press, 1990), at 172: "The cure, for Freud and Lacan, is an after-effect (aprés coup) of discourse—the talking cure—it can never be a goal, or 'object.'"

7. *See* Miller, supra note 6, at 16: "Interpretation could not cure anyone if we did not define the subject fundamentally by its dependency on language and speech.
   ... In psychoanalysis we keep ourselves outside everything else except the speech; what the subject is telling us."
8. Ellie Ragland-Sullivan, "Stealing Material: The Materiality of Language According to Freud and Lacan," in *Lacan and the Human Sciences*, ed. A. Leupin (Lincoln: University of Nebraska Press, 1991), at 80; *see also* Lacan, "On a question," supra note 2, at 193 ("the unconscious is the discourse of the Other").
9. *See, e.g.,* Elizabeth Wright, Psychoanalytic Criticism: Theory in Practice (New York: Methuen, 1987) (discussing the aesthetic implications of various schools of psychoanalysis, including Lacanian approaches).
10. *See* Lacan, "On a Question," supra note 2, at 214: "It would be better to confine this schema [of the structure of the subject at the termination of the psychotic process] to the waste-bin, if, like so many others, it was to lead anyone to forget in an intuitive image the analysis on which it is based."
11. Ellie Ragland-Sullivan, *Jacques Lacan and the Philosophy of Psychoanalysis* (Chicago: University of Illinois Press, 1987), x.
12. *See* Stephen Frosh, *The Politics of Psychoanalysis: An Introduction to Freudian and Post-Freudian Theory* (London: Macmillan Education, 1987), 1 (Freudian "concepts of repression, sexual desire and the unconscious [are] often implicit in [our] 'common sense' understandings of ourselves and each other.").
13. *See* Sigmund Freud, *Five Lectures on Psycho-Analysis*, ed. and trans. J. Strachey (New York: W. W. Norton, 1957), 42: "A child has its sexual instincts and activities from the first; it comes into the world with them; and, after an important course of development passing through many stages, they lead to what is known as the normal sexuality of the adult."
14. *See* Frosh, supra note 12, at 46 (Freud describes "the way society enters into the essence of the human individual, organizing the instincts where usually we consider that we are most privately ourselves").
15. *See* Freud, *Five Lectures*, supra note 13, at 40–41: "This assertion of [the predominance of erotic life] will not be willingly believed. Even workers who are ready to follow my psychological studies are inclined to think that I over-estimate the part played by sexual factors."
16. *See id.* at 21–28. Freud identified, in his early studies of patients suffering from hysteria, "a wishful impulse which was in sharp contrast to the subject's other wishes and which proved incompatible with the ethical and aesthetic standards of his personality.... [The] idea which had appeared before consciousness as the vehicle of this irreconcilable wish fell a victim to repression, was pushed out of consciousness with all its attached memories, and was forgotten.... [Repression] was thus revealed as one of the devices serving to protect the mental personality."
17. *See* Sigmund Freud, *An Autobiographical Study*, trans. J. Strachey (New York: W. W. Norton, 1952), 77: "The analyst, who listens composedly but without any constrained effort to the stream of associations and who, from his experience, has a general notion of what to expect, can make use of the material brought to light by the patient ... to infer the

unconscious material itself; or if the resistance is stronger he will be able to recognize its character from the associations, as they seem to become more remote from the subject, and will explain it to the patient."
18. Frosh, supra note 12, at 11: "[Psychoanalysis] contains the possibilities for an approach that analyzes the mechanisms by which the social world enters into the experience of each individual, constructing the human 'subject' and reproducing itself through the perpetuation of particular patterns of ideology." That is, our social relations are "themselves only available because of the particular ideological structures that dominate within a society.... [Social] structures are incorporated into individual consciousness and have a formative role on the ordering of the psyche." Id. at 47, 48.
19. See Jerome Frank, *Law and the Modern Mind* (New York: Tudor, 1930), 8–9, 13–31.
20. See id. at 31–32.
21. See id. at 13–31.
22. See, for example, Joseph Goldstein, "Psychoanalysis and Jurisprudence," *Yale L.J.* (1968): 1053, 1054. (Integration of psychoanalysis and law "is not close at hand, and the scant beginning has occurred only at a relatively superficial descriptive level.")
23. See, for example, id. at 1060–64, 1071.
24. See generally Sander Gilman, "The Struggle of Psychiatry with Psychoanalysis: Who Won?" *Critical Inquiry* 13 (1987): 293.
25. See, for example, Goldstein, supra note 22, at 1076–77.
26. See Charles G. Schoenfeld, *Psychoanalysis and the Law* (Springfield, Ill.: Thomas, 1973). Psychoanalytic explanations are acknowledged to be "at best *partial*." Id. at 7.
27. Id. at 114.
28. Id.
29. Charles Lawrence, "'Justice' or 'Just Us': Racism and the Role of Ideology" (book review), *Stan. L. Rev.* 35 (1983): 831 (hereafter cited as "Justice"); "The Id, the Ego, and Equal Protection: Reckoning with Unconscious Racism," *Stan L. Rev.* 39 (1987): 317 (hereafter "Equal Protection").
30. An unfinished manuscript on psychoanalysis and law by Franz Rudolf Bienenfeld (1886–1961) was published in two parts entitled "Prolegomena to a Psychoanalysis of Law and Justice," *Calif. L. Rev.* 53 (1965): pt. 1, 957; pt. 2, 1254.
31. See Albert Ehrenzweig, *Psychoanalytic Jurisprudence: On Ethics, Aesthetics, and "Law"—On Crime, Tort, and Procedure* (Leiden: Sijthoff 1971).
32. Lawrence, "Justice," supra note 29, at 841–42.
33. Id. at 842, 848.
34. Lawrence, "Equal Protection," supra note 29, at 322–23, 329.
35. Herbert Marcuse, *Eros and Civilization, A Philosophical Inquiry into Freud* (Boston: Beacon Press, 1955), 16.
36. Lawrence, "Equal Protection," supra note 29, at 331 n. 55.
37. See Peter Gabel, "Dukakis's Defeat and the Transformative Possibilities of Legal Culture," *Tikkun* (March/April 1989), at 16; see also id. at 14 (acknowledging that Lacanian "psychoanalysis is based on a fundamental split between the subject and the knowledge he has of himself").
38. See R. D. Laing, *The Politics of the Family and Other Essays* (New York:

Vintage Books, 1971), 3–19; Ragland-Sullivan, supra note 11, at 62: "Laing (following Winnicott) makes a Rousseauesque division between true and false images of self ('true' belonging to the natural and good inner self and 'false' to the distorting, repressive effects of the social realm).... Lacan's subject, on the other hand, is a paradox of true and false.... No final separation exists, therefore, between the inside and outside realms."

39. Gabel, supra note 37, at 16.
40. Id.
41. Id. at 15.
42. Id. at 107–8.
43. Id. at 108–9.
44. See, for example, David Trubek, "Where the Action Is: Critical Legal Studies and Empiricism," *Stan. L. Rev.* 36 (1984): 575, 607.
45. See, for example, Mark Kelman, "Trashing," *Stan. L. Rev.* 36 (1984): 293, 304.
46. See Gabel, supra note 37, at 15–16.
47. See Peter Gabel, "The Phenomenology of Rights-Consciousness and the Pact of the Withdrawn Selves," *Tex. L. Rev.* 62 (1984): 1563, 1565 n. 3.
48. Schema L appears in (1) *The Seminar of Jacques Lacan, Book 2: The Ego in Freud's Theory and in the Technique of Psychoanalysis 1954–1955*, ed. J.-A. Miller and trans. S. Tomaselli (New York: W. W. Norton, 1988), at 243; in (2) *The Seminar of Jacques Lacan, Book 3: The Psychoses 1955–1956*, ed. J.-A. Miller and trans. R. Grigg (New York: W. W. Norton, 1993), at 14; and in (3) "Le séminaire sur 'La lettre volée,'" in *Écrits* (Paris: Editions du Seuil, 1966), at 53; a simplified version appears in Lacan, "On a question," supra note 2, at 193, to signify "that the condition of the subject S (neurosis or psychosis) is dependent on what is being unfolded in the Other O."
49. See "Le séminaire," supra note 48, at 9 (as translated by Anthony Wilden in his notes following Lacan's "The Function of Language in Psychoanalysis," in Lacan, *Speech and Language in Psychoanalysis*, trans. Wilden (Baltimore: Johns Hopkins University Press, 1968), at 107 n. 48: "Thus it is if man comes to thinking the Symbolic order, it is because he is caught in it from the first in his being. The illusion that he has formed it by his consciousness results from the fact that it was by way of a *béance* specific to his Imaginary relation to his counterpart, that he was able to enter into this order as a subject. But he was only able to make this entrance by the radical defile of [*parole*] ... which ... is reproduced each time that the subject addresses himself to the Other ... who can nullify the subject himself ... by making himself an object in order to deceive him. This dialectic of intersubjectivity, whose use I have shown to be necessary—from the theory of transference to the structure of paranoia, itself—... is readily backed up by the [*Schema L*] which has long been familiar to my students.... The two middle terms represent the coupled reciprocal Imaginary objectification which I have emphasized in the *stade du miroir*").

For Lacan's description of the mirror stage, see Lacan, "The mirror stage as formative of the function of the I as revealed in psychoanalytic experience," in *Écrits*, supra note 2, at 1–7. Briefly, when an infant

(6–18 months old) sees her image in the mirror, she identifies with its totality and experiences herself as a unified body: "But this early identification also constitutes the first alienation, a split between outer form (big and symmetrical) and an inner sense of incoherence and dissymmetry."

Ragland-Sullivan, supra note 11 at 25. Note that "Lacan used solid lines to depict the unconscious relationship between *Autre* and *moi*, and between *autre* and *moi*. The broken lines ... infer the unconscious acting directly upon speech, writing, and human interrelations." Id. at 3.

50. *See* Alexandre Leupin, "Introduction: Voids and Knots in Knowledge and Truth," in *Lacan and the Human Sciences*, supra note 8, at 12–16, for a discussion of the deficiencies of Schema L and Lacan's later, improved topologies.
51. Refer to note 10 supra (Lacan's statement regarding another diagram, his Schema I).
52. "Introduction of the Big Other," Seminar 19 in *Book 2 of the Seminar*, supra note 48, at 235–47.
53. Id. at 236; *see Book 2 of the Seminar*, at 321: "[The other] isn't an other at all, since it is essentially coupled with the ego, in a relation which is always reflexive, interchangeable—the *ego* is always an *alter-ego*."

In an earlier (1954) seminar, Lacan remarked that the "I is an other," and then warned: "Don't start spreading it around that *I is an other*—... it doesn't mean anything. Because, to begin with, you have to know what an other means.... The subject as such [is not] an organism which adopts itself. It is something else ... something other than the axis we can grasp when we consider it as a function of an individual.... [The] subject is decentered in relation to the individual. That is what *I is an other* means." Id. at 7, 9.
54. "Introduction of the Big Other," supra note 52, at 243.
55. Id. at 244.
56. Id.
57. Id. at 244, 246.
58. Lacan, "On a Question," supra note 2, at 194.
59. Ragland-Sullivan, supra note 11, at 7.
60. Refer to note 50 supra.
61. In the epigraph, the phrase "where it was" refers to Freud's "Wo es war, soll Ich werden," translated as "where id was, there shall ego be," in *New Introductory Lectures on Psycho-Analysis* (1933), in *22 Complete Psychological Works of Sigmund Freud*, ed. J. Strachey (New York: W. W. Norton, 1966), at 80. *See* "The Freudian Thing, or the Meaning of the Return to Freud in Psychoanalysis," in *Écrits*, supra note 2, at 128–29.
62. *See* Lacan, "Aggressivity in Psychoanalysis," in *Écrits*, supra note 2, at 22.
63. *See* Stuart Schneiderman, *Jacques Lacan: The Death of an Intellectual Hero* (Cambridge: Harvard University Press, 1983), 151 ("Almost by definition, the ego can never be the master of the short session"). Id. at 134.
64. Gabel, supra note 37, at 106.
65. Peter Gabel, "A Critical Anatomy of the Legal Opinion," *ALSA Forum* (Fall 1980): 5, 10.
66. *See* Ragland-Sullivan, supra note 11, at 2: "The terms 'ego' or 'self' are misleading in understanding Lacan's concept of the subject, since they

imply a wholeness or totality that he refuted by his literal reformulation of the Freudian idea of *Ichspaltung* or a splitting of the subject."
67. Lacan, *Book 2 of the Seminar*, supra note 48, at 52–53 ("The ego makes itself manifest [in analysis] as defence, as refusal").
68. *See* id. at 194: "The ego is deprived of its absolute position in the subject. The ego acquires the status of a mirage, as the residue, it is only one element in the objectal relations in the subject."
69. *See* id. at 282: "The image of the ego—simply because it is an image, the ego is an ideal ego—sums up the entire imaginary relation in man."
70. *See* Goodrich, supra note 1, at 281–82: "Ego ... is in law a lack, an absence that is filled by entry into the symbolic. ... The entry of the individual into the symbolic, the transition from zero to one, from lack to identity, is the condition of institutional existence, the capture of the subject by law."
71. *See* Ragland-Sullivan, supra note 11, at 42–43.
72. Id. at xii ("This *Autre* ... intervenes in Lacan's theory on several levels, but all of which distinguish themselves by a dimension of exteriority and a determining function in relation to the human subject").
73. *See* Lacan, "The Function and Field," supra note 2, at 67 ("It is in the *name of the father* that we must recognize the support of the symbolic function which, from the dawn of history, has identified his person with the figure of the law").
74. *See* Ragland-Sullivan, supra note 11, at 16, citing Stuart Schneiderman, "Psychoanalysis and *Hamlet*," *DAI* 72 (1975): 23503A.
75. *See* Lacan, "On a Question," supra note 2, at 193: "What is being unfolded [in the Other for the subject] is articulated like a discourse (the unconscious is the discourse of the Other), whose syntax Freud first sought to define for those bits that come to us in certain privileged moments, in dreams, in slips of the tongue."
76. *See* Ragland-Sullivan, supra note 11, at 38 (clarity and "truth" reside in the unconscious Other(A)").
77. Wilden, supra note 49, at 266.
78. Id.
79. Id. at 264, 268. Sometimes "Other" will "simply mean the category of 'Otherness,' a translation Lacan himself has employed." Id. at 264.
80. Id. at 265, 269.
81. Lacan, *Television*, supra note 6, at 6.
82. Lacan, *The Four Fundamental Concepts of Psychoanalysis*, ed. J.-A. Miller and trans. A. Sheridan (New York: W. W. Norton, 1978), 203, 207.
83. *See* Ragland-Sullivan, supra note 11, at 53 (Lacan "collapsed the Freudian id and ego into the *moi*").
84. Id. ("The identificatory *moi* is repressed as an ideal ego and the social *je* is formed, and thus [the superego is] a part of both subjects.")
85. Id. at 57.
86. Id. at 56 (when an infant submits "to the laws that structure its particular social network and [internalizes] them, it has acquired a superego").
87. Lacan, *The Four Fundamental Concepts*, supra note 82, at 207.
88. Id; *see also* Lacan, "The Subversion of the Subject," supra note 1, at 316.
89. Mark Bracher, "Lacanian Theory and the Future of Cultural Criticism," *Newsletter of the Freudian Field* 3, nos. 1/2 (1989): 102, 103.

90. Ragland-Sullivan, supra note 11, at 228.
91. Id. at 38.
92. Lacan, "On a Question," supra note 2, at 217.
93. Russell Grigg, "The Function of the Father in Psychoanalysis," *Aust. J. Psychotherapy* 5, no. 2 (1986): 120–21.
94. Jane Flax, "Signifying the Father's Desire: Lacan in a Feminist's Gaze," in *Criticism and Lacan*, supra note 6, at 111.
95. Wilden, supra note 49, at 188.
96. Lacan, *The Four Fundamental Concepts*, supra note 82, at 251.
97. Id. at 63–64 ("Language ... imprints the cultural myths which adults later assume they have consciously deduced or learned").
98. J. Lacan, *The Seminar of Jacques Lacan, Book 1: Freud's Papers on Technique 1953–1954*, ed. J.-A. Miller and trans. J. Forrester (New York: W. W. Norton, 1988), at 177.
99. Ragland-Sullivan, supra note 11, at 59: "As the subject of linguistic distinctions and differences, the [speaking subject] stabilizes the *moi* by anchoring its sliding identifications and spontaneous fusions by naming and labeling these responses."
100. Lacan, *Book 1 of the Seminar*, supra note 98, at 171.
101. *See* Lacan, *Four Fundamental Concepts*, supra note 82, at 70 (signifiers structure and shape human relations).
102. *See* Lacan, *Four Fundamental Concepts*, supra note 82, at 142.
103. Id. at 126.
104. *See* id.
105. *See* Jacques-Alain Miller, "The Analytic Experience: Means, Ends, and Results," in *Lacan and the Subject of Language*, ed. E. Ragland-Sullivan and M. Bracher (New York: Routledge, 1991), at 85: "Why would anyone be interested in anything if not for its usefulness ...? ... 'I use Lacan.' Every time I hear that phrase, I am reminded that Freud's discovery stems from the useless, as you know, from the unusable, from the leftover of our conscious and purposeful activities."
106. *See* Goodrich, supra note 3, at 193. A commentary on Goodrich's work appears in C. Douzinas, R. Warrington, and S. McVeigh, *Postmodern Jurisprudence: The Law of the Text in the Texts of Law* (New York: Routledge, 1991), 124–35.
107. *See* Goodrich, supra note 3, at 197 (the subject's defenses as "the first obstacle of any analytic or therapeutic relation").
108. Id. at 196 ("analysis is led eventually to question an order of repression ... in which the laws governing the forms of discourse are inscribed in the very constitution of subjectivity."); 200 ("the student of law internalizes the limits of legal argument"); 201 ("The essence of any grammar [is] to standardize and control meaning."); 205: "It is the subject that fabricates the law through an act of denial, through a non-recognition or repression of subjectivity and desire in favor of entry into the symbolic as the fiction of law."
109. *See* id. at 198: "In analytic terms ... it is the teaching relationship, the form of language of the substantive disciplines, the methodologies of argument and the structures of evaluation and examination that are all at some point to be questioned, in terms of their internal and external disciplinary functions."

110. *See* Goodrich, supra note 1, at 179–86. The Haida Indians interfered with and stopped the logging activities even though a "valid" license had been issued, thus they became defendants in an injunction action.
111. Id. at 180.
112. Id.
113. Id. at 182. "The evidence presented as to the Haida title to and relationship with the islands was not legally relevant to the case being heard, which simply concerned interference [by the Haida] with a valid logging license." Id. at 183.
114. Id.
115. *See* id. at 185. Historically, the legal profession was seen to be "possessed of a hidden wisdom (*arcana juris*) and its task [was] to mediate that wisdom, to insert it in social speech as the absolute boundary of what it is humanly possible to say." Id. at 273.
116. *See* id. at 282.
117. "The Lost Temporality of Law: An Interview with Pierre Legendre," conducted by P. Goodrich and R. Warrington, *Law & Critique* 1 (1990): 3, 18.
118. Id. Goodrich remarks that Legendre's contributions to a Lacanian theory of legal processes are "no more than elements of a much larger philosophical project, that of the genealogy of legal institutions." Goodrich, supra note 1, at 262.
119. Interview with Legendre, supra note 117, at 18–19. "The Metaphor of the Reference . . . is the principle of division of the categories, in other words, the absolute. . . . Within the institutional assembly of the West, a father . . . incarnates the founding reference of which he is necessarily the intermediary."
120. *See* William T. Bray, David Caudill, and Jack Owen, "Once Again, the Trilogy in Retrospect: An Essay on the Virtues of Development Agreements in Texas," *S. Tex. L. Rev.* 32 (1990): 14–26, for a discussion of numerous such articles.
121. *See* Goodrich, supra note 1, at 273.
122. Id. at 26–28, citing Robert A. Williams Jr., "Legal Discourse, Social Vision and the Supreme Court's Land Use Planning Law: The Genealogy of the Lochnerian Recurrence in First English Lutheran Church and Nollan," *U. Colo. L. Rev.* 59 (1988): 427, 428–29, 446–73 (Judicial adoption of a particular "social vision" as determinative; two competing discourses—property as a fundamental right *versus* judicial deference in socioeconomic matters—reflect such visions); Gregory S. Alexander, "Takings, Narratives, and Power," *Colum. L. Rev.* 88 (1988): 1752, 1752–68 ("narratives of power" lie below abstract, doctrinal analyses).
123. Joan Copjec, "Dossier on the Institutional Debate: An Introduction," in *Television*, supra note 6, at 52.
124. Id.; refer to text accompanying note 46 supra.
125. Mortgage loan borrowers, particularly commercial borrowers, invariably can read, and after consulting with their attorney, can understand standard loan documents and give what is known as an informed and voluntary consent. Such a borrower presumably has bargaining power, equal to the lender, so as to eliminate unacceptable provisions in loan documents through negotiation. *See generally* John Calamari and Joseph Perillo,

Contracts, 3rd ed. (Minneapolis: West Publishing, 1987), 418–24. Those who have represented borrowers know, however, the difficulties in negotiating against a bank's "standard documentation"; often, nowadays, the initial loan commitment signed by a borrower *is* an agreement which limits the terms of the loan to the bank's "standard documentation." In real estate law practice, loan documents are seldom "negotiated" in the manner of (even "form") sale agreements, leases, or easements.

126. *See*, for example, *Lovell v. Western Life Insurance Co.*, 754 S.W.2d 298 (Tex. App.—Amarillo, 1988), a case involving a claim of breach of good faith and fair dealing brought by a borrower-mortgagor against a lender: "The duty of good faith and fair dealing does not exist in Texas unless intentionally created by express language or unless a special relationship of trust or confidence exists between the parties to the contract. *Arnold* . . . 725 S.W. 2d 165, 167 (Tex. 1987). 'In the insurance context, a special relationship arises out of the parties' unequal bargaining power.' 725 S.W.2d at 167. In analyzing the transaction in the instant case, we find [no] imbalance of bargaining power." 754 S.W.2d at 301–2.

127. *See* Interview, "Juror Comments on $46 Million Judgment," *Lender Liability Law Report*, January 1988, at 4: "Well, what was it that convinced the remainder of the jury that Bank of America (in *Kruse v. Bank of America*, 248 Cal. Rptr. 217 [Cal App. 1988]) was liable?"

[Jury Foreman:] "The fact that the bank's witnesses lied so much. . . . Every bank witness testified he had not instituted the loan request, even though three . . . had signed the loan request. One of [those who signed the request and approved it] testified . . . that in 'bank jargon,' an approval doesn't mean the bank actually approved the request, it means something else."

128. Lacan, *Book 1 of the Seminar*, supra note 98, at 178.

> For the human being the word or concept is nothing other than the word in its materiality. It is the thing itself. It is not just a shadow, a breath of virtual illusion of the thing, it is the thing itself.
>
> [For example, it] is owing to the fact that the word *elephant* exists in their language, and hence that the elephant enters into their deliberations, that men have been capable of . . . decisions which are more far-reaching for these pachyderms than anything else that has happened to them throughout their history.

Id.

129. *See* Zizek supra note 2, at 46: "Lacan's last word would be a radical alienation of the subject [if the subject's] content [was] determined by an exterior signifying network. . . . But Lacan's basic thesis, at least in his last works, is that there is a possibility for the subject to obtain some contents, some kind of positive consistency, also outside the big Other, the alienating symbolic network."

130. Goodrich, supra note 3, at 195, 210.
131. *See* Ragland-Sullivan, supra note 11, at 273.
132. *See* Zizek, supra note 2, at 68.

CHAPTER 3

This chapter is a substantially modified version of an article that appeared in *LAW & CRITIQUE* 3 (1992): 169.

1. This distinction was introduced and developed in part by Elizabeth Wright in *Psychoanalytic Criticism: Theory in Practice* (New York: Methuen, 1987) (a comparative study of the major schools of psychoanalytic criticism of art and literature—namely classical Freudian, ego-psychology, Jungian, object-relations theory, structuralist [e.g., Lacan], poststructuralist [e.g., Derrida], and antipsychoanalysis).
2. See Ellie Ragland-Sullivan, *Jacques Lacan and the Philosophy of Psychoanalysis* (Chicago: University Illinois Press, 1987), 87: "It is hard for [philosophers] to accept that the surface (text) does not *contain* meaning (as bottles contain wine), but takes on meaning only to conceal a deeper gap: standing behind the text is an unconscious system of repressed meanings."
3. See Susan Tiefenbrun, "Legal Semiotics," *Cardozo Arts & Ent. L. J.* 5 (1986): 89, 152: "[Lacan's] concept of hidden meanings and the distortion which comes about by the use or misuse of words is the very stuff with which lawyers grapple on a daily basis."

   Tiefenbrun briefly discusses Lacan in her comprehensive survey of legal semiotics, and concludes: "The law, which has begun to adopt if not a Lacanian then a psycholinguistic approach to legal issues, could benefit from more explicit applications of semiotic principles." Id. (footnote omitted).
4. See Jacques-Alain Miller, "How Psychoanalysis Cures According to Lacan," *Newsletter of the Freudian Field* 1, no. 2 (1986): 27: "The way [Lacan] uses terms, things do not always fit. You always have to re-think the way he is using the terms."
5. Id. at 26.
6. See Patrick Colm Hogan, "Structure and Ambiguity in the Symbolic Order: Some Prolegomena to the Understanding and Criticism of Lacan," in *Criticism and Lacan: Essays and Dialogue on Language, Structure, and the Unconscious*, ed. P. Hogan and L. Pandit (Athens: University Georgia Press, 1990), at 6–7, 9: "[A] critical or dialectical engagement with Lacan's text . . . would neither repress nor idealize Lacan. But . . . neither would it result in a haphazard eclecticism, a mere raiding of Lacan's text for 'useful' tidbits. . . . [The] practice of 'using' some particular and isolated idea, or even phrase or word, from some theorist . . . betrays a cavalier attitude and an intellectual slovenliness."
7. This aversion to "draftsmanship" is a recognition that the "thickening" of legal language beyond ordinary language, explained by lawyers as essential to clarity, results often in a lack of clarity. See Brenda Danet, "Language in the Legal Process," *L. & Society Rev.* 14 (1980: 445, 540–41. See also David Mellinkoff, *The Language of the Law* (Boston: Little, Brown, 1963), 11–12 (gulf between ordinary and legal language; each has its peculiar meanings), 290ff (belief in precision), 304ff (vague archaisms of legal language) (1963). The illusion of certainty here is on the part of lawyers, not their clients.
8. See generally Robert Hillman, "The Crisis in Modern Contract Theory," *Tex. L. Rev.* 67 (1989): 103, 104–13, for a discussion of the attack on contract doctrine as indeterminate.
9. Terry Eagleton, *Literary Theory: An Introduction* (Oxford: Blackwell, 1983), 168–69.
10. Randy Barnett, speech to AALS Contracts Section, January 2–6, 1991, Washington, D.C.

11. Id.
12. Ian Ayres and Robert Gertner, "Filling Gaps in Incomplete Contracts: An Economic Theory of Default Rules," *Yale L. J.* 99 (1989): 87.
13. Id. at 91 and n. 24.
14. Id. at 89–90, citing (inter alia) Frank Easterbrook and Daniel Fischel, "The Corporate Contract," *Columbia L. Rev.* 89 (1989): 1416. A variation on this justification is the majoritarian approach, *i.e.*, implying terms that *most* parties would want. See Ayres and Gertner, supra, note 12, at 93.
15. Charles Goetz and Robert Scott, "The Limits of Expanded Choice: An Analysis of the Interactions Between Express and Implied Contract Terms," *Calif. L. Rev.* 73 (1985): 261: "Terms of trade may *intentionally* be left imprecise as a 'lesser of evils' expedient. The obvious solution to incompleteness—express particularization—incurs great risks of misinterpretation. It may therefore be preferable to allow the parties to employ deliberately indeterminate formulations, which implicitly instruct the dispute-resolver to construe the contract equitably . . . [i.e.,] an equitable 'filling in the blanks' in light of conditions that were either difficult to anticipate or impractical to describe in advance." Id. at 317, cited in Ayres and Gertner, supra note 12, at 90 n. 23. *See also* Lawrence Friedman, "Law and Its Language," *Geo. Wash. L. Rev.* 33 (1964): 563, 578: "Standardized language . . . could lead to reliable and predictable standardized interpretation. Courts taking this approach sometimes paid inordinate attention to words and phrases and to changes in words and phrases. To depart from a conventional way of saying something was to invite unwelcome inquiry."
16. Ayres and Gertner, supra note 12, at 91. For example, if a buyer does not disclose potential losses that will result from the seller's nondelivery, the buyer will be penalized by limiting the damages for nondelivery to foreseeable damages. Note that Ayres and Gertner argue for "penalty defaults" only where information revelation is efficient, as in the case where a more knowledgeable party strategically decides "not to contract around even an inefficient default." Id. at 127.
17. *See* Hadley and Baxendale, 9 Ex. 341, 156 Eng. Rep. 145 (1854), discussed in Ayres and Gertner, supra note 12, at 101–16, and in Jason Johnston, "Strategic Bargaining and the Economic Theory of Contract Default Rules," *Yale L. J.* 100 (1990): 615, 620–39.
18. *See* Goetz and Scott, supra note 15, at 311: "Because of the inherently uncertain mediation of words, errors are inevitable in the process of defining the meaning of different combinations of terms." *See also* George Christie, "Vagueness and Legal Language," *Minn. L. Rev.* 48 (1964): 885, 911 ("Vagueness is an inescapable aspect of our language").
19. *See* Hillman, supra note 8, at 117: "Judges fill gaps based both on the presumed intentions of the parties and on their own views of fairness. . . . [O]ne can safely say only that . . . the recognition of court's important gap-filling role [provides a criterion] for determining the rights and obligations of interacting parties in a complex society. It is worth repeating, however, that although contract law affords judges some discretion, it often gives ample guidance to courts, lawyers, and parties."
20. *See* E. Allan Farnsworth, *Contracts*, 2d ed. (Boston: Little, Brown, 1990), para. 7.16; *but see* Goetz and Scott, supra note 15, at 276 ("Courts experience

grave difficulty determining the degree of repetition necessary to establish a 'course' of conduct.").
21. *See*, for example, *Lewis v. Benedict Coal Corp.*, 361 U.S. 459, 469 (1960).
22. *See*, for example, Randy Barnett, "A Consent Theory of Contracts," *Columbia L. Rev.* 86 (1986): 269, 320; Goetz and Scott, supra note 15, at 322. Briefly, default rules that imply terms most parties want will reduce transaction costs. I will not here add to the criticism of "the law and economics colonialism of legal discourse." *See* Judith Koffler, "Forged Alliance: Law and Literature" (review essay), *Columbia L. Rev.* 89 (1989): 1374, 1391. Regarding control of the vocabulary of legal discourse, it seems that "No matter what the human problem that gives rise to a legal issue . . .[,] market-talk refuses to go away. Volumes of critical attacks in the law reviews . . . have failed to stop the spread of the contagion." Id.

Professor Johnston adequately "demystifies" the economic analysis of law: "Common law doctrines are overdetermined—they can be explained from a variety of perspectives. 'Explaining' the common law from an economic point of view can therefore mean simply choosing a set of assumptions and notions of efficiency." Johnston, supra note 17, at 649 ("My goal . . . has been to expose this choice.").
23. *See generally* Clare Dalton, "An Essay in the Deconstruction of Contract Doctrine," in *Interpreting Law and Literature: A Hermeneutic Reader*, ed. S. Levinson and S. Mailloux (Evanston, Ill.: Northwestern University Press, 1988).
24. Goetz and Scott, supra note 15, at 306–9.
25. Id. at 309.
26. Id.
27. Id.
28. Id. at 322.
29. *See* Frank Lentricchia, *After the New Criticism* (Chicago: University of Chicago Press, 1980), xii (those listed above, together with Northrop Frye, Wallace Stevens, Frank Kermode, and Georges Poulet, "largely set the terms and themes of recent critical controversies in this country").
30. Id. at 326.
31. *See* Jacques Lacan, "Seminar on 'The Purloined Letter,'" *Yale French Studies* 48 (1972): 39, trans. J. Mehlman; and "Seminar of 21st January 1975," in *Feminine Sexuality: Jacques Lacan and the École Freudienne*, ed. J. Mitchell and J. Rose (New York: W. W. Norton, 1975), 166 (from Ornicar? 3: 104); *see also* Jacques Lacan, "Of Structure As an Inmixing of an Otherness Prerequisite to Any Subject Whatever," in *The Structuralist Controversy: The Languages of Criticism and the Sciences of Man*, ed. R. Macksey and E. Donato (Baltimore: Johns Hopkins University Press, 1972), 186.
32. Dennis Porter, "Psychoanalysis and the Task of the Translator," *MLN* 104 (1989): 1066, 1079.
33. Id. at 1078–79 ("A thinker whose written works and recorded seminars could be used for . . . training students in the recognition of the tropes of traditional rhetoric . . . seems to be self-consciously literary, to associate himself less with science than with our so-called humanities").
34. *See*, for example, Ragland-Sullivan, supra note 2.
35. *See*, for example, Sebastiano Timpanaro, *The Freudian Slip* (London: New Left Books, 1974), 58 (Lacan's "charlatry and exhibitionism" exposed);

Norman Holland, *The Critical I* (New York: Columbia University Press, 1992), 192–208 (while Lacan's foregrounding of the function of language is admirable, Lacan's linguistic and psychological assumptions are outdated and inconsistent with current developments in psycholinguistics).
36. David Ellis, *Wordsworth, Freud and the Spots of Time: Interpretation in "The Prelude"* (Cambridge: Cambridge University Press, 1985).
37. Id. at 3.
38. Id. at 4.
39. Id. at 3. Significantly, while Lacan was committed to rediscovery of (and reestablishing as central to theory) the *true* Freud, one would not characterize his work as a "wholesale acceptance" of either Freud's entire *corpus* (i.e., the later Freud is not essential to Lacanian theory) or Freud's scientism.
40. Jacques Lacan, "The Agency of the Letter in the Unconscious or Reason since Freud," in *Écrits: A Selection*, trans. A. Sheridan (New York: W. W. Norton, 1977), 148.
41. Id.
42. Id.
43. Id. at 149 and n. 8.
44. Malcolm Bowie, *Freud, Proust, and Lacan: Theory as Fiction* (Cambridge: Cambridge University Press, 1987), 102.
45. Recall that Lacan explicates three "orders" of human cognition—the Symbolic, the Imaginary, and the Real. As discussed in Chapter 2, Freud's topology of the human psyche is completely re-worked to include both a *moi* and a *je* in the place of the ego, but both functions participate in the unconscious; Lacan also revises Freud's "four fundamental concepts"—drive, the unconscious, repetition, and transference—and thereafter introduces a new conception of Desire. Moreover, Lacan formulates numerous techniques for clinical analysis and criticizes the psychiatric and psychoanalytic establishments in Europe and North America. See *generally* Ragland-Sullivan, supra note 2.
46. Lacan, "The Function and Field of Speech and Language in Psychoanalysis," in *Écrits*, supra note 40, at 57.
47. See A. A. Brill, "Introduction," in *The Basic Writings of Sigmund Freud*, ed. and trans. A. A. Brill (New York: Modern Library, 1938), at 13: "Freud became convinced that there is nothing arbitrary or accidental in psychic life, be it normal or abnormal.... For the very unconscious forces which he found in the neuroses he also found in the common faulty actions of everyday life,... which had hitherto been considered accidental and unworthy of explanation."
48. Lacan, "The Function and Field of Speech and Language in Psychoanalysis," in *Écrits*, supra note 46, at 59. *See also* Miller, supra note 4, at 25: "[It] is very difficult to understand how analysis works without taking into account that it is chiefly speech: speech and interpretation.... [T]he subject of your 'operation' as analyst is completely speech."
49. Lacan, "The Function and Field," supra note 46, at 60 (discussing Freud's *Jokes and their relation to the unconscious*).
50. Lacan, "The Function and Field," supra note 46, at 60–61; *see also* Anthony Wilden's commentary on this passage in *Jacques Lacan, Speech and Language in Psychoanalysis*, ed. and trans. A. Wilden (Baltimore: Johns Hopkins

University Press, 1968), at 268: "Lacan ... turns to [Freud's] work on jokes and reads it seriously, because the joke is not only structurally equivalent to a derivative of the unconscious, employing mechanisms similar to those involved in any kind of symptom, including the dream, but it also necessarily involves someone to which it must be told ..., without which it may be comic, but cannot be a joke. Lacan's introduction of the notion of the other is of value here, since Freud expressly says ... that jokes are of a social nature, whereas dreams are not."
51. Lacan, "The Function and Field," supra note 46, at 64.
52. Id. at 66.
53. Id. at 66, 68.
54. Wilden, supra note 50, at 270.
55. Bice Benvenuto and Roger Kennedy, *The Works of Jacques Lacan: An Introduction* (New York: St. Martin's Press, 1986), 81.
56. Alan Sheridan, "Translator's Notes," in Lacan, *Écrits*, supra note 40, at ix.
57. *See generally* Ragland-Sullivan, supra note 2, at 162–83.
58. Lacan, "Seminar on 'The Purloined Letter,'" supra note 31, at 40. In April 1955, Lacan gave a workshop in Paris on "The Purloined Letter," which is now translated in *Book 2 of the Seminar of Jacques Lacan: The Ego in Freud's Theory and in the Technique of Psychoanalysis 1954–1955*, ed. J.-A. Miller and trans. S. Tomaselli (New York: W. W. Norton, 1988), at 191–205. Bruce Fink, in his review of Books 1 and 2 of *The Seminar*, remarks that "Book II ... affords the reader a glimpse into Lacan's 'purloined letter' workshop, showing his essay on Poe to have arisen, not like Athena from Zeus' head, all in one piece, but rather gradually." Bruce Fink, "The Seminar of Jacques Lacan: A Critical Review," *Lit. & Psych.* 36, no. 4 (1990): 69, 72. The text of the short story, which appears in most Poe anthologies, is reprinted in *The Purloined Poe*, *infra* note 161, at 6–27.
59. *See* Benvenuto and Kennedy, supra note 55, at 92 (discussing Freud's *Beyond the Pleasure Principle* and Lacan's seminar that appears in Book 2, supra note 58).
60. *See* Benvenuto and Kennedy, supra note 55, at 93: "Lacan used the word 'insistence' to express the notion of the repetition compulsion ...: the meaning of the unconscious subject is pressing or *insisting* on being expressed."
61. Sigmund Freud, *The Interpretation of Dreams* (1900), vol. 5 of the *Standard Edition of The Complete Works of Sigmund Freud* (London: Hogarth, 1955), 528, cited and discussed in Benvenuto and Kennedy, supra note 55, at 93: "Thus, in analysis, the chain of unconscious purposive ideas (or, in linguistic terms, the signifying chain) insists on being expressed and heard."
62. Lacan, "Seminar on 'The Purloined Letter,'" supra note 31, at 60.
63. Id.
64. *See* Lacan, "The Subversion of the Subject and the Dialectic of Desire in the Freudian Unconscious," in *Écrits*, supra note 40, at 316; *see also* Ragland-Sullivan, "Stealing Material: The Materiality of Language according to Freud and Lacan," in *Lacan and the Human Sciences*, ed. A. Leupin (Lincoln: University of Nebraska Press, 1991), at 60.

65. Ragland-Sullivan, supra note 2, at 223.
66. Mark Bracher, "Lacanian Theory and the Future of Cultural Criticism," *Newsletter of the Freudian Field* 3, nos. 1/2 (1989) 102, 103 ("individual subjects meet only through *their* representatives: signifiers").
67. Id. at 103, 105.
68. Id. at 105.
69. Lacan, "Desire and the Interpretation of Desire in Hamlet," trans. J. Hulbert, *Yale French Studies* 55 (1977): 11, 28, quoted in Bracher, supra note 66, at 105.
70. Bracher, supra note 66, at 105.
71. Bowie, supra note 44, at 155.
72. Lacan, "Seminar on 'The Purloined Letter,'" supra note 31, at 60.
73. Id. at 66.
74. Much more could be said about the significance of the Poe essay in Lacanian theory. Benvenuto and Kennedy identify the King in his blindness with the ego "which feels itself invulnerable and omnipotent"—the illusion of autonomy in the ego is fundamental to Lacanian theory. Benvenuto and Kennedy, supra note 55 at 97; *see also* Jacques Lacan, "The mirror stage as formative of the I as revealed in psychoanalytic experience," in *Écrits*, supra note 40, at 6 ("Our experience shows that we should start ... from the *function of mèconnaissance* that characterizes the ego in all its structures"). Lacan remarks that the Queen and then the Minister are "trapped in the typically imaginary situation of seeing that she/he is not seen [and misconstruing] the situation in which she/he is seen." Lacan, "Seminar on 'The Purloined Letter,'" supra note 31, at 61, *quoted in* Benvenuto and Kennedy, supra note 55, at 98. Elizabeth Wright finds implications in Lacan's reading of Poe for the process or reading and writing generally, and she also points out that Lacanian conceptions of "Unconscious and repression, desire and lack ... [are] present in every visual recognition" in the story. *See* Wright, supra note 1, at 116. Malcolm Bowie identifies the purloined letter as "a pure migratory signifier [that] attracts different meanings to itself, mediates different kinds of power relationships and determines subjects in what they do and are." Bowie, supra note 44, at 124. Perhaps most significant, Derrida questioned Lacan's method and undisclosed presuppositions in an essay that has received much attention. *See* Derrida, "The Purveyor of Truth," *Yale French Studies* 52 (1975): 31, discussed in Barbara Johnson, *The Critical Difference: Essays in the Contemporary Rhetoric of Reading* (Baltimore: Johns Hopkins University Press, 1980), 114–17, and in Christopher Norris, *Derrida* (London: Methuen, 1987), 114–17.
75. Lacan, "The Agency of the Letter," supra note 40, at 147.
76. Id.; *see generally* Ragland-Sullivan, supra note 64, for an extensive commentary on the materiality of language; *see also* Benvenuto and Kennedy, supra note 55, at 108, who explain that the "material support is indeed well illustrated by Poe's purloined letter: though the letter is material, it cannot be found by the police looking for it. The letter is treated ... as a signifier, something which takes its value from representing games of power and intrigue. [Thus the letter] is only really the *place* where the letter should be, whether or not it is subsequently found."
77. Lacan, "The Agency of the Letter," supra note 40, at 148.

78. Id.
79. Id. at 149; *see generally* the discussion in Benvenuto and Kennedy, supra note 55, at 110–12 (commentary on Lacan's essay); *see also* Wright, supra note 1, at 109–10: "Saussure expresses the combination [of signified and signifier] by the formula s/S.... Lacan begins his critique by throwing doubt upon the security [, the bond,] of the combination.... Lacan inverts Saussure's formula [, suggesting] the place of unconscious desire as beneath the range of the conscious level of language, out of sight and unnoticed, yet able to shift unpredictably."
80. Lacan, "The Agency of the Letter," supra note 40, at 151.
81. Id.
82. Benvenuto and Kennedy, supra note 55, at 112. Recall that "Saussure claimed that meaning is generated by signifiers, not just in relation to their signifieds but also according to their position in the sentence in relation to other signifiers. So, too, Lacan will liken the unconscious to the movement of the signifier which generates meaning according to its place in the 'signifying chain.' It is this view which allows for Lacan's idea of the primacy of the signifier; what matters, in other words, is the meaning generated by the position of the signifier, not the usual meaning (signified) associated with it." Françoise Meltzer, "Unconscious," in *Critical Terms for Literary Study*, ed. F. Lentricchia and T. McLaughlin (Chicago: University of Chicago Press, 1990), at 159.
83. Benvenuto and Kennedy, supra note 55, at 113–14, citing Frederick de Saussure, *Course in General Linguistics*, ed. Charles Bally and Albert Sechehaye, trans. R. Hollis (La Salle, Ill.: Open Court, 1986) (originally published in 1915 by students who compiled lecture notes).
84. Lacan, "The Agency of the Letter," supra note 40, at 154. While Saussure drew dotted lines of correspondence between the mass of ideas and the mass of sound images, Lacan remarks that "all our experience runs counter to this linearity, which made me speak once ... of something more like 'anchoring points' (*'points de capiton'*) as a scheme for taking into account the dominance of the letter in the dramatic transformation that dialogue can effect in the subject." Id. (footnote omitted).
85. Id. at 156 and n. 20, 160.
86. *See* Bowie, supra note 44, at 12, citing Jakobson's "Two Aspects of Language and Two Types of Aphasic Disturbances," pt. 2 of Roman Jakobson and Morris Halle, *Fundamentals of Language* (The Hague: Mouton, 1956), 94–95: "Freud's 'displacement' and 'condensation' were both based on the principle of continuity, the one being metonymic and the other synecdochic; his 'identification' and 'symbolism' were based on similarity, and are hence metaphoric." *See also* Russel Grigg, "Metaphor and Metonymy," *Newsletter of the Freudian Field* 3, nos. 1/2 (1989): 58–66.
87. Lacan, "The Agency of the Letter," supra note 40, at 156. "On metonymy, ... Lacan appears to be quite standardly adopting Jakobson's analysis." Grigg, supra note 86, at 67.
88. Wilden, supra note 50, at 241, paraphrasing Lacan, supra note 40, at 156.
89. Lacan, "The Agency of the Letter," supra note 40, at 157. This passage "grasps the crucial element lacking from Jakobson's account ... [For Lacan, the] occurrence of the metaphor depends upon the relations that the

latent signifier maintains, not with the signifier that has replaced it, but with the other signifiers in the chain to which it is related by contiguity." Grigg, supra note 86, at 69; *see also* Ragland-Sullivan, supra note 2, at 234: "The supplemented signifier, in other words, falls from the level of consciousness to the level of unconsciousness, where it acts as a kind of latent unconscious signifier grafted onto an unconscious chain of associations."

Lacan's example of a metaphor is Victor Hugo's "His sheaf was neither miserly nor spiteful" from "Booz endormi." Lacan, supra at 156 and n. 21. "His sheaf" refers to Booz, who has been replaced—"usurped"—"in the signifying chain." Id. at 157. "'Booz' remains present not through a relation of semantic similarity with [sheaf] (there is none), but through its link, which Lacan calls metonymic, with the rest of the chain. The predicate clearly refers to Booz, which illustrates how the substitution metaphor is well able to function without there being any semantic relation between the two signifiers involved." Grigg, supra note 86, at 69.

90. For a more comprehensive and technical discussion of these two tropes in Lacanian theory, *see* Grigg, supra note 86. Significantly, Lacan's account (and use) of metaphor and metonymy is but one of many accounts.
91. Lacan, "The Agency of the Letter," supra note 40, at 160.
92. Freud, *Introductory Lectures on Psycho-Analysis*, in vol. 15, *Standard Edition*, supra note 61, at 18.
93. Wright, supra note 1, at 21.
94. Lacan, "The Agency of the Letter," supra note 40, at 160.
95. Wright, supra note 1, at 22. "Dreams are brief, meager and laconic in comparison with the range and wealth of dream thoughts." Benvenuto and Kennedy, supra note 55, at 120.
96. Lacan, "The Agency of the Letter," supra note 40, at 160.
97. Benvenuto and Kennedy, supra note 55, at 121, paraphrasing Lacan, "The Agency of the Letter," supra note 40, at 161.
98. *See* Bowie, supra note 44, at 113: "The unconscious, in so far as it becomes visible and audible in speech, symptoms, dreams and involuntary acts of omission or commission, is governed by the same rules as all other systems: the rules that Lacan has expressed in summary form as the 'logic of the signifier.'"
99. *See* Louise Halper, "Tropes of Anxiety and Desire: Metaphor and Metonymy in the Law of Takings," *Yale J. L. & Humanities* 8 (1995): 101.
100. Bowie, supra note 44, at 111.
101. Id. at 121.
102. Id. Bowie also acknowledges the utility for analysts of remaining alert to rhetoric in order to understand more clearly the discourse and thus the suffering of "nameable individuals." Id.
103. *See* Elizabeth Roudinesco, *Jacques Lacan & Co.: A History of Psychoanalysis In France, 1925–1985*, 390–98, trans. J. Mehlman (Chicago: University of Chicago Press, 1990), for a humorous account of Lacan's feud with Ricoeur, as well as a response to Ricoeur (who made the above accusation): "As far as linguistics was concerned, Lacan did nothing of what Ricoeur claimed. [Lacan] employed certain concepts from linguistics to effect a rearticulation of Freud's texts, but never did he implement the

slightest 'linguistic conception of the unconscious.'" Id. at 395.
104. See Jean-Françoise Lyotard, *Discours, Figure* (Paris: Klinksieck, 1971), 270, ("it is the effect on language of the force exerted by the figural (as image of form)"). Lacan deflects the critique essentially by agreeing that he has not locked himself into the laws of linguistics: "[Lyotard] discovers that what I describe as the effect of the signifier does not correspond to the signified delineated by linguistics, but well and truly to the subject." Lacan, "Points," the introduction to *Écrits* (Paris: Editions du Seuil, 1970), at ii, cited *in* G. Bennington, *Lyotard: Writing the Event* (Manchester: Manchester University Press, 1988), 90. The debate between Lyotard and Lacan is summarized well by Bennington, supra at 81–91, and by Peter Dews in "The Letter and the Line: Discourse and Its Other in Lyotard," *Diacritics* 14, no. 3 (1984): 40–49. See also Grigg, supra note 86, at 67: "In my opinion . . . the difference between [Lacan and Lyotard] is . . . the result of different views of how best to categorize metaphor and metonymy."
105. David Ingleby, "Understanding 'Mental Illness,'" in *Critical Psychiatry: The Politics of Mental Health*, ed. D. Ingleby (New York: Pantheon Books, 1980), at 64.
106. Ragland-Sullivan, supra note 2, at 169–70.
107. Bowie, supra note 44, at 113, quoting Lacan, "Of Structure," supra note 31, at 188. *See also* Lacan, "Science and Truth" (transcript of a 1965 seminar), *Newsletter of the Freudian Field* 3, nos. 1 & 2 (1989): 4, 15 ("the unconscious is language").
108. *See* id. at 167.
109. *See* Ragland-Sullivan, supra note 2, at 259.
110. Sigmund Freud, *Five Lectures on Psycho-Analysis* ed. and trans. J. Strachey (New York: W. W. Norton, 1977), 16, 27, 35.
111. Ragland-Sullivan, supra note 2, at 260–61.
112. Wilden, supra note 50 at 225.
113. *See* id.
114. *See* Ragland-Sullivan, supra note 2, at 68–89. The term Other (*Autre*) has various meanings in Lacan's texts; in chapter 2 above, I explain that it is a reference to that which is determinative and *exterior* in the psyche, thus at times one's parents, one's language, one's culture, etc.; the term "other" (autre) often refers to other people or to our projected images of ourselves.
115. Meltzer, supra note 82, at 159. "Metonymy is the signifier of desire for Lacan. What is desired is always displaced, always deferred, and reappears endlessly in another guise." Id. at 160.
116. Id. at 160–61.
117. For example, Lyotard; *see* Ragland-Sullivan, supra note 2, at 87 for a discussion of such critiques.
118. Id. at 87–88.
119. As a final warning against conceiving Lacanian theory as an uncritical and reductionistic commitment to a linguistic paradigm, consider the following remarks of Jacques-Alain Miller (responding to the misconceptions, among others, that psychoanalysis is for Lacan an exercise in hermeneutics, that Lacan is a poststructuralist, and that Lacan's seminars and theory were surrealistic, un-clinical):

What did Lacan do in his lifetime? There is one answer. He saw patients... so keep that in mind. Lacan was a practicing psychoanalyst....
You know the important interest that Lacan elicits among... literary critics.... But he was a practicing psychoanalyst....
Lacan tried to reformulate what Freud had said in *his* (Freud's) language, but with the scientific references [Lacan] had at his disposal.... Lacan's point of view is that... Freud was saying something other than what he seems to mean on a first reading. As such, [Lacan] tried to recapture the original inspiration of psychoanalysis before it was distorted.

Miller, supra note 4, at 6–7, 9. *Compare* Holland, supra note 35, at 217: "Lacanians, although they claim to be psychoanalytic, reason their psychology out of Saussure and philosophy, not the experience of couch and clinic."

120. My colleague, L. H. LaRue, does not find the analogy between legal texts and scripture, often found in law and literature analyses, very helpful in understanding how we interpret law. *See* LaRue, "Dissecting Interpretation" (book review), *Tex. L. Rev.* 68 (1990): 1073, 1079–80. I do not disagree; my section title is intended only to suggest a focus on law as language and legal analysis as a work in language, similar to Lacan's focus on the unconscious as language, although I do think the term "scripture" highlights the perceived importance to our lives of the text under consideration (i.e., it is a text not to be ignored).

121. Hogan, supra note 6, at 8–9: "In my reading of Lacan I find fairly consistent, if implicit use of a juridical model for psychoanalysis.... Lacan's juridical model asks us to think of [analyst and analysand] as dialecticians in [a sort of inquest]. Where the medical model turns our attention to diagnostic tests, Lacan's juridical model returns us to speech."

122. The term "phallic division" refers to the function of the "Name-of-the-Father," discussed in chapter 6 of this book.

123. *See* Ragland-Sullivan, supra note 2, at 135, 278; *see generally* id. at 258–308.

124. *See* Lacan, "The Subversion of the Subject" supra note 64, at 311 (translating *demande* as "demand"); *see also* Ragland-Sullivan, supra note 2, at 69, 85:

> Demande... is not a traditional psychoanalytic concept. Its usual translations—request or appeal—can be found, however, in law....
>
> [The term *demande* in Lacan's three-tiered explanation of drive—need, desire, and *demande*—] is usually rendered into English as "demand," although the French word meaning "to demand" is *exiger*.... Desire certainly entails a sense of urgency. But the word *demande* would be correctly translated from French as "appeal" or "request," [since] *demande*... asks a question.

125. *See* Lacan, "The direction of the treatment and the principles of its power," in *Écrits*, supra note 40, at 263 (Desire is "what is invoked by any demand beyond the need that is articulated in it"); "The Subversion of the Subject," supra note 64, at 311: "Desire begins to take shape in the margin in which demand becomes separated from need: this margin being that which is opened up by demand [toward]... the Other."

126. Lacan, supra note 125, at 263; *see* "Translator's Notes," *supra* note 56, at

xi (*Manque* translated as lack, "except in the expression, created by Lacan, '*manque-à-être*,' for which Lacan himself has proposed the English neologism 'want-to-be'").
127. "Translator's note," supra note 127, at viii.
128. *See* Ragland-Sullivan, supra note 2, at 69, 89.
129. *See* Lacan, "The Subversion of the Subject," supra note 64, at 314.
130. *See* Ragland-Sullivan, supra note 2, at 84 ("The Lacanian analyst [listens for] an intrasubjective dialogue with the Other[A]").
131. *See* id. at 86 (Demand "aims for something specific, some substitute object"); *see also* "Translator's Notes," supra note 56, at viii (Desire is insatiable, "a perpetual effect of symbolic articulation").
132. *See* Lacan, "The Subversion of the Subject," supra note 64, at 312: "[The] unconscious is . . . discourse of the Other. . . . But we must also add that man's desire is . . . the desire of the Other."
133. *See*, for example, Bernard Jackson, *Semiotics and Legal Theory* (London: Routledge, 1985) and *Law, Fact and Narrative Coherence* (Merseyside: Deborah Charles, 1988); R. Kevelson, *The Law as a System of Signs* (New York: Plenum Press, 1988); Tiefenbrun, supra note 3; J. M. Balkin, "The Hohfeldian Approach to Law and Semiotics," *U. Miami L. Rev.* 44 (1990): 1119.
134. *See* Balkin, supra note 133, at 1120 (before showing that Hohfeld is a semiotician, Balkin notes the affinity between Saussure's semiology and critical legal studies); *see also* Balkin, "The Promise of Legal Semiotics, *Tex. L. Rev.* 69 (1991): 1831, 1839: "[Some] will surely exclaim that what I have been describing as 'legal semiotics' is no more than a process of good old-fashioned legal analysis. I think this is partly true, but only partly."
135. Ragland-Sullivan, supra note 2, at 195.
136. Id. at 232. Lacan "said repeatedly that he did not like semiotics." Id., referring to J. Lacan, *Le Séminaire, Livre 20, Encore 1972–73*, ed. J.-A. Miller, 1975.
137. Ragland-Sullivan, supra note 2, at 210 ("some semioticians in France have become theoretical Lacanians, if not psychoanalysts").
138. *See* Dragan Milovanovic, "Law and the Challenge of Semiotic Analysis," *Leg. Stud. Forum* 14 (1990): 71 (review essay of Bernard Jackson's *Law, Fact and Narrative Coherence*, supra note 133).
139. Id. at 74–75, citing Jackson, supra note 138, at 27 (in the nonreferential view, "meaning consists in relations *within* a particular system of signification, and does not depend upon a relationship of reference to the outside world"). Note that the syntagmatic and paradigmatic axes of language are also at the basis of Saussure's and Jakobson's theories. *See* Grigg, supra note 86, at 58–59.
140. Milovanovic, supra note 138, at 75.
141. Id. at 76. "Whereas Jackson focuses on the grammatical-logical structures, the rhetorical structures which consist of tropes (metaphor, metonymy . . . etc., in other words where reference is to something outside of language itself), perpetually undermine the "truth" being constructed." Id. at 76–77.
142. Id. at 76. *Compare* Douzinas and McVeigh, book review of Jackson's *Semiotics and Legal Theory* (1985), *Int'l J. Sociology of Law* 16 (1988): 127, 128 (contrasting functionalist referentiality—signs refer to something out-

side themselves—with structuralist non-referentiality—signs refer to other signs or meaning-contents).
143. Milovanovic, supra note 138, at 78–79. In juridic discourse, "the syntagmatic and paradigmatic framework that creates a narrative indeed produces a narrow frame, one well suited to maintaining given dominant understandings of reality." *See also* Douzinas and McVeigh, supra note 142, at 132 (discussing Jameson's appropriation of Greimasian semiotics "to show how ideological closure operates ").
144. Milovanovic, supra note 138, at 81.
145. Much has been written about the centrality of metaphor to legal institutions and processes. Steven Winter argues that neither traditional "objectivists" nor critical subjectivists (or relativists) have captured the "largely imaginative and metaphoric" aspect of the law. Winter, "Transcendental Nonsense, Metaphoric Reasoning, and the Cognitive Stakes for Law," *U. PA. L. Rev.* 137 (1989): 1105, 1112; *see generally* id. at 1162–71 (discussing Felix Cohen's critique, and use of, legal metaphor). The "Answerer" in Jan Deutsch's fictional dialogue (concerning law as metaphor) remarks, in response to the question of how judicial precedent is compelling if not through verifiable doctrine, "that a judicial opinion works the way a metaphor works." Deutsch, "Law as Metaphor: A Structural Analysis of Legal Process," *Geo. L. J.* 66 (1978): 1339, 1346. James Murray, drawing on the work of James B. White and G. Joseph Vining, suggests that a focus on metaphor could lead to "a new dimension of understanding law." Murray, "Understanding Law as Metaphor," *J. Legal Educ.* 34 (1934): 714, 730.

Thomas Ross describes the power of legal metaphors, including the power to hide paradoxes "in the shelter of our metaphors." Ross, "Metaphor and Paradox," *Ga. L. Rev.* 23 (1989): 1053, 1084. An example of "hiding" a paradox in a metaphor is found in Farnsworth's study of contract interpretation, "'Meaning' in the Law of Contracts," *Yale L. J.*, 76 (1967): 939. The "grip" of the "meeting of the minds" metaphor was so strong in nineteenth century "will theory" that a buyer's acceptance by mail of a seller's mailed offer (where the goods had already been sold) was validated not because the seller did not notify the buyer of revocation, but because the seller's offer was made continuously as it travelled to the buyer. Id. at 945, citing *Adams v. Lindsell*, 106 Eng. Rep. 683 (K. B. 1818).

Finally, Brenda Danet, in her comprehensive analysis of the ordering function of legal language in social relations, writes that "metaphorical uses of language are not mere decorations but one more kind of creative use of language. . . . To speak, to interact with others verbally, is to construct the world, to constitute it, not merely to mirror it in words." *Language in the Legal Process*, supra note 7, at 456–57 (1980). *See*, for example, Ryan, "Comment," *Canad. Bar Review* 47 (1969): 318, 321–22 ("Commerce" in U.S. Supreme Court jurisprudence metaphorically reified as a "current," a "flow," or a "stream"). *See also* Nedelsky, "Law, Boundaries, and the Bounded Self," in *Law and the Order of Culture*, ed. R. Post (Berkeley: University of California Press, 1991), at 169: "Metaphors inevitably distort or shape our perceptions in the sense that they hide some dimensions of the phenomenon and highlight others. And it is,

146. further, not an option simply to avoid metaphors.... [A]ll our thinking is metaphoric in structure. [footnote omitted]."
146. Id. at 1176; see also Clare Dalton, supra note 23, at 291–92.
147. Gary Peller, "The Metaphysics of American Law," *Calif. L. Rev.* 73 (1985): 1151, 1213.
148. Id. at 1192–93. "The participants in the legal discourse socially constructed a language of representation and then collectively imagined that the metaphors were real." Id. at 1206.
149. Id. at 1243–44.
150. Id. at 1165.
151. *See* id. at 1164 n. 13 and 1165 n. 14.
152. Ragland-Sullivan, supra note 2, at 234–35 ("These meanings reappear at the surface as linguistic... repetitions, reversals, and so on"). "Lacan renewed the search for the foundations of logic and language beyond propositional logic, demonstrating how an unconscious dialectic overdetermines conscious meaning in its allusion to a repressed discourse. Here Lacan went beyond Jacques Derrida, who stopped at metaphor and was content to show the substitutive interchangeability of binary opposites." Id. at xix.

Again, "Lacan parts company with... Derrida... by postulating a true text which 'knows'—the unconscious—and in the elaboration of which all conscious use of knowledge and language is already interpretation." Id. at 90. Lacan begins to explain "*why* the mind works metaphorically [and] *how* the symbol system resides in the brain." Id. at 104.
153. Id. at 234, citing Lacan, "The Agency of the Letter," supra note 40, at 157; refer to note 96 supra and text accompanying.
154. *See* Ragland-Sullivan, supra note 2, at 234 (citing Lacan, Écrits (Paris: Editions du Seuil, 1966), 91 ("behind the [surface] text is an unconscious system of repressed meaning").
155. Nancy Harrowitz refers to "Poe the Semiotician" in her essay "The Body of the Detective Model: Charles S. Peirce and Edgar Allan Poe," in *The Sign of Three: Dupin, Holmes, Peirce*, ed. U. Eco and T. Sebeok (Bloomington: Indiana University Press, 1983), at 187.
156. Lacan, "Seminar on 'The purloined letter,'" supra note 31, at 62.
157. Id. at 69.
158. Eagleton, supra note 9, at 173 (discussing Lacan).
159. Refer to note 107 supra and text accompanying.
160. *See* Shoshana Felman, "On Reading Poetry: Reflections on the Limits and Possibilities of Psychoanalytical Approaches," in *The Purloined Poe: Lacan, Derrida, and Possibilities of Psychoanalytic Reading*, ed. J. Muller and W. Richardson, with notes by T. Mabbot (Baltimore: Johns Hopkins University Press, 1988), at 149 (Lacan's reading of texts "is methodologically unprecedented in the whole history of literary criticism").
161. Ragland-Sullivan, supra note 2, at 251.
162. Id. at 257.
163. *See* Felman, supra note 160, at 149.
164. Eagleton, supra note 9, at 169.
165. Lacan, *Book 1 of the Seminar of Jacques Lacan: Freud's Papers on Technique 1953–1954*, ed. J.-A. Miller and trans. J. Forrester (New York: W. W. Norton, 1988), 2.

166. *See* Danet, supra note 7, at 531 ("Silences, in context, can be as meaningful as speech").
167. *See* Slavoj Zizek, *The Sublime Object of Ideology* (London: Verso, 1989), 68.
168. Lacan, *Book 2 of The Seminar*, supra note 58 at 195.
169. Id. at 196–97.

CHAPTER 4

This chapter is a modified version of an article that appeared in CARDOZO LAW REVIEW 15 (1993): 707.
1. Pierre Schlag, "The Problem of the Subject," *Tex. L. Rev.* 69 (1991): 1627. The article appears in a symposium issue entitled "Beyond Critique: Law, Culture, and the Politics of Form," *Tex. L. Rev.* 69 (1991): 1595–2041
2. Id. at 1629.
3. Id. at 1621: "The effort here is to retrieve a whole set of critical inquiries from their presently concealed condition so that we might begin to think about them."
4. *See* id. at 1629 n. 7, citing works that explore "the various ways in which the legal and social formation of subjects contributes to the production of law and legal thought," including articles by Boyle, Coombe, Minow, Winter, and Schlag himself.
5. Id. at 1629.
6. Id. at 1629.
7. Id. at 1633–34 (footnotes omitted): "Whenever Chris[topher Langdell] addresses a matter of pedagogy in his preface [to his contracts casebook], the 'I' is all over the place. And yet, quite mysteriously, as soon as the law makes its appearance in the preface, the 'I' vanishes. Chris disappears. Dean Langdell is removed."
8. Id. at 1627–38.
9. Id. at 1639.
10. Id. at 1639–40: "Object-forms such as rules, doctrines, and principles are worshipped in the manner of a fetish precisely because the Langdellian thinker never apprehends the moment of self-objectification."
11. Id. at 1640: "The sublimation of the subject into the order of the object and the resulting fetishism is a move that is replayed endlessly in American legal thought."
12. Id. at 1641. The breakdown in Langdellian transcendental object strategies "is classic: first, the subject becomes aware that he is on the scene. Second, the subject notices that he is not just a spectator, but is actively contributing to the construction of what was supposed to be a self-sufficient transcendental order of the object. Finally, the subject comes to understand that the order of the object is his own creation." Id. (footnotes omitted).
13. Id. at 1642–43. For example, Langdell, Bork, Fiss, and Dworkin, "*at different conceptual points*, [each refuse] to accept critical moves that would refer the order of the object back to the actions of a constituting subject." Id. at 1643.
14. Id.
15. Id.

16. Id. at 1646.
17. Id. at 1647: "Indeed, in Langdellian discourse the doctrines seem to negate, convert, modify, and limit each other without the apparent assistance of any social actor, not even the author."
18. Id. at 1655: "[We] are primed to focus on whatever occupies the conventional space of objectivity and to simultaneously elide the problem of the subject.... Our intellectual conventions in legal thought repeatedly direct our attention toward that which is already represented or easily representable as an object-form."

    Schlag details various effects of a breakdown of formalist strategies, including *disintegration* of subject-form and object-form distinctions, *reconstruction* of new arrangements of the distinctions, and *collapse* of the distinctions to avoid strong specifications. *See* id. at 1656–62.
19. *See* id. at 1663–67.
20. Id. at 1685–86.
21. Id. at 1695–97.
22. Id. at 1697.
23. Id.
24. Id. at 1698.
25. Id. at 1699.
26. Id. at 1702.
27. Id. at 1709.
28. Id. at 1717.
29. Id. at 1717–18 and 1721 n. 371.
30. Id. at 1724, discussing Anthony Kronman, "Precedent and Tradition," *Yale L. J.* 99 (1990): 1029.
31. Schlag, supra note 1, at 1625–26.
32. Id. at 1730.
33. Id.
34. Id. at 1739–40.
35. Id. at 1742.
36. Id.
37. Pierre Schlag, "'Le Hors De Texte, C'est Moi'": The Politics of Form and the Domestication of Deconstruction," *Cardozo L. Rev.* 11 (1990): 1631.
38. Id. at 1631–32.
39. Id. at 1632.
40. Id. at 1633.
41. Id. at 1634.
42. Id.
43. Id. at 1638.
44. For example, in Jack Balkin's description of deconstruction, Schlag finds "an ideology which at once depicts and constitutes morally charged individual subjects as competent choosers of normatively empty intellectual techniques ... this ideology puts the individual self in charge of choosing when to deploy deconstruction, [thus insulating] the self, and the rhetoricity of the self from the subversive reach of deconstruction." Id. at 1641–42, citing J. M. Balkin, "Deconstructive Practice and Legal Theory," *Yale L.J.* 96 (1987): 743.
45. Schlag, supra note 37, at 1647–48.
46. *See* Ellie Ragland-Sullivan, *Jacques Lacan and the Philosophy of Psychoanalysis* (Chicago: University of Illinois Press, 1987), x (explaining Lacan to many

Anglophone readers "on their own terms ... is simply impossible").
47. Schlag, supra note 37, at 1651: "To 'apply' deconstruction on the model of contemporary interdisciplinary work would succeed in putting beyond reach much of what deconstruction would like to challenge and engage."
48. Id. at 1653.
49. Id. at 1656.
50. Id. at 1660.
51. Id.
52. Id. at 1667.
53. Id. *See* my discussion of Zizek's views, in chapter 7, for another version of this argument.
54. Schlag contrasts the myth of the individual self with the "rhetorical, psychological, social, and political" context; when his focus narrows, he is concerned with the self as "one of the rhetorical spaces when ideology does its work—unquestioned"; the reproduction of the "self" as autonomous and integrated is political—"a politics of form." Id. at 1670.
55. Refer to my discussion of Derrida at the outset of chapter 3.
56. *See* Schlag, supra note 37, at 1671: "The difficulty with discourse in the legal academy currently is that the self of the legal thinker is so vastly overinflated in importance—that it has failed to recognize that it has been largely replaced as a decisional site by bureaucratic forms of organization, linguistic structures, mass communication, etc. In other words, this prototypically academic self has failed to recognize that it is largely a language game run by bureaucratic, institutional, and linguistic practices."
57. Schlag, supra note 1, at 1650.
58. Id. at 1673.
59. Id. at 1698–99.
60. Id. at 1738.
61. *See* Anthony Wilden's commentary in Jacques Lacan, *Speech and Language in Psychoanalysis*, trans. Wilden (Baltimore: Johns Hopkins University Press, 1968), at 266.
62. Jacques Lacan, *The Four Fundamental Concepts Of Psycho-Analysis*, ed. J.-A. Miller and trans. A. Sheridan (New York: W. W. Norton, 1978).
63. *See* Lacan, "The Agency of the Letter in the Unconscious or Reason since Freud," in *Écrits: A Selection*, trans. A. Sheridan (New York: W. W. Norton, 1977), 148.
64. *See* Lacan, "The Function and Field of Speech and Language in Psychoanalysis," in *Écrits*, supra note 63, at 57.
65. Id. at 66–68.
66. *See* Bice Benvenuto and Roger Kennedy, *The Works of Jacques Lacan: An Introduction* (London: Free Association Books, 1986), 81.
67. Ragland-Sullivan, supra note 46, at 7.
68. Id. at 10.
69. Lacan, "The Subversion of the Subject and the Dialectic of Desire in the Freudian Unconscious," in *Écrits*, supra note 63, at 297.
70. Id. at 298.
71. John Mowitt, "Foreword: The Resistance in Theory," in Paul Smith, *Discerning the Subject* (Minneapolis: University of Minnesota Press, 1988), at xi.

72. Mowitt, supra note 71, at ix.
73. Smith, supra note 71, at xxviii.
74. Id. at xxx.
75. *See* id at xxxi: "A theory of resistance... becomes possible only when we take into account the specific history of the 'subject' and its implications into systems of knowledge, power, and ideology."
76. Id. at 3–11.
77. Id. at 18–21.
78. Id. at 21–22.
79. Id. at 32.
80. Id. at 40.
81. Id. at 51.
82. Jacques Derrida, *Writing and Difference* (Chicago: University of Chicago Press, 1978), 229, cited in Smith, supra note 71, at 46.
83. Smith, supra note 71, at 49.
84. Schlag, supra note 1, at 1740–41.
85. Smith, supra note 71, at 68.
86. Id. at 75.
87. Id. at 78.
88. Id. at 82.
89. Id. at 94–99.
90. Id. at 96.
91. Id. at 78–79.
92. *Tex. L. Rev.* 67 (1989): 1195.
93. Id. at 1205.
94. Id. at 1246.
95. Id.
96. Id. at 1246–47. Schlag is concerned that his own and any "broader" definition of cognition tends to privilege thought over being, a rationalist move toward stability.
97. Id. at 1196, 1213, and 1222.
98. Schlag, supra note 1, at 1742.
99. *See*, for example, Leonard Kaplan and Vincent Rinella, "Jurisprudence and the Appropriation of the Psychoanalytic: A Study in Ideology and Form," *Int'l J. L. & Psychiatry* 11 (1988): 215, 248.
100. Patricia Williams, *The Alchemy of Race and Rights* (Cambridge: Harvard University Press, 1991), 11. Objectifying legal authority "is an extremely common device by which not just subject positioning is obscured, but by which agency and responsibility are hopelessly befuddled." Id.
101. Id. at 46.
102. Id. at 56.
103. Id. at 62.
104. *See* id at n. 9, citing Lacan, "Aggressivity in Psychoanalysis," in *Écrits*, supra note 63, at 23–24.
105. Williams, supra note 100, at 62.
106. Schlag, supra note 1, at 1742.
107. Smith, supra note 71, at 102; *compare* Steven Winter, "Foreword: On Building Houses," *Tex. L. Rev.* 69 (1991): 1595, 1607 (foreword to the symposium in which Schlag's *The Problem of the Subject* appears): "If we are to understand the subject as socially situated and socially constructed

in any meaningful sense, we must be careful to avoid re-inscribing the distinction between the internal and the external—which is to say, between the subject and its objects."

CHAPTER 5

This chapter is a modified version of an essay that appeared in *Law & Critique* 5 (1993): 31.

1. See Paul Slavney, *Perspectives on "Hysteria"* (Baltimore: Johns Hopkins University Press, 1990), at 2: "Thus, in the *Diagnostic and Statistical Manual of Mental Disorders* 3d edition (DSM-III), what had been known... as *conversion hysteria* was renamed *conversion disorder*, and the personality type formerly designated as *hysterical* was retitled *histrionic*."
2. Regarding the controversy over the place of women in Lacanian theory, *see*, for example, *Feminine Sexuality: Jacques Lacan and the École Freudienne*, ed. J. Mitchell and J. Rose, trans. J Rose (New York: W. W. Norton, 1982) (which includes, at 61–73, Lacan's "Intervention on Transference," a reconsideration of Freud's "Dora" case); *In Dora's Case: Freud-Hysteria-Feminism*, ed. C. Bernheimer and C. Kahane (New York: Columbia University Press, 1985); Martha Evans, *Fits and Starts: A Genealogy of Hysteria in Modern France* (Ithaca: Cornell University Press, 1991). Regarding recent feminist interest in hysteria generally, *see*, for example, Beret Strong, "Foucault, Freud, and French Feminism: Theorizing Hysteria as Theorizing the Feminine," *Lit. & Psych.* 35 (1989): 10; and Jennifer Pierce, "The Relation Between Emotion Work and Hysteria: A Feminist Reinterpretation of Freud's Studies on Hysteria," *Women's Studies* 16 (1989): 225.
3. See Slavney, supra note 1, at 2–3. Significantly, despite condemnation from physicians and feminists, "the concept of 'hysteria' is alive and well in the practice of medicine. No term so vilified is yet so popular; none so near extinction appears in better health." Id. at 3.
4. See id. at 111–20.
5. Pierce, supra note 2, at 266 ("Freud and Breuer failed to see that their women patients' seemingly personal troubles were intimately linked to a larger social, cultural and historical context").
6. Denis Brion, "The Hidden Persistence of Witchcraft," *Law & Critique* 4 (1993): 227.
7. *See* Slavney, supra note 1, at 3.
8. *See* for example, Murray Levin, *Political Hysteria in America: The Democratic Capacity for Repression* (New York: Basic Books, 1971).
9. *See* Charles Bernheimer, "Introduction: Part One," in *In Dora's Case*, supra note 2, at 2–7; Evans, supra note 2, at 1–50.
10. *See* Josef Breuer and S. Freud, *Studies on Hysteria*, trans. J. Strachey (New York: Basic Books, 1953) (debt to Charcot is acknowledged; *see* id. at 17); Sigmund Freud, *Dora: An Analysis of a Case of Hysteria* (New York: Macmillan, 1963).
11. Sigmund Freud, *Group Psychology and the Analysis of the Ego*, trans. J. Strachey (New York: W. W. Norton, 1959). *See also* Jean-Martin Charcot, *Clinical Lectures on Diseases of the Nervous System*, trans. T. Savill, 3 vols. (London: New Sydenham Society, 1889), at 71, 86 (epidemic "hysteria" in factories and schools as disease-simulating behavior).
12. Id.

13. Id. at 40.
14. See Theodor W. Adorno, "Freudian Theory and the Pattern of Fascist Propaganda," in *Sigmund Freud*, ed. P. Roazen (Englewood Cliffs, N.J.: Prentice-Hall, 1987), at 82–102.
15. Id. at 84.
16. See *Dora*, supra note 10, at 39, 123.
17. Adorno, supra note 14, at 102.
18. Id.
19. *Diagnostic and Statistical Manual of Mental Disorders* (DSM-III) § 300.11 (New York: American Psychiatric Association, 1980).
20. See, for example, *Ruse v. Sedgwick County*, 708 P.2d 216 (Kan. Ct. App. 1984); *Guillory v. Travelers Ins. Co.*, 326 So. 2d 914 (La. Ct. App. 1976).
21. 473 N.W.2d 451 (N.D. 1991).
22. 130 F. Supp. 270 (M.D. Pa. 1955).
23. Id. at 274.
24. See *Darcy v. Handy*, 351 U.S. 454 (1955).
25. 100 A.2d 257 (Md. Ct. App. 1952).
26. Id. at 260.
27. Id.
28. See, for example, *Achesa v. Murakami*, 176 F.2d 953 (9th Cir. 1979).
29. See, for example, *Yates v. U.S.*, 227 F.2d 851 (9th Cir. 1955) (communism hysteria); *Aaron v. Cooper*, 257 F.2d 33 (8th Cir. 1958) (dissent recognizing hysteria over integration).
30. See, for example, *Ginsburg v. New York*, 390 U.S. 629 (1968) (dissent addressing hysteria over pornography); *Kline v. Mass. Ave. Apt. Corp.*, 439 F.2d 477 (D.C. Cir. 1970) (dissent acknowledges hysteria of apartment dwellers over inner city crime); *Stevens v. U.S.*, 440 F.2d 144 (6th Cir. 1971) (emotional hysteria leading to gun control legislation).
31. See *Littleton v. Berbling*, 468 F.2d 389 (7th Cir. 1972).
32. *Richards v. Mileski*, 662 F.2d 65 (D.C. Cir. 1981) (claim of hysterical overreaction of government to charges of homosexuality); *Child v. Spillane*, 866 F.2d 691 (4th Cir. 1988) (AIDS hysteria); *Public Citizen v. Young*, 831 F.2d 1108 (D.C. Cir. 1987) (hysteria over cancer); *Transport Workers' Union of Phila. Local 234 v. Southeastern Pa. Transp. Auto.* 863 F.2d 1110 (3rd Cir. 1988) (hysteria over drug and alcohol use viewed by the court as well founded, not exaggerated); *U.S. v. Hammer*, 916 F.2d 186 (4th Cir. 1990) (potential hysteria over product tampering); *Kucharek v. Hanaway*, 902 F.2d 513 (7th Cir. 1990) (censorship of textbooks and reading lists flavored with hysteria); *Dartmouth Review v. Dartmouth College*, 889 F.2d 13 (1st Cir. 1989) (hysteria against student publication arising from its alleged harassment of black professor).
33. Judith Koffler and Bennett Gershman, "The New Seditious Libel," *Cornell L. Rev.* 69 (1984): 816, 862–63.
34. Note, "American Dreammasters v. The Cocaine Cowboys: Caplin, Monsanto, and the New Cold War," *Tex. L. Rev.* 69 (1990): 169, 200–203.
35. See Brian Levack, *The Witch-Hunt in Early Modern Europe* (London: Longman, 1987), 137.
36. Id. at 222.
37. Id. at 160.
38. Id.

39. Id. at 160–61.
40. Id. at 161.
41. *See* Sigmund Freud, "Extracts from the Fliess Papers 1892–1899," in *I Standard Edition* (1966), supra note 12, at 242 (Letter 56).
42. Sandra Gilbert, "Introduction: A Tarantella of Theory," in Hélène Cixous and Catherine Clement, *The Newly Born Woman*, trans. B. Wing (Minneapolis: University of Minnesota Press, 1986), at xiii.
43. Cixous, "Part I: The Guilty One," in *The Newly Born Woman*, supra note 42, at 10.
44. Evans, supra note 2, at 209.
45. Cixous, supra note 43, at 5.
46. Slavoj Zizek, *The Sublime Object of Ideology* (London: Verso, 1989), 113.
47. Cixous, supra note 43, at 25.
48. Evans, supra note 2, at 239–41, citing E. Trillat, *Histoire de L'Hystérie* (Paris: Seghers, 1986), and B. Simon, *Mind and Madness in Ancient Greece: The Classical Roots of Modern Psychiatry* (Ithaca: Cornell University Press, 1978).
49. Evans, supra note 2, at 241.
50. Strong, supra note 2, at 23–24.
51. Id. at 24.
52. *See* Jacques Lacan, "Intervention on Transference," trans. J. Rose, in *In Dora's Case*, supra note 2, at 93: "What needs to be understood regarding psychoanalytic experience is that it proceeds entirely in a relationship of subject to subject—which means that it preserves a dimension irreducible to all psychology considered as the objectification of certain properties of individuals."
53. Evans, supra note 2, at 178; *see* id. at 178–99 for a summary of Lacan's "phases" of theoretical reflection on hysteria.
54. Id.
55. Freud, supra note 41, at 242.
56. Evans, supra note 2, at 209, citing D. Carrer and A. Venard, "Les Mythe et les parfait petites sorcières," *Sorcières* 22, 4–11.
57. Cixous, supra note 43, at 14.
58. Jacques Lacan, *The Seminar Of Jacques Lacan, Book II: The Ego in Freud's Theory and in the Technique of Psychoanalysis 1954–1955*, trans. S. Tomaselli (New York: W. W. Norton, 1988), at 262.
59. Evans, supra note 2, at 189; *see* Jacques Lacan, "L'envers de la psychanalyse," unpublished transcript of 1969–70 seminar, at 83 (hysteria as refusal to follow master signifier).
60. *See* Slavney, supra note 1, at 146–49 (describing psychiatric studies establishing that sociocultural forces account for many instances of clinical "hysteria").
61. Freud, supra note 11, at 61. The "ego ideal" is an agency that can come into conflict with the ego, and its functions include "self-observation, the moral conscience, the censorship of dreams, and the chief influence in repression." Id. at 42.
62. Lacan, supra note 58, at 167.
63. Freud, supra note 11, at 12.
64. Lacan, supra note 52, at 103.
65. Evans, supra note 2, at 241.

66. Id.
67. Pierce, supra note 2, at 265.
68. Id.
69. Jacques Lacan, *The Four Fundamental Concepts of Psycho-Analysis*, trans. A. Sheridan (New York: W. W. Norton, 1981).
70. See Sigmund Freud, *An Autobiographical Study*, trans. J. Strachey (New York: W. W. Norton, 1952), 63–64.
71. Pierce, supra note 2, at 267.
72. See for example, Jeffrey Masson, *The Assault on Truth: Freud's Suppression of the Seduction Theory* (New York: Farrar Strauss, 1984).
73. See Frederick Crews, "The Revenge of the Repressed: Part II," *N.Y. Rev. Books*, Dec. 1, 1994, at 52.
74. Freud, supra note 70, at 63.
75. Id. at 30.
76. See Charles Lawrence, "The Id, the Ego, and Equal Protection: Reckoning with Unconscious Racism," *Stan. L. Rev.* 39 (1987): 317 (legal recognition of racism on the basis of a finding of discriminatory intent essentially denies the reality of unconscious racism).
77. Brion's study can be usefully compared and contrasted with two books on false accusations of child abuse by Richard A. Gardner. *True and False Accusations of Child Sex Abuse* (Creskill, N.J.: Creative Therapeutics, 1992), is a comprehensive (700+ pages) study of the interview techniques used to validate child abuse allegations and of the phenomenon of suggestibility among alleged victims (both children and adults who belatedly "realize" they were abused). *Sex Abuse Hysteria: Salem Witch Trials Revisited* (Creskill, N.J.: Creative Therapeutics, 1991), catalogues numerous psychological and social factors that ground child abuse hysteria, including a relatively recent openness to discuss sexuality, our tendency to indulge children, media frenzy, the economic gains to experts and validators, projection on the part of accusers (of their own repressed fantasies), and so forth.
78. See Gardner, *True and False Accusations*, supra note 77, at 650 (legal system provides a vehicle for false accusations of child abuse).

CHAPTER 6

This chapter is a modified version of an essay that appeared in Legal Studies Forum 16 (1993): 421.
1. Charles Dickens, *Bleak House* (Garden City, N.Y.: Literary Guild, 1953), 164–65: "Mr. Chadband is attached to no particular denomination, and is considered by his persecutors to have nothing so very remarkable to say . . .; but he has his followers, and Mrs. Snagsby is of the number."
2. All of Chadband's speeches in *Bleak House* are circular and empty. I do not believe Lacan's seminars are without substance, but the criticism has been made. See Sebastiano Timpanero, *The Freudian Slip* (London: New Left Books, 1974), 58 (Lacan's "charlatry and exhibitionism" prevail over his comprehensibility; "behind the smoke-screen . . . there is nothing of substance").
3. Jacques Lacan, *Television*, ed. J. Copjec and trans. D. Hollier, R. Krauss, and A. Michelson (New York: W. W. Norton, 1990), 3: "I always speak the truth. Not the whole truth, because there's no way to say it all. Saying it all is literally impossible: words fail."

4. J. Lacan, "On a Question Preliminary to Any Possible Treatment of Psychosis," in *Écrits: A Selection*, trans. A. Sheridan, at 199.
5. *See* Leopold Pospisil, *The Ethnology of Law*, 2d ed. (London: Cummings, 1978), 2: "An ethnologist studies a given culture as a functionally and structurally related whole and does not *a priori* exclude any segment of it as non-relevant. Law to him is not an autonomous institution but rather an integral part of a culture."
6. *See* Jacques Lacan, *The Four Fundamental Concepts of Psycho-Analysis*, trans. A. Sheridan and ed. J.-A. Miller (New York: W. W. Norton, 1981), 203: "The Other is the locus in which is situated the chain of the signifier that governs whatever may be made present of the subject—it is the field of that living being in which the subject has to appear."
7. *See* Catherine Clément, *The Lives and Legends of Jacques Lacan*, trans. A. Goldhammer (New York: Columbia University Press, 1983), 132: "[The] Other is a location, a place from which the human subject can draw what it needs to express its desire.... The expression of desire is to be read literally, letter by letter—again we encounter the letter, which takes us back to the elementary component of language, the signifier.... [The] Unconscious is thus the discourse of the Other,... [but the] Other is also the law, the Father, the repository of language and culture.... [The Other] represents the phallus, the ultimate symbol ... of human Law in phallocratic societies."

    Regarding feminist criticism of Lacanian theory as phallocentric, refer to text accompanying notes 40–45 infra.
8. For a more detailed account of Lacan's three orders (symbolic, imaginary, real), *see* Ellie Ragland-Sullivan, *Jacques Lacan and the Philosophy of Psychoanalysis* (Chicago: University of Illinois Press, 1987), 130–95.
9. The epigraph is the report of the attending physician, in Daniel Paul Schreber, *Memoirs of My Nervous Illness*, trans. I. McAlpine and R. Hunter (Cambridge: Harvard University Press, 1955), at 386.
10. *See* William Richardson, "Lacan and the Problems of Psychosis," in D. Allison, P. De Oleivera, M. Roberts, and A. Weiss, *Psychosis and Sexual Identity: Towards a Post-Analytic View of the Schreber Case* (Albany: SUNY Press, 1988), at 24.
11. *See* "Psycho-Analytic Notes on an Autobiographical Account of a Case of Paranoia (*Dementia Paranoides*)" (1911), in vol. 12 of *Standard Edition of the Complete Psychological Works of Sigmund Freud*, trans. J. Strachey (New York: W. W. Norton, 1958), at 9. *See also* Gerard Pommier, "Psychosis and the Signifier," *PsychCritique* 2 (1987): 35: "It first appears that there should be no ... reason to psychosis, as by definition it is unreasonable. However, ... when we take a closer look at its phenomena ... they do not happen in disorder. In fact, they are arranged with great precision."
12. *See* Lacan, supra note 4, at 183, 187.
13. Id. at 199.
14. Id. (refer to text accompanying note 4 supra).
15. *See* Clément, supra note 7, at 171: "Foreclosure is a legal term implying the forfeiture (*déchéance*) of a right not exercised within the prescribed limits.... The father is there in flesh and blood. But paternal authority can nevertheless be lost in various ways, so that the Father forfeits his symbolic right."

16. Lacan, supra note 4, at 217.
17. Id. at 203. *See* Willy Apollan, "Theory and Practice in the Psychoanalytic Treatment of Psychosis," in *Lacan and the Subject of Language*, ed. E. Ragland-Sullivan and M. Bracher (New York: Routledge, 1991), at 121: "[Psychosis] always presupposes the presence or the undiscernible action of voices.... Psychosis is characterized by the unchaining and disenthralling of the voices, which function as detached from language."

    See also Michael Walsh, "Reading the Real in the Seminar on the Psychoses," in *Criticism and Lacan: Essays and Dialogue on Language, Structure, and the Unconscious*, ed. P. Hogan and L. Pandit (Athens: University of Georgia Press, 1990), at 71: "[The] whole text of *Les Psychoses* attests to a notion of fundamental signifiers which remain unassimilated [,] which the subject cannot accommodate.... In effect, there can be no question of a diagnosis of psychosis in the absence of a disturbance in the subject's relationship with language. Thus the ... initial attention to the characteristically psychotic phenomenon of verbal hallucination."

    The fundamental signifiers, excluded or refused in the symbolic, return or reappear in the real in the form of a psychotic hallucination, a "return from the exterior" of that which was rejected. Id. at 72–74, quoting and translating Jacques Lacan, *Le Séminaire*, vol. 3, *Les Psychoses* (1981), at 21, 22, 57.
18. Lacan, supra note 4, at 206.
19. Jeffrey Mehlman, "Trimethylamin: Notes on Freud's Specimen Dream," in *Untying the Text: A Post-Structuralist Anthology*, ed. R. Young (New York: Routledge, 1981), at 179.
20. Lacan, supra note 4, at 200; *see also* Clément, supra note 7, at 168–69: "For Lacan the Real is a concept that cannot exist without the barrier of the Symbolic, which.... forms the basis of the subject's perception of the world [—] for the Real, when it really does rear its head, is terrifying. This can happen, for example, when the subject ... hallucinates the Real where it does not exist and thinks that it is "seeing."
21. Id. at 219.
22. Apollon, supra note 17, at 119. *See also* Lacan, supra note 4, at 216: "That [a social] psychosis [like half the world gathering under the symbol of Father Christmas] may prove to be compatible with what is called good order is not in question, but neither does it authorize the psychiatrist, even if he is a psychoanalyst, to trust his own compatibility with that order to the extent of believing that he is in possession of an adequate idea of the *reality* to which his patient appears to be unequal."
23. *See* Ragland-Sullivan, supra note 8, at 269, 285.
24. *See* Apollon, supra note 17, at 119.
25. Ragland-Sullivan, supra note 8, at 249, 270–71.
26. Apollon, supra note 17, at 120.
27. In the Lacanian notion of cure, "there will always be a fundamental division within the subject"—there is no such thing as a total person or total self. *See* David Fisher, "Introduction," in *Lacan and Theological Discourse*, ed. E. Wyschograd, D. Crownfield, and C. Rasche (Albany: SUNY Press, 1989), at 8.
28. Jacques Lacan. "Introduction to the Names-of-the-Father Seminar," in *Television*, supra note 3, at 81. *See* Samuel Weber, *Return to Freud: Jacques*

Lacan's Dislocation of Psychoanalysis, trans. M. Levine (Cambridge: Cambridge University Press, 1991), 137 n. 26: "The 'father' is guardian of the law.... But if the father can exercise this function, it is less as a person than through his name.... [In] the place of a *dead* father... this name assumes its structuring power.... It is therefore of more than anecdotal interest that... Lacan interrupted the seminar... as a response to the exclusion of his name from the list of training analysts." Lacan's seminars, by the way, continued under other auspices.

29. Id. at 84–90.
30. Id. at 91.
31. Edith Wyschogrod, "Re-marks," in *Lacan and Theological Discourse*, supra note 27, at ix.
32. Lacan, "Introduction," supra note 28, at 92.
33. *See* David Crownfield, "Summary," in *Lacan and Theological Discourse*, supra note 27, at 38 (response to Charles Winquist, "Lacan and Theological Discourse," in id. at 26–33). As discussed in chapter 3 of this book, metaphor and metonymy here correspond to Freud's condensation and displacement, which are re-articulated to constitute language itself.
34. Lacan, supra note 6, at 34.
35. Charles Scott, "The Pathology of the Father's Rule: Lacan and the Symbolic Order," in *Lacan and Theological Discourse*, supra note 27, at 80.
36. John Forrester, *The Seductions of Psychoanalysis: Freud, Lacan and Derrida* (Cambridge: Cambridge University Press, 1990), 130.
37. *See* Jacques Lacan, "Of structure as an inmixing of an Otherness prerequisite to any subject whatever," in *The Languages of Criticism and the Sciences of Man*, ed. R. Macksey and E. Donato (Baltimore: Johns Hopkins University Press, 1972), at 188.
38. Lacan, supra note 4, at 217.
39. Malcolm Bowie, *Lacan* (Cambridge: Harvard University Press, 1991), 109–10; refer to note 20 supra (Clément's commentary).
40. *See*, for example, Ragland-Sullivan, supra note 8, at 267–308.
41. *See* id. at 271. *See also* Slavoj Zizek, "'Woman is one of the names-of-the-father': or, How Not to Misread Lacan's Formulas of Sexuation," *Lacanian Ink* 10 (1995): 24.
42. Id. at 298.
43. *See* for example, Luce Irigaray, *The Sex Which Is Not One*, trans. C. Porter (Ithaca: Cornell University Press, 1985), 86–105.
44. Id. at 86. *See also* Drucilla Cornell, "Re-thinking the Beyond of Real," *Cardozo L. Rev.* 16 (1995): 729, for a critical perspective on Lacan's phallic orientation; *see generally* Elizabeth Grosz, *Jacques Lacan: A Feminist Introduction* (New York: Routledge, 1990), 147–87, for a detailed account of feminist responses to Lacanian theory.

Another version of this critique is found in Adrian Dannatt's "La Can-Can Française," *Lacanian Ink* 10 (1995): 97, who notes that "Psychoanalysis is not outside geography or beyond natural characteristics," and that we perhaps "do not sufficiently take into consideration the cultural context of Lacan's ideas." Id. at 97. "Lacan moved in a Mediterranean, a Latin world, where external differences between men and women were at a maximum; and his construction of femininity cannot but be related to the assumptions of such societies." Id. at 99.

45. *See* Ragland-Sullivan, supra note 8, 277, 307.
46. *See* Pommier, supra note 11, at 42–44; *See also* Jacques Lacan, *The Seminar of Jacques Lacan, Book 3: The Psychoses 1955–1956*, ed. J.-A. Miller and trans. R. Grigg (New York: W. W. Norton, 1993), at 319: "[It] is not a question of a mother-father-child triangle, but a triangle (father)-phallus-mother-child. Where is the father in this? He is the ring that holds all this together."
47. Paul Smith, *Discerning the Subject* (Minneapolis: University of Minnesota Press, 1988), 94–97.
48. Id. at 99.
49. Id.; *see also* id. at 88.
50. *See Lucas v. South Carolina Coastal Council*, 112 S.Ct. 2886 (1992).
51. Id. at 2895–2900. On remand, the background principles of property law and nuisance prevention did not justify the prohibition against construction on Lucas's lots. Note that this holding allows both sides in the takings controversy to claim a victory. Those in favor or highly restrictive environmental regulation now say that only a "total" loss of use constitutes a compensable taking, while property rights advocates opine (a) that loss of economically beneficial uses can occur even when some uses remain, and (b) that the holding is narrow due to the facts in Lucas (i.e., general takings jurisprudence does not require a total loss like Lucas suffered).
52. *See* "Pay Me, or Get Off My Land," *Newsweek*, March 9, 1992, at 70.
53. *See Pennsylvania Coal v. Mahon*, 260 U.S. 393, 415 (1922) ("while property may be regulated to a certain extent, if regulation goes too far it will be recognized as a taking").
54. 404 S.E.2d 899 (S.C. 1991), rev'd, 112 S.Ct. 2886 (1992).
55. 404 S.E.2d at 905 (Harwell, J., dissenting).
56. *See* Richard Epstein, "Ruminations on Lucas," *Loy. L.A. L. Rev.* 25 (1992): 1226.
57. Id.: "To see how extreme [Lucas's] position is, [suppose] that the only use for a parcel of land is as a dump site for waste materials, which ... poison underground waters. ... [The] State would be required to pay full value to the owner of the dump site in order to shut it down."
58. *See* "Pay Me" supra note 52.
59. Briefly, the Court adopted a rule that is limited to total loss cases. Property rights advocates remain concerned about partial restrictions, and critics of the "total loss" rule view it as illusory—the exception for background principles of nuisance law threatens to swallow the new "rule." Arguably, "this imaginary world in which clear and specific rules are supposedly settled prior to the onset of government regulation is merely a small-scale version of the property-rights pipe dream that the Court has consistently and correctly rejected over the last 70 years." Jeremy Paul, "Scalia's Pursuit of Property's Holy Grail Has Its Price," *Conn. L. Tribune*, July 20, 1992.

CHAPTER 7

Page references to *Bleak House* (Garden City, N.Y.: Literary Guild, 1953) appear in parentheses in the text of this chapter.
1. *See* Edgar Johnson, "The Anatomy of Society" (1952), in *Charles Dickens,*

"*Bleak House*": *A Selection of Critical Essays.* ed. A. E. Dyson (Nashville: Aurora, 1969), at 145: "Nor are these sharp and bitter strictures unjustified by the actualities. The Day case, nowhere near settled at the time Dickens wrote, dated from 1834, had always involved seventeen lawyers and sometimes thirty or forty, and had already incurred costs of [70,000 pounds].... Jarndyce and Jarndyce was suggested by the notorious Jennings case, involving the disputed property of an old miser of Acton who had died intestate in 1798, leaving [1,500,000 pounds]. When one of the claimants died *in 1915* the case was still unsettled and the costs amounted to [250,000 pounds]."

See also "Some Account of the Proceedings in a Common Chancery Suit, and the Probable Time of its Duration, c 1828," in *Sources of English Legal and Constitutional History,* ed. M. Evans and R. Jack (Sydney: Butterworths, 1984), 383–85 (a common suit takes over five years due to procedural delays; during those delays, some parties become insolvent or die, new cross-actions arise, the pleadings increase in bulk, and a large part of any estate is swallowed up in fees).

2. See Neil Gow, "No Chance in Chancery," *J. L. Society of Scotland,* Dec. 1990, at 518–19: "The real *Jennens* case became the fictitious *Jarndyce v. Jarndyce.*... A more modern case in the *Jarndyce* mould is *Diplock's* case in 1945 [lasting nine years].... In re *Theobald Mathew's Estate* [another such case,] is still running after six years.... [Mr. Mathew's eldest brother] has spent a total of six months in court and chambers in 249 appeals as applicant, respondent, plaintiff, defendant and appellant in proceedings over his brother's estate. As a litigant in person he claims... that he has appeared variously before thirty-three High Court judges, fourteen registrars, twenty-six masters, four stipendiary magistrates and four JPs.... [S]ome [286,000 pounds] has already been incurred in legal costs.

3. See Robert Barnard, *Imagery and Theme in the Novels of Dickens* (New York: Humanities Press, 1978), 74–75: "*Bleak House* is not so much a warning to society to reform itself as a picture of a society long past the stage at which reform is still possible.... [S]uggestions of rot and approaching collapse... permeate the novel.... Mines, or trails of gunpowder, are under Chancery.... The explosion, soon to come, will indeed be a 'good one,' destroying not partially but totally.... Nevertheless, it is certainly true that, in those parts of the novel that were intended to be prophetic, the prophecies have been proved false."

4. See for example, Raymond William, *The English Novel from Dickens to Lawrence* (London: Hogarth, 1984), 32–33: "[Dickens] is uniquely capable of expressing the experience of living in cities.... [His characters act out] the real and inevitable relationships and connections, the necessary recognitions and avowals of any human society."

See also Julia Prewitt Brown, *A Reader's Guide to the Nineteenth-Century English Novel* (New York: Macmillan, 1985), xix ("However engaging [Dickens'] novels are as independent verbal structures... their relation to real life cannot be dismissed so easily").

5. See Anita L. Allen, "The Jurisprudence of Jane Eyre," *Harv. Women's L. J.* 15, 173, 178–82 (describing the law and literature movement, including efforts to explicate law in, as, and through literature).

6. See Jacques Lacan, "Seminar on 'The Purloined Letter'" trans. J. Mehlman,

Yale Fr. Stud. 48 (1972), 39–72 discussed in chapter 3 of this book.
7. *See* Slavoj Zizek, *The Sublime Object of Ideology* (London: Verso, 1989).
8. This chapter includes, for purposes of clarifying Zizek's notion of ideology, character analyses.

> Character analysis, however, has a bad reputation.... [By treating] characters like people,... analysts... are perhaps enriching psychoanalysis but only at the price of misreading literature.
> [Some critics treat] a literary text... all too much like the raw materials of an actual analysis—... when they ignore the literal story or manifest argument in a text and try instead to see into it or through it and to relate its structure and conflicts to a drama within some human mind.

Meredith Anne Skura, *The Literary Uses of the Psychoanalytic Process* (New Haven: Yale University Press, 1981), 29, 32. My intention, like Joyce Wexler's in her recent reading of Conrad, is not to "use psychoanalytic theory to illuminate [a literary text, but to use] literature to clarify theory." *See* Joyce Wexler, "Conrad's Dream of a Common Language: Lacan and 'The Secret Sharer,'" *Psychoanalytic Rev.* 78 (1991): 599: "Lacan's use of fiction to articulate his theories offers a precedent for examining the connections between theory and text in either direction.... [While] it would be absurd to argue that Lacan is the key to understanding [Conrad's short story,] I would claim instead that the story helps us understand Lacan's theory of the subject's entry into the Symbolic order."

9. *See* Jay Clayten, "Dickens and the Genealogy of Postmodernisn," *Nineteenth-Century Literature* 46 (1991): 181: "[Postmodernism] has no single, stable meaning. It refers to so many different things... that the multiplicity of references has itself been theorized as a major 'lesson' of postmodernism: 'that terms are by no means guaranteed their meanings, and that these meanings can be appropriated and redefined for different purposes, different contexts, and, more important, different causes.'" Id. at 184, quoting Andrew Ross, "Introduction," in *Universal Abandon? The Politics of Postmodernism*, ed. A. Ross (Minneapolis: University of Minnesota Press, 1988), xi.
10. My "dear Mother, I'll be as tractable and obedient as you can wish.... So now I am ready even for the lawyers." *Bleak House*, at 516.
11. "Viewed by this light it becomes a coherent scheme and not the monstrous maze the laity are apt to think it." Id. at 371.
12. *See* id. at 375, 376.

> "When will he awake from his delusion!"...
> "The more he suffers, the more averse he will be to me—having made me the principal representative of his suffering."...
> "So unreasonably!"
> "Ah... what shall we find reasonable in Jarndyce and Jarndyce! Unreason and injustice at the top... at the heart and at the bottom."

Id. at 557.
13. Joseph Gold, *Charles Dickens: Radical Moralist* (Minneapolis: University of Minnesota Press, 1972), 1, citing (at n. 2) medical and psychiatric authorities on Dickens.
14. Id. at 188.
15. Gordon Hirsch, "The Mysteries in Bleak House: A Psychoanalytic Study,"

in *Dickens Studies Annual* 4, ed. R. Partlow (Carbondale: Southern Illinois University Press, 1975), at 132–33. Richard, for example, is indecisive about his future occupation, which frequently stems from inhibition of aggressiveness, which is a defense against rage, which is occasioned by frustration of infantile sexual desires. Id. at 144, citing Otto Fenichel, *The Psychoanalytic Theory of Neurosis* (1945), 178–83.
16. Id. at 143–46.
17. New York: St. Martin's Press.
18. Id. at 2, 89.
19. Id. at 89; Morris acknowledges that Lacan's notions of desire and lack provide "a point of fracture within the total determinism Althusser seems at times to imply." Id. at 5.
20. Audrey Jaffe, *Vanishing Points: Dickens, Narrative, and the Subject of Omniscience* (Berkeley: University of Calif. Press, 1991), 137.
21. Id.
22. Id.
23. Id. at 19.
24. *See* Louis Althusser, *Lenin and Philosophy and Other Essays* (New York: Monthly Review Press, 1971).
25. *See* Ellie Ragland-Sullivan, *Jacques Lacan and the Philosophy of Psychoanalysis* (Chicago: University of Illinois Press, 1987), 272 (In "Althusser's famous misreading of Lacan, ... the conscious subject is both master of Desire and of language!"); Paul Smith, *Discerning the Subject* (Minneapolis: University of Minnesota Press, 1988), 14–23:

> It is easy to see what is attractive to Althusser in Lacan's ... symbolic order [which] seems to be offered as an overarching, even inescapable monolith having everything in common with the discursive formations which work ideologically....
>
> Such a view, however, misappropriates Lacan's concept of the symbolic which ... does not take on the characteristics of the historical real as Althusser wants it to.

Id. at 20.
26. Zizek, supra note 7, at 34.
27. Id. Recall Schlag's critique, discussed in chapter 4, of theorists who acknowledge our social constructedness and then forget that acknowledgment in their theorizing.
28. Id. at 13.
29. Id. at 14–15.
30. Id. at 47, 33, 48.
31. Refer to text accompanying note 28 supra.
32. Id. at 32. One of Zizek's major theses, not discussed in this book but implied in the above passage, is that traditional critiques of ideology presume that the "spell" of ideology is broken upon disclosure or enlightenment; such critiques are ineffective, however, in light of today's cynical subjects who are quite willing to acknowledge the falsity or illusivity of ideology even as they fail to renounce it—even while they act as if it is not an illusion. *See* id. at 28–33. Thus when Zizek suggests that ideology depends upon non-knowledge of "*its essence*," id. at 21, he is not saying that the cynical subject is outside the social effect of ideology, because just as the traditional subject of ideology does not know about

his illusion, the cynical subject does not know *what he is doing*. Thus an ideological distortion is "already at work in the social reality itself, at the level of what individuals are *doing*, and not only what they *think* or *know* they are doing. When [for example] individuals use money, they know very well that there is nothing magical about it—that money, in its materiality, is simply an expression of social relations.... The problem is that in their social activity itself, in what they are *doing*, they are *acting* as if money ... is the immediate embodiment of wealth as such." Id. at 31.
33. Id. at 44 (fantasy in Lacan as "the support that gives consistency to what we call 'reality'").
34. Id. at 48.
35. Id.
36. Id. at 49.
37. Id. at 126.
38. Id.
39. Id.
40. Id.
41. Less complicated reasons for Richard's seduction by Chancery can be offered: he is rebelling against his guardian (father-figure) and makes the conflict a legal one (Richard asserts that he is not accountable "to Mr. Jarndyce, or Mr. Anybody"); he is careless, impulsive and lacks commitment; and his fantasy is to avoid work and recuperate his class status, the pursuit of which leads to increasing desperation as he loses power and control over his life—this latter explanation is consistent with the analysis, above, of Richard's "object" of desire in Chancery. *See generally* Barbara Bottfried, "Fathers and Suitors: Narratives of Desire in Bleak House," *Dickens Studies Annual* 17, ed. M. Timko, F. Koplan, and E. Guiliano (New York: AMS Press, 1990), 169–203.
42. Refer to note 41 supra.

CHAPTER 8

The first part of this chapter is a modified version of a symposium article published in *Cardozo Law Review* 16 (1995): 793; the remainder of the chapter is a modified version of an article published in *The Psychoanalytic Review* 82 (1995): 683.
1. *See*, for example, Louis B. Schwartz, "With Gun and Camera Through Darkest CLS-Land," *Stan. L. Rev.* 36 (1984): 413, 446, 453 (CLS'ers unjustifiably assume that their own souls survive "uncorrupted").
2. *See*, for example, James Boyle, "The Politics of Reason: Critical Legal Theory and Local Social Thought," *U. PA. L. Rev.* 133 (1985): 685, 740, 749, 769–78.
3. *See* Janet Malcolm, *Psychoanalysis: The Impossible Profession* (New York: Vintage Books, 1982), 27–28: "[Freud] never changed his profoundly amoral view of psychoanalytic therapy [,but an] atmosphere of the sermonette pervades the writings of today's *nouvelle vague* neo-Freudians, Kernberg and Kohut. Kernberg's 'clinical descriptions' of narcissistic patients are like passages from a nineteenth-century novel cataloguing the ethical deficiencies of its villains and villainesses. Kohut adopts a more pastoral tone toward *his* 'shallow,' 'grandiose,' 'self-centered,' 'envious,' 'ex-

ploitative,' 'empty' patients, but his intention seems no less reproving and improving."
4. Id. at 3 ("Aaron Green [as I shall call him] is a forty-six-year-old psychoanalyst who practices in Manhattan in the East Nineties").
5. Id. at 73, 76.
6. See id. at 4.
7. Refer to epigram of this chapter; see also John Rajchman, *Truth and Eros: Foucault, Lacan, and the Question of Ethics* (New York: Routledge, 1991), 43: "In Lacan's eyes, analysis would be a form of love which never supposes that it knows what is good for someone else."
8. Jacques Lacan, *The Seminar of Jacques Lacan, Book 7: The Ethics of Psychoanalysis*, ed. J.-A. Miller and trans. D. Porter (New York: W. W. Norton, 1992).
9. Id. at 1: "Given all that is implied by the phrase, the ethics of psychoanalysis will allow me, far more than anything else, to test the categories that I believe enable me to give you through my teaching the most suitable instruments for understanding what is new both in Freud's work and in the experience of psychoanalysis that derives from it."
10. Id. at front-inside jacket ("Lacan clarifies many of his key concepts").
11. See for example, Rajchman, supra note 7; Jonathan Scott Lee, *Jacques Lacan* (Amherst: University of Massachusetts Press, 1990), 161-70; Marcelle Marini, *Jacques Lacan: The French Context*, trans. A. Tomiche (New Brunswick, N.J.: Rutgers, 1992), 171-74.
12. Lacan's primary "texts" are the transcripts from his seminars from 1953-1980; for a summary of the seminars and earlier works, see Marini, supra note 11, at 139-249.
13. Lacan, supra note 8, at 251-52.
14. See Michael Walsh, "Reading the Real in the Seminar on the Psychoses," in *Criticism and Lacan: Essays and Dialogue on Language, Structure, and the Unconscious*, ed. P. Hogan and L. Pandit (Athens: University of Georgia Press, 1990), at 68-69: "[Lacan's] value lies less in his availability to appropriation as an orthodoxy and more in the openness of the question he raises: if he valued such openness in the texts of Freud, then we should [look] beyond the dictae and formulae for what remains radical and provocative."
15. See generally David S. Caudill, "Freud and Critical Legal Studies: Contours of a Radical Socio-Legal Psychoanalysis," *Ind. L.J.* 66 (1991): 651, 674-76 (citing Gabel, Trubek, Kelman, and Boyle).
16. See id. at 667-69 for a general discussion of the efforts in Frankfurt School Critical Theory to appropriate Freud. Lacan's return to Freud, by contrast, takes place within the tradition of French structuralism, wherein the influence of Marx is less direct. See id. at 669-74. Significantly, however, American critical legal studies is an heir to both Critical Theory and structuralism. See generally David Kennedy, "Critical Theory, Structuralism and Contemporary Legal Scholarship," *New Eng. L. Rev.* 21 (1985-86): 209.
17. See generally Ellie Ragland-Sullivan, *Jacques Lacan and the Philosophy of Psychoanalysis* (Chicago: University of Illinois Press, 1987) (summary of Lacan's theory of the human subject), 1-67: "Lacan's subject of the unconscious..., as a mirror of its own structuration,... interacts with its

environment to change its own reflection. It then resurfaces through the speaking subject and in relationship dynamics. The kaleidoscopic shifts in social conceptions of the 'self' as revealed in history will bear out Lacan's claim that the subject is a network of identificatory and linguistic relations formed by the effects of the external world as they correspond to survival needs and demands for recognition." Id. at 7; *see also* id. at 187 (Lacan "maintained that mind is not a unity; personal reality is built up by structures, effects, and the fragments of perceived fragmentations").

18. *See,* for example, William Kerrigan, "Terminating Lacan," *S. Atlantic Q.* 88 (1989): 993, 1007: "As a postmodernist..., I have been attacking the popular assumption that someone with postmodern sympathies who also wants to do psychoanalytic literary criticism should as a matter of course, on the grounds of common sense, work in the name of Lacan or the movement he inspired. Most of that work is on another road altogether. It leads straight back to the bogs and mires of philosophy. It is logophallocentric, nostalgic countertransference to rationalism, a marked regression from Freud's prescient distaste for philosophy."

19. *See* Mikkel Borch-Jacobsen, "The Freudian Subject, from Politics to Ethics," in *Who Comes after the Subject?*, eds. E. Cadava, P. Connor, and J.-L. Nancy (New York: Routledge, 1991), at 63–66. "Freud himself had enormous trouble in dealing with this problem. For Freud also most frequently interpreted this narcicissm, this desire-to-be-oneself that so radically disrupts any notion of the 'self,' as a desire of oneself *by oneself*—in short, as a subject's auto-affirmation, its auto-position, as its circular auto-conception.... [Lacan,] by retaining, if not the ego, at least its *image*, [also] has evidently allowed himself to be won over, in an apparent reversal, by the auto-representative structure of narcissistic desire." Id. at 67–68.

20. *See* Lacan, supra note 8, at 8–10 (analytic ideals); 115–17 (Kleinian technique); 291–325 (two lectures under the heading "The Tragic Dimension of Psychoanalytic Experience").

21. *See* id. at 22–23, 221, 257–60 (Plato and Aristotle on "the good"); 12, 228–29 (Bentham's theory of fictions); 11, 235 passim (Hegel's master-slave analysis *and* his view of *Antigone*); 249 passim (Kant on the "beautiful"); 78–80, 219 passim (Sade's ethics).

22. *See* id. at 26–34 (pleasure principle and reality principle); 66–70 (super-ego and prohibition of incest); 87–90 (sublimation); 91–95 (the drives—*Triebe*); 207–17 (the death drive); 304–8 (Oedipus complex).

23. *See* id. at 135 (anamorphosis); 139–40 (cave drawings); 141 (Cézanne).

24. *See* id. at 243–87.

25. *See* id. at 237–40.

26. *See* id. at 129–31.

27. *See* Rajchman, supra note 7, at 15; *see also* Marini, supra note 11, at 171 ("until his death, [Lacan] always wanted to write the message of the seminar himself; however, the quasi-legacy remained unfinished").

28. *See,* for example, Lacan, supra note 8, at 70: "The step taken by Freud at the level of the pleasure principle is to show us that there is no Sovereign Good—that the Sovereign Good, which is *das Ding*, which is the mother is also the object of incest, is a forbidden good, and that

Notes to Pages 131–33

there is no other good. Such is the foundation of the moral law as turned on its head by Freud." *See also* id. at 95 ("Freud is telling us the same thing as Saint Paul, namely, that what governs us on the path of our pleasure is no Sovereign Good").

29. *See* id. at 76: "[Ethics] begins at the moment when the subject poses the question of that good he had unconsciously sought in the social structures. And it is at that moment, too, that he is led to discover the deep relationship as a result of which that which presents itself as a law is closely tied to the very structure of desire."

30. *See* id. at 218, 230, 232.

31. *See*, for example, id. at 208–9 (regarding the bourgeois State, founded on need and reason, and the goal of non-alienated human emancipation in Marx): "Freud shows us—and it is in this sense that he doesn't go beyond Marx—that, however far the articulation of the problem has been taken by the tradition of classical philosophy, the two terms of reason and of need are insufficient to permit an understanding of the domain involved when it is a question of human self-realization. It is in the structure itself that we come up against a certain difficulty, which is nothing less than the function of desire."

32. Refer to note 29 supra; *see* id. at 83–84 ("dialectical relationship between desire and the Law causes our desire to flare up only in relation to the Law"); *see also* id. at 260: "It isn't for nothing that crime is one boundary of our exploration of desire or that it is on the basis of a crime that Freud attempts to reconstruct the genealogy of the law." Regarding the law of desire beyond morality, *see* id. at 270–83 (Antigone's appeal to an-Other "good," "beyond νόμιμα, the laws").

33. *See* id. at 3–4. ("We do not find ourselves in the presence of a man less weighed down with laws and duties than before the great critical experience of so-called libertine thought.")

34. *See* id. at 28.

35. *See* id. at 10; *see also* id. at 219: "One might [even] be paradoxical or trenchant and designate our desire [as analysts] as a non-desire to cure. Such a phrase is meaningful only insofar as it constitutes a warning against the common approaches to the good that offer themselves with a seeming naturalness, against the benevolent fraud of wanting-to-do-one's-best-for-the-subject."

36. *See* id. at 237: "He who comes to seek you out, does so in order to feel good, to be in agreement with himself, to identify with or be in conformity with some norm. Now you all know what we nevertheless find in the margin [—] the subject reveals himself to the never entirely resolved mystery of the nature of desire." *See also* id. at 99 (on sublimations).

37. *See* id. at 302–4.

38. *See* id. at 182–83.

39. *See* id. at 183 (in leftist weeklies, "what is affirmed concerning the horrors of Mammon on the first page leads, on the last, to purrs of tenderness for this same Mammon").

40. *See* id. at 20 ("moral law . . . is structured by the symbolic").

41. *See* id. at 224 (In the "signifying chain . . . our subject has a place in history that is quite solid and almost locatable"); 236 ("human desire is situated in the relationship of man to the signifier"); 321–22 (desire located

"not simply [in] the modulation of the signifying chain, but [in] that which flows beneath it as well [—] what we are as well as what we are not, our being and our non-being").
42. *See* id. at 313 (regarding action and desire—"the former's fundamental failure to catch up with the latter"); *see also* id. at 72: "Everything that qualifies representations in the order of the good is caught up in refractions, in the atomized system that the structure of the unconscious facilitations impose, in the complex mechanisms of a signifying system of elements. It is only in that way that the subject relates to that which presents itself on the horizon as his good. His good is already pointed out to him as the significant result of a signifying composition that is called up at the unconscious level ... where he has no mastery over the system of directions and investments that regulate his behavior in depth."
43. *See* id. at 230. "Traditional morality concerned itself with what one was supposed to do 'insofar as it is possible,' as we say, and as we are forced to say. What needs to be unmasked here is the point on which that morality turns. And that is nothing less than the impossibility in which we recognize the topology of our desire." Id. at 315.
44. *See* id. at 58–68.
45. *See* id. at 90–99.
46. *See* id. at 107–13.
47. *See* id. at 130–31.
48. *See* id. at 139–240 (Lectures XI–XVIII).
49. *See* Jorge De Gregorio, "The Unconscious and the Law, the Law in the Unconscious," *Cardoza L. Rev.* 16 (1995): 1023, 1038–41 (the legal/ethical models in *Oedipus* and *Antigone*).
50. *See* Lacan, supra note 8, at 243–87. "The text of *Antigone* ... will enable us to point to a fundamental moment, to reach an essential reference point in our investigation of what it is man wants and what he defends himself against. We will see what an absolute choice means, a choice that is motivated by no good." *See* id. at 240.
51. *See* id. at 243–48. "In effect, *Antigone* reveals to us the line of sight that defines desire." *See* id. at 247.
52. *See* id. at 258–59, 263.
53. *See* id. at 264–69.
54. *See* id. at 277–80.
55. *See* id. at 293, 300.
56. *See* id. at 303.
57. Ernest Wallwork, *Psychoanalysis and Ethics* (New Haven: Yale University Press, 1991).
58. *See* id. at x, 1, 230, 288–89.
59. *See* id. at 311–14.
60. *See* id. at 314–15, 319.
61. Mark Bracher, *Lacan, Discourse, and Social Change: A Psychoanalytic Cultural Criticism* (Ithaca: Cornell University Press, 1993).
62. *See* id. at 74.
63. *See* id. at 74–75.
64. *See* id. at 75–76.
65. *See* id. at 76–78.
66. *See* id. at 83–102.

67. See id. at 103–18 (analysis of antiabortion discourse).
68. See id. at 119–37 (analyses of Ronald Reagan's and of Jesse Jackson's speeches).
69. See id. at 138–67.
70. See id. at 168–89 (focusing on Keats's "To Autumn").
71. Id. at 75.
72. Id.
73. Id.
74. Id. at 77.
75. Id. at 79. "Like the discourse of the Analyst in individual psychoanalytic treatment, such a procedure would promote change without offering advice.... Any change that might occur would result from the use that the analysands made of the insights attained concerning their own conflicting desires." Id. at 78.
76. Refer to text accompanying note 2.
77. "Religion and Television," in *Lacan and Theological Discourse*, ed. E. Wyschogrod, D. Crownfield, and C. A. Rasche (Albany: SUNY Press, 1989), at 148.
78. Id. at 136.
79. Id. at 139.
80. See E. K. Coughlin, "Social Scientists Again Turn Attention to Religion's Place in the World," *Chron. Higher Educ.*, Apr. 1, 1992, at A6; J. L. Guth, "Secular Scholars and the Religious Right," *Chron. Higher Educ.*, Apr. 7, 1993, at B3; S. Hart, *What Does The Lord Require?: How American Christians Think About Economic Justice* (New York: Oxford University Press, 1992).
81. James Skillen, *Scattered Voices: Christians at Odds in the Public Square* (Grand Rapids: Zondervan, 1990), 201.
82. Kent Greenawalt, *Religious Convictions and Political Choice* (New York: Oxford University Press, 1988), 166–67.
83. David Tracy, "Mystics, Prophets, Rhetorics: Religion and Psychoanalysis," in *The Trials of Pscyhoanalysis*, ed. F. Meltzer (Chicago: University of Chicago Press, 1988), at 259.
84. K. Gergen, "Exploring the Postmodern: Perils or Potentials?" *Am. Psychologist* 49 (1994): 412–15.
85. For a recent summary of the Frankfurt School's appropriation of Freud, see Eli Zaretsky, "Psychoanalysis and Critical Theory," *Constellations: An Int'l Journal of Critical and Democratic Theory* 2 (1995): 280–86 (part of a review symposium of Rolf Wiggershaus's *The Frankfurt School: Its History, Theories, and Political Significance* (Cambridge: MIT Press, 1994)).
86. See generally Caudill, "Freud and Critical Legal Studies," supra note 15.
87. Tim Dean, "The Psychoanalysis of AIDS," *October* 63 (1993): 83–116.
88. Lawrence Solum, "Constructing an Ideal of Public Reason," *San Diego L. Rev.* 30 (1993): 729–62.
89. Steven K. White, *Political Theory and Postmodernism* (Cambridge: Cambridge University Press, 1991), 128.
90. Michael Sandel, *Liberalism and the Limits of Justice* (Cambridge: Cambridge University Press, 1982).
91. C. Kukathos and P. Pettit Rawls: *"A Theory of Justice" and Its Critics* (Stanford: Stanford University Press, 1990), 100.

92. Sandel, supra note 90, at 172–73.
93. Kukathos and Pettit, supra note 91, at 105.
94. Id. at 106.
95. Id. at 108.
96. Id. at 109.
97. Id.
98. C. Fred Alford, *Melanie Klein and Critical Social Theory* (New Haven: Yale University Press, 1989), 14–15.
99. Id. at 15.
100. Id. at 179–83.
101. T. Hoy. "Derrida: Postmodernism and Political Theory," *Phil. and Soc. Criticism* 19 (1993): 243, 244.
102. Id. at 247.
103. J. M. Balkin, "Transcendental Deconstruction, Transcendent Justice," *Mich. L. Rev.* 92 (1994): 1131, 1137.
104. Jane Flax, *Disputed Subjects: Essays on Psychoanalysis, Politics and Philosophy* (New York: Routledge, 1993), 111.
105. C. Elder, Book Review, *J. Religion* 74 (1994): 289, 291.
106. T. Nagel, "Freud's Permanent Revolution," *N.Y. Rev. Books*, May 12, 1994, at 38.
107. Flax, supra note 104, at 38.
108. Id.
109. Id. at 48–50.
110. H. Foster, "Postmodernism in Parallax," *October* 63 (1993): 3, 10–11.
111. Flax, supra note 104, at 56.
112. Earle, supra note 77, at 141.
113. David Crownfield, "Summary," in *Lacan and Theological Discourse*, supra note 77, at 158.
114. Skillen, supra note 81, at 200.
115. G. Warnke, *Justice and Interpretation* (Cambridge: MIT Press, 1993), 42.
116. F. Richardson and J. Christopher, "Social Theory as Practice: Metatheoretical Options for Social Inquiry," *J. Theoretical and Philosophical Psych.* 13 (1993): 137, 142.
117. B. Fay, *Critical Social Theory* (Ithaca: Cornell University Press, 1987), 182.
118. Id. at 182–83.
119. Jacques Derrida, "Force of Law: The Mystical Foundation of Authority," *Cardozo L. Rev.* 11 (1990): 919.
120. Balkin, supra note 103, at 1158.
121. S. Hendley, "Liberalism, Communitarianism and the Conflictual Grounds of Democratic Pluralism," *Phil. and Soc. Criticism* 19 (1993): 293, 294.
122. Lacan, supra note 8, at 321.
123. Slavoj Zizek, *Looking Awry: An Introduction to Jacques Lacan Through Popular Culture* (Cambridge: MIT Press, 1991), 156.
124. Id. at 156.
125. E. Ragland, "Editorial: L'envers de la Psychoanalyse," *Newsletter of the Freudian Field* 6 (1992): 1.
126. Jacques-Alain Miller, "Duty and the Drives," *Newsletter of the Freudian Field* 6 (1992): 5.
127. Dean, supra note 87, at 96.
128. Id.

129. Zizek, supra note 123, at 163–65.
130. *See* P. Halder, "Myth-Understood," *Law and Critique* 5 (1994): 113; P. Fitzpatrick, *The Mythology of Modern Law* (London: Routledge, 1992), ix.
131. Flax, supra note 104, at 113.
132. Ragland, supra note 125, at 4.
133. Zizek, supra note 123, at 164.
134. See Eugene Webb, "The New Social Psychology of France: The Heritage of Jacques Lacan," *Religion* 23 (1993): 61; "The New Social Psychology of France: The Girardian School," *Religion* 23 (1993): 255.
135. White, supra note 89, at 117–18.
136. Id. at 120.
137. J. J. DiCenso, "Symbolism and Subjectivity: A Lacanian Approach to Religion," *J. Religion* 74 (1994): 45, 59.
138. Id. at 47.
139. Refer to text accompanying note 13 supra.
140. Webb, supra note 134 (*The Girardian School*), at 255–56.
141. R. Girard, *Generative Scapegoating*, in *Violent Origins: Walter Burkert, René Girard, and Jonathan Z. Smith on Ritual Killing and Cultural Formation*, ed. R. Hammerton-Kelly (Stanford: Stanford University Press, 1987), at 122.
142. Skillen, supra note 81, at 197.

INDEX

Alford, C. Fred, 142
Althusser, Louis, 11–12, 123

Barnett, Randy, 45
Bleak House (Charles Dickens), 101, 116–28
Bowie, Malcolm, 9, 10, 56
Bracher, Mark, 53, 134–35
Brenkman, John, 12
Brion, Denis, 86–88, 97, 99–100

child abuse, false accusations of, 87–88, 188 n. 77
Cixous, Hélène, 94–95, 96
contracts, law of, 39, 43–47, 64–65
Copjec, Joan, 39
Critical Legal Studies, ix, 29, 62, 69, 72, 129, 139, 152

deconstruction, 70–71, 76
Derrida, Jacques, 21, 71, 143, 147
desire, 58–60, 122, 131–36, 147

Earle, William James, 136
Ego, the, 34, 81
Ellis, David, 49
Evans, Martha, 95–96

feminism, Lacan and, 108–9, 185 n. 2
formalism, legal, 68, 70
Frank, Jerome, 27–28
Freud, Sigmund, 8, 14–15, 19, 58, 74, 79, 88–89, 96–99, 105, 123, 136, 145; legal theory based on the work of, 27–30

Gabel, Peter, 12, 29–30
Goodrich, Peter, 36–39, 40–41

Halper, Louise, 56
Hogan, Patrick Colm, 23, 59
Holland, Norman, 16, 21
hysteria, xiv, 85–86, 88–100; legal conceptions of, 89–92

imaginary, the, 8, 12, 103, 107, 150
Ingleby, David, 56

Jackson, Bernard, 60–61
Jacobson, Roman, 9, 54

Kerrigan, William, 14, 16, 17, 21

law and economics, 46, 47–48, 170 n. 22
law and literature, 116–17
law and religion, 136–53
law practice, 38–40, 44
law school, 36–37
Lawrence, Charles, 28–29
legal ideology, critique of, xiv, 129–30, 139–41, 149
Legendre, Pierre, 38–39
Levack, Brian, 93
Lyotard, Jean-Françoise, 56, 176 n. 104

MacCabe, Colin, 22
metaphor and metonymy, xiii, 53–58, 174–75 n. 89, 179 n. 145
metonymy. *See* metaphor and metonymy
Miller, Jacques-Alain, 11, 130
Milovanovic, Dragan, 12–13, 61

Name-of-the-Father, 102–3, 105–8, 109–10
neopragmatism, legal, 69

Other, the, 7–8, 32–33, 59, 77, 103, 106, 158–59 n. 2; law as, 31–32, 36–37, 73

Peller, Gary, 61–62
pluralism, 136–39, 145–47, 149
postmodernism, xi, 18, 131
poststructuralism, 19–20
psychosis, 106, 109–15, 120, 190 n. 17
"Purloined Letter, The" (Edgar Allan Poe), 51–53, 62–63, 173 n. 74

Ragland, Ellie, 10, 13, 26, 53, 108–9
rationality, critique of, xii, 74
Rawls, John, 137–39, 141–43, 145–47
real, the, 9, 103
regulatory takings, law of, 111–15

Sandel, Michael, 141, 143
Saussure, Ferdinand, 9, 16, 54
Schema L, Lacan's, xiii, 30–31, 73
Schlag, Pierre, 66–72, 75–81
Schoenfeld, Charles G., 27–28

Schreber, Daniel Paul, 104–8, 113–14
semiotics, 60
Sheridan, Alan, 59
signifier, the, 33–34, 51–57, 58, 63, 102, 107, 108
Smith, Paul, 11–12, 13, 75–78, 81, 110
Speaking Subject, the, 35, 74
subject, problem of the, xi, 7, 13, 66–81, 144, 150
Sussman, Henry, 5, 13, 18–19
symbolic, the, 8–9, 11–12, 50–51, 102, 107, 150
symptom, the, 57

unconscious, the, 5; discourse of, 5, 33, 42, 49–50, 73–74, 103

Wallwork, Ernest, 134
Weber, Samuel, 10–11
White, Stephen K., 148
Wilden, Anthony, 11
Williams, Patricia, 79–81
witch-hunts, 87, 92–93

Zizek, Slavoj, 19–20, 122–25, 127, 147–48